ALWAYS ALABAMA

A HISTORY OF
CRIMSON TIDE FOOTBALL

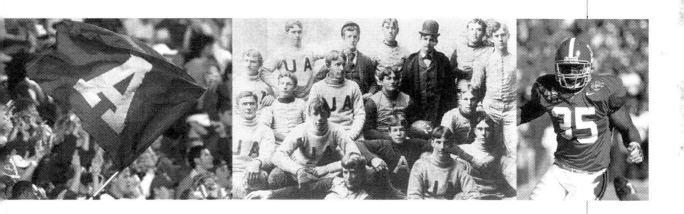

DON WADE

A FIRESIDE BOOK
PUBLISHED BY SIMON & SCHUSTER
NEW YORK LONDON TORONTO SYDNEY

FIRESIDE
Rockefeller Center
1230 Avenue of the Americas
New York, NY 10020

For information regarding special discounts for bulk purchases,
please contact Simon & Schuster Special Sales at
1-800-456-6798 or business@simonandschuster.com

Designed by Susan Walsh

Manufactured in the United States of America

1   3   5   7   9   10   8   6   4   2

Library of Congress Cataloging-in-Publication Data is available.

ISBN 978-1-4767-9271-2

For Mom and Dad, for all you've done.

ACKNOWLEDGMENTS

Writing is a solitary pursuit. It's true, certainly, that I wrote every word in this book. Yet not a single word could have been written without the support, guidance, and inspiration I received from so many other people, some of whom I didn't even know before this project started.

For a book like this, my personal thanks must begin with all the Alabama players and coaches who have made Crimson Tide football the most tradition-rich program in college football history. They made the great plays, games, and seasons that produced so many stories worth telling. At the beginning of this project, however, I encountered a few well-meaning skeptics. These people warned me that Alabama players, particularly those who had played for Bear Bryant, had grown tired of talking about the good old days. Almost unanimously, this turned out to be false. I interviewed nearly one hundred people for this book—many of them former Alabama players and coaches—and they were gracious with their time and their insight. Many of them even helped me connect with other former players. It's impossible in this space to thank them all, but I do want to give special appreciation to two former players who seldom grant interviews but did extend that courtesy to me for this book: Tommy Lewis and Darwin Holt.

My agent, Bob Mecoy, was in many ways my coach. He knew just when to pat me on the back and kick me in the backside, kept me looking downfield, and always gaining ground against the ever-present deadline. Brett Valley, my editor, balanced our race against the clock with a dedication to ensuring the book would be the best it could possibly be.

George Schroeder, my good friend and the author of a fine book chronicling the history of Arkansas Razorbacks football, talked me down from numerous ledges and at times had more faith in me than I had in myself. Gary Robinson, my sports editor at the *Commercial Appeal* in Memphis, went beyond all reason in his understanding of the scope of this project and also acted as a valuable sounding board at various points in the process; other editors at the newspaper also supported this effort, and I thank them as well. John Pruett, long-time sports editor of the *Huntsville Times,* not only contributed some good stories for these pages, but also was kind enough to read the manuscript and saved me from several errors.

It's probably not possible to express how much the help I received from director Ken Gaddy and his staff at the Paul W. Bryant Museum meant. Ken and his crew were tireless in their efforts to assist me in finding all the information I needed. Taylor Watson and Gary Shores were always available to answer questions or cue a tape, and Brad Green went above the call of duty to help me select photos from the museum's vast archives. The museum's oral history archives also were a crucial source for tapping into the thoughts and feelings from players, coaches and others from long ago, as were the newspaper clippings that go back to the football program's early days.

I'm indebted to Alabama athletic director Mal Moore, who embraced and encouraged the writing of this book from the beginning. I'm grateful to Charlie Fiss, vice president of communications for the AT&T Cotton Bowl, for generously contributing photos that make this book that much better. I'm also thankful for all the authors who have written all the books on Alabama football and Bear Bryant that came before this one. Each of them helped light the way. Likewise, I'm appreciative of the fine work by so many daily sportswriters who have covered Alabama football through the years. Thanks, too, to a young sportswriter with the *Decatur Daily News,* Kyle Veazey, who assisted with a couple of interviews for this project.

If this book had a soundtrack, it would be the band Third Day's "Wherever You Are" CD, which literally helped me drive forward as I was reporting and researching. Thanks, guys, you helped me see the light at the end of this tunnel. Most of all, I'm thankful to my Heavenly Father for the blessing of being able to write this book.

Finally, while writing is indeed a solitary pursuit, an author who is married with three children does not live in isolation. If anybody had to endure a "gut-check" during this process, it was my beautiful wife, Deb. She had to live with me at my worst, and yet was a constant source of encouragement and unwavering support. An excellent writer and editor, she provided essential feedback throughout. My sons, Stephen, Matthew, and Jonathan, tired of hearing Dad say, "I can't right now, I have to work on the book," but now can't wait to go to Tuscaloosa and watch the start of Alabama's next season, which is the glory in all of this: The story goes on.

ACKNOWLEDGMENTS

CONTENTS

ix

CONTENTS

ALWAYS ALABAMA

RISING TIDE

INSIDE the Bryant Museum, history has a way of changing.

It changes just about every time another fan watches the video of Alabama's famous goal line stand against Penn State in the 1979 Sugar Bowl at the Louisiana Superdome. The result of that play is always the same: Bear's boys in the red jerseys deny Joe Paterno's boys in the white jerseys and take home another national championship.

But fans' memories are sort of like the running of Alabama's old wishbone offense: full of options.

At the museum on the campus of the University of Alabama in Tuscaloosa, that play is always just a touch of a button away. Clem Gryska, who played at Alabama in the 1940s and was a longtime assistant under Bryant, still keeps an office at the museum. He is often nearby when fans revisit the glorious moment, and watch their beloved Crimson Tide stuff that Penn State running back as he tries to leap into the end zone.

▲ PREVIOUS PAGE
Alabama fans have
had a lot to cheer
about, including
twelve national
championships.

"I bet one hundred thousand people have come up to me and said, 'Coach, I know they didn't score because I was in that section on the goal line,' " Gryska says and laughs.

"I don't know that they're lying, really, they just want to be a part of it."

Not that Gryska's blaming them. In their way, those fans are just displaying the same passion that got hold of Tommy Lewis on January 1, 1954, in the Cotton Bowl. That's when Lewis came roaring off the Alabama sideline, sans helmet, to tackle a Rice player he feared was going to run for a touchdown. Lewis's enduring line afterward:

"I'm just too full of Alabama."

More than a half-century later, it still describes the depth of sentiment for Crimson Tide football, which is the proud owner of twelve national championships and no fewer than five national championship near-misses.

Six of those national titles were won by Bryant's teams, one by protégé Gene Stallings in 1992, and five during the Wallace Wade and Frank Thomas eras, which stretched from 1923 through 1946.

Clearly, winning never became old hat; certainly not to the man on the sideline in the houndstooth hat. Once, after Bryant had won his three national titles in the 1960s, someone asked him what was left to do. His answer was quick and sure.

"A fourth," he said, "and then a fifth, and a sixth."

For players—and Bryant was one of these, too, helping the Crimson Tide to the 1934 national championship—representing Alabama football always has meant reaching within themselves to that far place losers just won't go.

Bryant did this when he played the 1935 Tennessee game with a broken leg, shrugging off the feat by saying, "It was just one little bone."

Young Boozer, a halfback and Bryant teammate on the '34 national championship team, captured the overriding credo perfectly.

"The ingrained philosophy at Alabama," Boozer said, "was to give a little more than you've got."

This is what Tommy Lewis was doing that day at the Cotton Bowl—staying in the game even when, well, he wasn't.

"My last game for Alabama, the school I grew up loving as a kid," Lewis says. "We took a good whipping that day [losing 28–6, Lewis scoring the only touchdown], and they'd brought the first team off the field and put the second team in there.

"The ball carrier broke into our secondary and I was standing on the sideline, had dropped my headgear to my side. I looked up and saw 'em knock our end down, knock our linebacker down, and the guy turned the corner and I turned to one of my teammates and

Rice's Dickie Moegle looked to be en route to a touchdown in the 1954 Cotton Bowl, when Alabama's Tommy Lewis (42) listened to his heart and not his head and came off the sideline to tackle Moegle. "If I could take back anything in my life," Lewis says, "it would be that play."

said, 'He's going all the way.' And my buddy said, 'Yeah, he sure is, Lew.'

"And then I looked back and he was almost right in my face," Lewis says, "and I unloaded on him. I didn't want to lose. It was my last game at Alabama. It all just came together in one whack.

"If I could take back anything in my life—I'm telling you, anything—it would be that play because it just won't ever go away."

He is not exaggerating. When Alabama played in the 2006 Cotton Bowl, Lewis's tackle was briefly covered during the television network's halftime show. Not that Lewis, who was in Florida, saw it.

"I took a walk on the beach at halftime," he says. "I wasn't going to watch that. I'm still embarrassed about it."

He needn't be.

What Lewis doesn't bring up himself is that he went to the Rice locker room and apologized. And, the next day, the *Dallas Morning News* absolved him in an editorial that called Lewis a "genuine competitor" and his infamous play a "forgivable error."

Lewis later went on the *Ed Sullivan Show* and it was there that he said, "I'm just too full of Alabama."

It was, of course, the way he was raised, the way so many Alabama players were raised. Lewis's father had an auto parts store in tiny Greenville, Alabama. On game days, that store was full of Alabama.

"Any Saturday," Lewis says, "the radio would be loud enough for all the customers to hear."

Yet, in the beginning, Alabama football made nary a sound.

FROM DIRT TO ROSES

Tradition can neither spontaneously invent itself nor just be dialed up on a radio. It has to be inspired, nurtured, maybe even pampered. In time, all that would come to fruition under Dr. George Hutcheson "Mike" Denny, who became school president in 1912.

For years, though, football at Alabama was rather like the South at large—fledgling, at times misunderstood, and fighting to make a place for itself.

In 1892, W. G. Little, a Livingston, Ala., native, would prove the first catalyst. He had attended the university before going off to Phillips Exeter Academy in Andover, Mass. The death of Little's brother brought him back to the university. Little carried with him the trappings of what, at the time, seemed as much a fad as a sport: cleats, a leather football helmet, and that oddly shaped pigskin.

Nevertheless, in 1892, Little formed Alabama's first team—called the Cadets, which was in line with Alabama's then-role as a military school. Little was the

Alabama's first football team in 1892 finished the season with a 2-2 record.

first-ever team captain. E. B. Beaumont was the first coach, and also the first coach to last but a season.

The first game, however, was a re-sounding triumph: 56–0 over Birming-ham High School, which was really a collection of players from several area high schools.

Not only were there no bye weeks then, there wasn't even a day of rest be-fore the next game. After debuting with a win on November 11, the Cadets, on November 12, lost 5–4 to the Birming-ham Athletic Club, despite a long touchdown run by Little (touchdowns were only worth four points at the time). A win in a rematch with the Birming-ham A.C. and a loss to Auburn meant a 2-2 finish to the first season.

From there, the program would build slowly. Simply known as the "Var-sity" or the "Crimson Whites," after the school colors, Alabama didn't win a game in two of the next three years.

Off the field, university trustees in-creasingly fretted that football and its in-herent roughness were compromising academics and the school's reputation. In 1897, the trustees prohibited playing games off campus; the season was re-duced to a single game. In 1898, there was no team at all.

Gradually, the trustees loosened their hold on the football program, and the team also got a new nickname—"The Thin Red Line"—courtesy of a sports-writer. By 1907, another sportswriter, apparently moved by Alabama's efforts

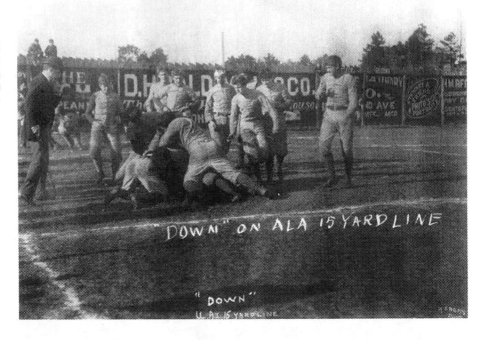

'Bama actually played the last game of the 1892 season in February 1893, losing to Auburn, 32–22.

"DOWN" ON ALA 15 YARD LINE

"DOWN"
AT 15 YARD LINE

in Birmingham when Alabama played Auburn to a 6–6 tie in a sea of mud, coined the phrase *Crimson Tide.*

Crimson Tide tradition would not begin in earnest until Mike Denny's arrival five years later. Denny often came to Alabama's practices, often got in the way, and occasionally would get run over. He didn't seem to mind.

"Dr. Denny genuinely loved football," says Alabama athletic director Mal Moore, who earned seven national championship rings as a player under Bryant and as assistant under Bryant and Stallings.

By 1915, Alabama had its first All-American: W. T. "Bully" VandeGraaff, a standout tackle on offense and defense. That year, Bully scored 17 points in a 23–10 win over Sewanee in Birmingham. It was a bigger game than one

might imagine, for Sewanee was a power and rival in those days, and Alabama had not defeated Sewanee since 1894.

A newspaper headline from the game read: VandeGraaff Snatches Victory from Defeat When He Intercepts Forward Pass and Goes for Touchdown.

At least one sportswriter believed this game offered clues of what was to come: "If the Alabama eleven of yesterday is any forecast of the future, it is easy to be seen that a new era of athletics has dawned at the university."

If anything, that writer may have undersold the changes. The 1915 season also was the team's first playing at Denny Field. Even more crucial, Denny made strong coaching hires, the boldest his often-overlooked 1919 decision to

bring in diminutive Cleveland horse-racing writer Xen Scott, who had played a little football at Cleveland's Western Reserve University.

In 1922, Scott's fourth and final season, the Crimson Tide carried a 2-2-1 record into Philadelphia and beat Penn 9–7; it was an upset of epic proportions, considering that no one had given a Southern team any chance at defeating an Eastern power.

Scott was in poor health——his physician had even ordered him not to make the trip. Zipp Newman, sports editor for the *Birmingham News,* reported Scott's pregame pep talk:

"Boys, things haven't gone well at Alabama this year. I have tried to give you my best, although as you know I have had to spend most of my time in bed. You, every one of you, has been criticized.

"I don't mind the abuse and criticism heaped upon my head, that all goes with the game. But for the sake of the boys back home, who are pinning their hopes in your ability, get in there and show them that Alabama has got a football team."

After the victory was secured, a joyous Scott hugged players as they came off the field; several players began singing "Dixie."

When the coaches and players returned home, a crowd in the thousands greeted them at Tuscaloosa's train depot. Students carried guard Ben Compton——a giant by the day's standards——on their shoulders. Bands played.

The sweet music of success was now

ALWAYS ALABAMA

in the air, the stage grandly set for larger glories to come under Wade, who would lead Alabama to its first national title in 1925, and a berth in the January 1, 1926, Rose Bowl against Washington.

At the Rose Bowl, they weren't just playing for themselves, their school, or their state.

In fact, so widespread was the support for Alabama that among the telegrams arriving at Pasadena's Huntington Hotel on game day was this one: "Husk and Shuck The Huskies, from Tuskegee Institute Football Team, National Colored Champions."

When Alabama defeated the Huskies, 20–19, the victory echoed all the way from sunny California to the coldest cotton field. It echoes still in the school fight song, "Yea, Alabama," which ends with these words: "You're Dixie's football pride, Crimson Tide!"

Even an impartial observer knew as much after the first Rose Bowl. Walter Eckersall, who refereed the historic game, said in a newspaper account that the "lads from Dixie" had "placed the southern brand of football on a par at least with that played in other sections of the country."

It was only the beginning. The Crimson Tide won the national championship the following year, even though the season ended with a 7–7 tie with Stanford in the Rose Bowl. Wade's third, and final, national title came in 1930 after announcing before the season that

he would leave the following year to become football coach and athletic director at Duke.

"He was pretty tough," 1926 All-American end Hoyt "Wu" Winslett said of Wade. "Some of the fellows called him the 'Bear.' "

This first Bear recommended Frank Thomas, who had played quarterback for Knute Rockne at Notre Dame, as his successor. Thomas's teams won the national title in 1934 and again in 1941. They probably deserved another in 1945, when they went 10-0 and finished the season on New Year's Day (1946) with a 34–14 spanking of Southern Cal.

It would be Alabama's final Rose Bowl appearance. The game was preceded by yet another memorable cross-country train trip and a chance to hang out with former 'Bama halfback turned Western star Johnny "Mack" Brown and to see how movies were made.

"What a trip, us rednecks in Holly-

Frank Thomas coached 'Bama's last Rose Bowl team on January 1, 1946, and it included All-Americans Harry Gilmer (52) and Vaughn Mancha (41).

wood," recalls salty All-American center Vaughn Mancha. "We went on the set and the guy that impressed me most was Errol Flynn. He was about 6-5 and had those tight pants on—he was Robin Hood—and son-of-a-gun, we wanted to dress him out."

THE BEST
IS YET TO COME

Although Alabama mostly continued to win during the Harold "Red" Drew era—from 1947 to 1954—the Tide would have welcomed a Robin Hood's help during the J. B. "Ears" Whitworth years of 1955-57 when Alabama was poor in wins: 4-24-2.

Upon Bear Bryant's return to his alma mater in 1958—when "Mama called" as Bryant described it—there was much work to do. Bryant rid himself of marginally motivated players. He realized the ceiling was higher here than at the other places he had been a head coach: Maryland, Kentucky, and Texas A & M.

"The tradition, Bryant talked about that every day," says Billy Neighbors, a freshman on Bryant's first team and an All-American lineman on the '61 national title team. "That's the reason he came back here. That's the reason I went there, that's the reason half the kids go there. Every team's not gonna win a national championship, every team's not gonna be good—that's the way life is. But you've got a better chance here than any other place in America.

"He talked about Frank Thomas and Wallace Wade. He talked about all the great players. I met a lot of those great players."

They included College Football Hall-of-Famers Pooley Hubert, a quarterback on the first Rose Bowl team; Harry Gilmer, a small but wiry halfback known for his jump passes in the 1940s; and Fred Sington, called the "greatest lineman in the country" by Knute Rockne.

"Bryant loved that tradition," Neighbors says. "He believed in that. He knew he could win a championship."

The Bear soon became more than merely a great coach with a clear vision and a dedicated plan. He became the Capstone's touchstone.

As University of Georgia coach and athletic director Wally Butts once famously said: "The definition of an atheist in Alabama is someone who doesn't believe in Bear Bryant."

Everyone knew of, and appreciated, his toughness. Still, the presence and power of the man, his genuine concern for the individual player, the ability to inspire with just a few well-timed words, all had to be experienced firsthand to be understood.

John Croyle, now better known as the father of 2005 senior 'Bama quarterback Brodie Croyle, was a defensive end for Bryant in the early 1970s. He tells the story of sitting in Bryant's office, at age nineteen, and outlining his life's plan——to operate a ranch where he could care for abused and neglected children.

It was perhaps the most important moment in young John Croyle's life. And suddenly, a secretary was politely interrupting to say there were people waiting.

"I've got Roone Arledge [president of ABC], Spiro Agnew [vice president of the United States] and Bob Hope [the king of comedy] all on hold," she said. "What do you want me to tell them?"

"Tell them I'll be with them in a minute," Bryant said.

"That's a lot if you're a nineteen-year-old kid," says Croyle, who still runs Big Oak Ranch in Springville, Alabama. "He made me feel as if I was more important than anything those men had to say."

To be sure, when Bryant talked, everyone listened. Even those on the other side of the competition welcomed a chance to get close to him. Bert Bank, a former state senator and producer of the Alabama football and basketball networks during Bryant's day, told of taking the coach to speak to the state legislature.

"Everybody—even the Auburn people—was elated to shake hands with him," Bank said.

Of himself, Bryant often said, "I ain't nothing but a winner." By the mid-1960s, this point was beyond dispute. His teams won back-to-back national titles in 1964 and 1965 and should have won a third in '66 when Alabama went 11-0.

"I've thought about that a lot because of Southern Cal's recent success," Moore says, referring to Texas spoiling USC's recent quest for three straight national championships. "To be the first team to threepeat, to be truthful, it's already been done.

"We were national champions in '64

◀FACING PAGE
Halfback Harry Gilmer played from 1944 to 1947 and twice led the team in rushing, and four times led it in passing.

Paul W. "Bear" Bryant won six national titles in his quarter-century as coach at Alabama.

and '65 and we did what we were supposed to do—we defended the national championship."

Alabama would win three more national titles under Bryant in the seventies ('73, '78, and '79) but, first, there would be a decline, at least by the special standards that now applied to Bryant and the Crimson Tide.

The team went 8-3 in 1968, the most losses since Bryant's first season in 1958, when a 5-4-1 record was considered an achievement given the program's losing ways under Whitworth.

The first of those three losses in 1968 came in the season's third week: 10–8 to Coach Johnny Vaught's Ole Miss Rebels in Jackson, Mississippi. The quarterback of that Ole Miss team was a red-haired sophomore named Archie

Manning, whose sons Peyton and Eli now throw footballs in the NFL.

Even more telling was what Ole Miss did, or didn't, do leading up to the 1969 game. Playing as a heavy favorite at Kentucky the week before their game with the Crimson Tide, the Rebels played coy on offense and were upset by the Wildcats.

"It was a bad loss," says Manning, recalling why their offense sputtered: "We saved our stuff for Alabama."

The Alabama-Ole Miss game proved a beauty, the Crimson Tide winning 33–32 in Birmingham. It was the first college football game televised nationally in prime time and 'Bama prevailed, despite Manning passing for 436 yards and three touchdowns and rushing for 104 yards.

Alabama's season, however, took an ugly turn, finishing at 6-5 with lopsided losses to rivals Tennessee and Auburn. A 6-5-1 season in 1970 signaled a need for a makeover.

No one thing had brought the program back down to earth, and Bryant easily could have clung to the past and resisted change.

Instead, he embraced it, and so began another decade of dominance.

MOVING AHEAD

In 1970, halfback Wilbur Jackson became the first African-American player to sign a football scholarship to play at Alabama. In the opening game of 1971 at Southern Cal, defensive end John Mitchell became the first African-American to play in a game for the Crimson Tide.

"Coach Bryant told me right in front of my mom and dad, 'You're probably going to have some problems coming here. I just want you to give me the first opportunity to solve those problems,'" Mitchell told a newspaper reporter in Pittsburgh, where Mitchell is now an assistant coach with the Steelers. "He said not to go to the press or anyone else but, you know, I never had to go to him."

A few years later Ozzie Newsome, an African-American who would go on to have a Pro Football Hall-of-Fame career as a tight end, was an All-American receiver for Bryant. Newsome remembers the coach as being blind to color, but eyes open wide to the kind of effort a player gave.

"It wasn't a black player or a white player, you were an Alabama player," says Newsome, now general manager for the Baltimore Ravens. "There was no status. The walk-ons got treated just as well as the so-called stars.

"Whatever ability you had, if you gave it to him all the time, then he was happy. But if you had ability and you gave it to him when you wanted to, you weren't going to survive there very long."

The first game in 1971 in Los Angeles was notable for another debut, too:

DON WADE

In 1970, Wilbur Jackson became the first African-American to sign a football scholarship to play at Alabama.

the wishbone offense, which Bryant had learned from University of Texas coach Darrell Royal, and which the Crimson Tide had been practicing in secret, right up to game day.

"He called me from out there on Friday night," Royal recalls. "I said, 'Coach, do you think it's a total secret and that California group expects you to come back with the same attack you had last year?' And he said he really believed that. I told him, 'I bet you have some fun.'"

And they did, too, beating USC 17–10. When the decade was over, Alabama had won 103 games, three national championships, and eight Southeastern Conference championships.

Actress Sela Ward (center) was an Alabama cheerleader in the 1970s.

"Alabama's just different," says Steadman Shealy, a quarterback from 1977 to 1979. "We're supposed to score touchdowns. We're supposed to win."

For the most part, that's what Alabama has continued to do since Bryant's retirement after the 1982 season and death just a few weeks later. But the immediate post-Bryant years, when first Ray Perkins and then Bill Curry coached the Crimson Tide, were not altogether smooth.

Perkins produced a 32-15-1 record, which would have been good enough most places. Curry went 26-10-0, which would have been good enough most places.

Alabama is not most places.

"Every time Ray lost, a lot of Alabama fans felt if Coach Bryant had still been coaching he'd have won that

game," says Gene Bartow, who followed John Wooden as basketball coach at UCLA, and later was basketball coach and athletic director at the University of Alabama-Birmingham. "At UCLA, people knew if Coach Wooden had been coaching they would have won that game.

"Even now," Bartow continues, "they're still following Wooden out there. And they're still following Bryant at Alabama."

They are not just following Bryant, though, because Bryant had a tradition to follow, too, a tradition that was planted in a simpler time, when as Fred Sington—"Football Freddie" in the old Rudy Vallee song—remembered it, "our president, Dr. Denny, knew everybody by their first name."

"The University of Alabama owes

Dr. Denny, Lord knows how much," All-American Wu Winslett once said.

Without question, Denny was the one dedicated to building the athletic program through football. Without question, he was the one that gave the coaches he hired and the players they recruited a chance to achieve remarkable feats.

"They won a bunch of Rose Bowls," says Roger Shultz, a center from 1987 to 1990. "It's unbelievable the foundation those guys set."

And, just as those early days of glory helped ease the pain of the post-Civil War South, helped soothe the collectively bruised self-image, success in the Bryant years gave Alabama an identity apart from the one being painted nationally during the civil rights movement.

In 1964, when three civil rights workers were murdered in Mississippi, an event that stained the entire South, the Crimson Tide was winning their second national championship of the decade.

In 1965, when they were winning another national title for the Bear, Dr. Martin Luther King, Jr., and more than two thousand others were being arrested in Selma, Alabama, during demonstrations against voter registration rules.

The news on the sports page was always better than the news on the front page.

"People loved Coach Bryant," says Linda Knowles, who was his secretary in the football office for much of his tenure in Tuscaloosa. "He gave us something to be proud of in this state. And there have been times we didn't have much to be proud of."

Which is why when Alabama foot-

'Bama fans pack Bryant-Denny Stadium in expectation of great things

Former Tide quarterback Mike Shula became coach under trying circumstances in 2003, and led Alabama to a 10-win season and Cotton Bowl victory in 2005.

ball goes through a down period, it perhaps feels so much worse. It feels like letting down the past, not merely the present and the future.

This is why the '92 national championship under Gene Stallings, who had played for Bryant at Texas A & M and been an assistant to him at Alabama, seemed to make the family whole again, restoring pride and future expectations to a place above the clouds.

"You never want to let go of that part of it," says Shultz, now associate athletic director at Troy University in Alabama. "I love the high expectations. I love walking around telling people I played for the University of Alabama.

"The good thing is people recognize its greatness. You brag so much that, when you're down, people are taking shots at you. Now, all of a sudden you rise up again, and you're the favorite person in your Sunday school class."

John Mauro was a defensive end on the 1978-79 national title teams. Today, he's back in his native northwestern Indiana—Notre Dame country—and spends some of his free time coaching youth football. Tony Rice, a former Notre Dame star, is one of his assistants.

Naturally, after Alabama's then-undefeated 2005 season took a little detour with losses to LSU and Auburn, Rice had some fun at Mauro's expense. Then, when Notre Dame lost its bowl game and Alabama beat Texas Tech in

the Cotton Bowl, Mauro got the last word.

"I just looked at Tony and said, 'Hey, you want an Alabama shirt?' "

That moment of redemption had been a long time coming. Too many coaches had failed to live up to the tradition. Too many coaches couldn't uphold their own dignity, much less the school's dignity. Then former Tide quarterback Mike Shula came home, and healing began anew because, again, there was a determined leader.

Back in the '79 Sugar Bowl, when Alabama had to make a goal-line stand to win the national championship, that same resolve bonded the defense into a single force.

"Gut check, this is what we play for," cornerback Don McNeal says, repeating what he remembers being said in the Alabama huddle.

And so, they held their ground that day in the Superdome. Just like Alabama football has held its ground no matter the time, place, or circumstance.

As then-Alabama president Dr. David Mathews said in a talk to the 1970 Crimson Tide football team: "Tradition like ours is a burden in many ways. To have a tradition like ours means that you can't quit. To have a tradition like ours means you always have to show class, even when you are not quite up to it. To have tradition like ours means you have to do some things that you don't want to do and some you even think you can't do, simply because the tradition demands it of you . . ."

"The legend still goes on," says Billy Neighbors, a member of the '61 national championship team who has sent two sons, Wes and Keith, to play football at Alabama. "It'll be there forever.

"You can't take it away."

2

BEFORE THE BEAR

COACH Tommy was in his last season, and probably knew it. Seven years earlier, in 1946, high blood pressure and a heart condition had forced Frank Thomas off the Crimson Tide sideline.

When he reluctantly relinquished his coaching duties after the '46 season, he was Alabama's all-time wins leader (115) and had two national championships to his credit. They were the fourth and fifth titles in school history, after three under Wallace Wade, the man who recommended Thomas succeed him.

Now it was 1953, and Coach Tommy's health was in serious decline. A year earlier, he had given up his role as athletic director. Still, he sometimes made it out to practices and games. On these good days, Coach Tommy would have someone drive him just beyond the corner of the end zone, where he could watch the game from the car.

Defensive back Hootie Ingram had grown up

▲ PREVIOUS PAGE
Frank Thomas
coached Alabama
from 1931 to 1946,
had a 115-24-7
record, and won
two national
championships.

as a friend of the family, often spending the night in the Thomas household; the coach had a son just about the same age.

Thomas had a soft spot for Ingram and he was just the kind of player Thomas would have loved to have had on one of his teams. Ingram had a knack for stealing passes, leading the nation with 10 interceptions in one season. On this day, he would intercept a pass and run it all the way back for a touchdown—to the end zone where Coach Tommy sat in his car.

"If the spike had been invented then, I'd have spiked the ball," Ingram says, eyes brightening at the memory.

As dramatic as the moment was, Ingram best remembers his quiet times with Coach Tommy. Every Thursday of Ingram's sophomore year it was the same: He'd have dinner on campus, then head over to Coach Tommy's house.

For more than an hour, the young player and the old coach would sit and talk football. Coach Tommy would ask about what they did in practice that day. They'd dissect the opponent, and discuss Coach Red Drew's game plan; Thomas had recommended Drew, a former assistant, replace him.

"He just wanted to keep his mind functioning in football," says Ingram, who decades later served as Alabama's athletic director. "He'd have me diagram defenses and plays."

They are bittersweet memories for Ingram because sometimes it feels like Thomas gets lost in latter-day glories. Any quick recounting of Alabama's football history has a tendency to begin and end with Paul W. Bryant.

"I'm glad Coach Bryant has got so much strong momentum. [His legacy] may never die," says Ingram. "But after a period of time, people like Wallace Wade and Frank Thomas can fade out.

"That's kind of a shame."

FORERUNNERS

It would be a shame—not to mention inaccurate—to believe Wade and Thomas were the only coaches before Bear Bryant to make significant contributions.

Moments in time are connected like links in a chain. Some of those links are strong, some are weak. All play a part in the larger story.

In 1892, Alabama's first coach, E. B. Beaumont, even had a part to play. He went 2-2, didn't come back in 1893, and became the first coach to take public—and some would say deserved—criticism.

The school yearbook, the *Corolla*, described his selection as coach as "unfortunate." The *Corolla* also said he had "very limited" knowledge of the game: "We therefore got rid of him."

No, coaching at Alabama was never going to be easy.

In the first twenty-six years of the football program, thirteen different men would assume the title of head coach. One man, Eli Abbott, who had been a tackle on Alabama's first team, would have two coaching stints. Neither was particularly successful as two of his four teams didn't win even one game.

To be fair, coaching a college football team often was a less than glamorous and profitable pursuit. In the early years, interference from university trustees was a major problem. In the mid-1890s, the trustees did not want Alabama playing games off-campus. The 1897 team played only one game, in Tuscaloosa.

Building any kind of momentum, much less tradition, was going to be almost impossible. The *Corolla* blasted the trustees, saying their no-travel rule had "handicapped" the football team and given the school "very little to be proud of."

As the situation improved, and the football team began to play more games, coaches began to stay longer. J. W. H. "Doc" Pollard, a Dartmouth alumnus, coached Alabama from 1906 through 1909, and brought with him a tricky little play called the "Pollard two-step."

Eventually ruled illegal, the Pollard two-step created an unbalanced line by essentially turning the linemen into big ballerinas. Holding hands, the linemen would approach the line of scrimmage and then hop or skip to one side or the other, opponents never knowing how many men would jump to the right, and how many would jump to the left.

Doc's four-year record: 21-4-6 and who knows how many calf strains from the Pollard two-step.

When Dr. Mike Denny arrived in 1912 as school president, D. V. Graves was in the second of his four years as coach. Graves, too, would win 21 games; Denny had loftier goals. In going 5-4 in 1914, Graves scored lopsided victories over Birmingham Southern (54–0), Tulane (58–0), and Chattanooga (63–0). He also lost the games that mattered most—17–7 to Tennessee and 18–0 to Sewanee, Alabama's biggest rival at that time. Just as Bill Curry couldn't beat Auburn in the 1980s, Graves couldn't beat Sewanee, going 0-3-1.

Nevertheless, after the 1914 season, Denny was telling sportswriters, on the record, that Graves would return for the next season. This turned out to be what is now known as the dreaded vote of confidence—a sure sign that change is coming.

In 1915, Denny brought in Thomas Kelly, a roll-up-his-sleeves, cigar-chomping man who had learned under the University of Chicago's Amos Alonzo Stagg—the all-time college football wins leader until Bear Bryant came along.

Denny's hire looked brilliant when Alabama began the 1915 season with four decisive wins, all of them shutouts. Just before *the* game—against Sewanee—Kelly contracted typhoid

fever. Athletics director Lonnie Noojin and Farley Moody, captain of the 1912 team, stepped in for Kelly. Alabama beat Sewanee, 23–10, and finished the season 6-2.

"This pair valiantly set their shoulders to the wheel and faithfully worked until the end," said Kelly, who lost 100 pounds off his 250-pound frame due to typhoid.

Kelly coached two more years, until 1918, when World War I ended the season before it started. When football resumed in 1919, Denny had made his most daring move yet: hiring Cleveland horse racing writer Xen Scott as Crimson Tide coach.

Scott was an immediate success. His first team, in 1919, began with five straight shutouts. He apparently was not the trickster that Kelly was. After a 27–0 win over Birmingham Southern in his debut, one newspaper account, noting the team had thrown just one pass, said: "Scott confined his attack to the simplest of formations."

After the fifth straight shutout—a 40–0 blowout of Sewanee—it was clear Scott was winning converts.

"Coach Scott's highly trained machine mows down purple warriors like a scythe would blades of grass" declared one headline.

The next year Scott guided Alabama to a 10-1 record. When Alabama finished that season in Cleveland, with a 40–0 drubbing of Case College, where Scott had previously coached, sportswriters there heaped lavish praise on him.

"He shakes a wicked typewriter during the summer months when the trotters and pacers are stepping along," said the *Cleveland Plain Dealer.* "And he can tell a good football player by talking to him over the telephone."

If true, recruiting must have been greatly simplified.

Scott's lasting achievement, however, would come in his final season in 1922, when the Crimson Tide, bobbing along with a 2-2-1 record, would go up to

Philadelphia to play Penn, a noted Eastern power.

Alabama had just lost to Texas, 19–10, in Austin. They had a long train ride and plenty of time to ruminate on the fact that, nationally, no one was giving them any shot at staying on the field with Penn, much less winning the game. Grantland Rice, one of the legendary sportswriters of the era, predicted Alabama wouldn't even score.

As for Scott, he had been sick enough that his doctor told him not to make the trip. Scott ignored this, of course and, on the journey up, included an important side trip to Washington, D.C., to see Navy play Penn State. His reasoning was simple: His boys needed to see Eastern teams up close to realize these guys were nothing special. They were just football players who had a different accent and a different history—

their forefathers had fought on the Union side.

In Philadelphia, some 25,000 fans filled Franklin Field and waited for the inevitable result—a resounding triumph for Pennsylvania. It never came.

After a scoreless first quarter, a Bull Wesley field goal gave Alabama a 3–0 lead in the second quarter. Penn seized the lead later in the period when George Sullivan ran 35 yards, reversing his direction on the play, for a touchdown. With the extra point, Penn took a 7–3 lead into halftime.

Alabama scored what proved to be the winning touchdown in the third quarter when Pooley Hubert went over the goal line, and fumbled. The Tide's Shorty Propst fell on the ball for a touchdown. Wesley missed the extra point, but it didn't matter. The 9–7 lead would hold up as the final score.

Penn couldn't crack the Alabama defense, though the game might have turned Penn's way had a player referred to in game stories only as Johnson hung onto a 40-yard pass. Accounts of the day indicate that had Johnson caught the ball, he would have had a clear field ahead of him.

"The ball was right in his hands," Penn coach John W. Heisman said after the game. "He didn't even have to reach for it."

Heisman (of Heisman Trophy fame) did not hesitate to reach for excuses to explain Alabama's victory: His players

In 1919, Dr. Denny made the bold decision to hire Cleveland horse-racing writer Xen Scott as Alabama's coach.

Wallace Wade was a no-nonsense coach who led the Crimson Tide to three national championships.

knew Georgia Tech had beaten Alabama, that Navy had beaten Georgia Tech, and that they had beaten Navy.

"Thus, they didn't see why we couldn't trim Alabama," Heisman said, adding, "It was a [natural] letdown in play and morale and Alabama caught us at the top of its form."

This comment perhaps got back to Scott, who days later didn't want to concede that last point.

"We did not prime especially for the Penn contest," Scott said, "but of course I would have rather won this game than any other."

It is not overstating things to say it was the game that first put Alabama football in the nation's consciousness or that Scott was the school's first great coach.

Scott, unfortunately, would not beat his biggest opponent: cancer. The 1922 season was his last and, in 1923, Wallace Wade became the Crimson Tide coach.

WADING IN

Wallace Wade had been assistant coach at Vanderbilt. Perhaps more relevant, he had been a cavalry captain in World War I.

Wade had some horses at Alabama, too. Pooley Hubert, Fred Sington, and Johnny Mack Brown are all in the College Football Hall of Fame. Four other

players under Wade made All-American, including Hoyt "Wu" Winslett.

Not only would Wade become the first Alabama coach to win the national championship (in 1925), he was the first one to be called the Bear. And like the Bear that came later, Wade always put the football team before everything else.

Sington found this out after pitching a no-hitter for the Crimson Tide baseball team one spring. He assumed his football coach would be proud of the accomplishment. Instead, Wade chewed him out.

"Where in the world were you yesterday when you were supposed to run the hurdles and get ready for football?" Wade told him more than asked him. "[Baseball's] secondary entirely."

Said Sington, years later, "It showed me that Coach Wade was sort of sincere about football." He also was sincere about how his players behaved off the field. Sington got to where he would keep one eye out for Wade's Chrysler Eight sedan.

"He used to ride up and down University Avenue meditating about the game, apparently, and if I came out of class and was walking along, and there were two or three co-eds on the same side of the street, I didn't know them," Sington said. "If I saw that Chrysler coming, I crossed the street because Coach Wade didn't believe you ought to go over to the circle and meet the sorority girls. He didn't like that at all."

He didn't like nonsense. He didn't even like Alabama's elephant mascot because he thought it was demeaning. Wade fancied his players as being more like cats—quick and cunning.

The coach believed in hard work. Wade's practices were tough, deliberate, painstakingly precise, and long. One practice ended up being especially drawn out.

Dave Sington, the son of Fred Sington, and an Alabama player in the 1950s, recounts a story that his father told him: It seems at practice one day Wade was informed he had a phone call. He left to take it and practice went on.

Maybe the phone call was of utmost importance, or maybe Wade just saw it as an opportunity to test his team. Whatever the reason, he didn't return.

"He just left 'em out on the field," Dave Sington says.

Finally, after about two hours, a team manager found Wade and asked if he wanted them to quit practicing.

"Nobody would stop," Dave Sington remembers his dad telling him. "They just kept on going. I guess they were just scared to death of him."

Wade could be brutally blunt, too. After the 1924 season, a mediocre one for Winslett, Wade bumped into him walking across campus. Wade had some advice:

"Hoyt, I believe if you want to make a letter at Alabama, you better go out for track."

"I resented that," said Winslett. "I never forgot it."

And he perhaps used it, just as Wade intended, for motivation. Two years later, when Winslett would be named All-American, he had a big day in a victory over Georgia Tech. As player and coach walked off the field together, Wade had a different message.

"Hoyt," Wade said, "I don't know whether the writers will give you credit or not, but you played the greatest game against Georgia Tech that any Alabama player ever played."

Winslett never forgot that moment, either, because it was the kind of thing Wallace Wade just didn't do.

"You could talk to Coach Bryant and Coach Thomas," said Fred Sington, who knew both men well. "I don't know that

anybody ever went in and actually spoke to Coach Wade, because if you walked in that door to speak to him, he said, 'How's that?' And that was the end of it."

But Wade was beloved by Alabama fans because he made the impossible possible. When Alabama accepted a Rose Bowl invitation after a 9–0 season in 1925, the assessment from the national press was that Wade was taking his boys all the way to California for a whipping.

While it was Alabama's first Rose Bowl trip—and the first for any Southern team—Wade had played for Brown University in the 1916 Rose Bowl. As one writer noted in the lead-up to the game: "He is in an ideal position to understand the mental and physical strain upon his players and the best method of

practicing his men upon arrival in the West."

After a 2,800 mile train trip that included a four-hour stop at the Grand Canyon, the team arrived in Pasadena on Christmas Eve. Wade decided the best plan was to go right to work: Alabama practiced on Christmas Day.

Players managed to have some fun—they visited movie studios and had their pictures taken with actress Bebe Daniels—then Wade more or less locked the boys in the Hotel Huntington the rest of the week.

Alabama had arrived a full week before game day, and it proved a wise idea, given that it took the team a while to get its legs back.

"After the first three workouts, we began to feel like ourselves again," said team captain Bruce Jones.

When the players entered the Rose Bowl on New Year's Day, they heard a familiar sound. The Elks Band of Pasadena was playing "Dixie." It would prove to be the theme of the day as the Crimson Tide beat the heavily favored Washington Huskies in a 20–19 thriller. The colorful Damon Runyon wrote in his dispatch how it happened and what it meant:

"The Crimson Tide of Southern football was on the ebb. Two touchdowns behind, and badly outplayed by the champions of the Pacific Coast all through the first half—that was the situation.

"And 45,000 spectators parked along the sloping tiers of the Rose Bowl were wondering just what excuse the Alabamans had for coming out here other than a desire to see the country.

"Then, suddenly, Alabama unleashed a species of human wildcat named 'Pooley' Hubert, quarterback of the Alabama team. Before the Washington lads fully realized what was happening, this 'Pooley' Hubert was all over them, kicking and scratching and throwing forward passes at them . . .

"It was a great team that the South sent to California . . . probably the greatest that ever came out of the South."

Alabama football was never the same. Wade's 1926 team went 9-0-1, playing Stanford to a 7–7 tie in the next Rose Bowl, and again was declared national champions.

It appeared Wade and Alabama had a dynasty on their hands. And then came a 5-4-1 season, a 6-3 season, another 6-3 season.

All the glorious winning had only made Dr. Denny and others around the Capstone want more; they became impatient through these comparatively ordinary years. The second-guessing, as it would be called now, didn't go over well with Wade.

"He didn't like criticism too much," Winslett said years later. "He had been criticized quite a bit from the 1927, 1928, and 1929 teams."

In the spring of 1930, a curious thing happened: Wade announced he would resign after the next football season to become coach and athletic director at Duke. He offered no explanation other than the end of the 1930 season also would represent the end of his five-year contract.

Dr. Denny had no comment, either, except to say, "It is for Mr. Wade to

Denny Stadium opened in 1929.

speak of his new contract and the personal reasons he has for accepting it."

Even before the 1930 season began, Denny had chosen a new coach—Frank Thomas, albeit with Wade's recommendation. Against this strange backdrop, the 1930 season began. And, against all reason, it ended with a 10-0 record, a 24–0 thumping of Washington State in the Rose Bowl, and a third national title in Wade's eighth and last season at Alabama.

When the Tide played Georgia at Birmingham's Legion Field in the last game before the Rose Bowl, fans knew they were getting a last look at their coach.

"Wade, Wade, Wade!" they chanted.

"Athletics as a whole are on a better plane than ever before at the Capstone," Wade had said just before the historic season began.

He couldn't have been more right.

PASSING THE BATON

When Wade's last team made the long trip to California for yet another Rose Bowl, it carried the coach-in-waiting, too.

"Coach Thomas was on that train with the team, but he never came up front and he never mingled with the team," Fred Sington said. "He stayed in the background very modestly."

The football program didn't skip a beat when Wade handed off to Thomas after the 1930 season.

His first season, in 1931, began with three wins. Then came a 25–0 loss to Tennessee. Thomas, who most recently had been backfield coach at Georgia and thus probably had heard the Crimson masses chanting Wade's name at Legion Field, felt the need to lend a little perspective.

"I am building for the future," Thomas said.

What else could he say? Wade had left behind a third national title as a parting gift and a lot of the players who made it happen were gone.

Furthermore, Denny earlier had made plain his views on the value of a coach. He told Thomas upon accepting the Alabama job that success in football was "ninety percent material" and "ten percent coaching" and that Thomas would be provided with all the material he needed.

"You will be held to strict accounting for delivering the remaining ten percent," Denny said, and in that moment Thomas perhaps better understood why Wade had left.

As for Thomas, his whole life had been building toward his future career as coach at Alabama. He was the son of Welsh immigrants; his father was an iron worker. The family never had much money and young Frank went to Notre Dame to play football for Knute Rockne and to make a better life.

Rockne loved him for his field presence, remarking after one Irish win: "That kid knows football. He's quick to spot a weakness. He's a fine field general." Rockne also predicted, accurately, that Thomas one day would make a fine coach.

Sadly, in Thomas's first year at the Capstone, Rockne died in a plane crash. That first season Thomas abandoned Wade's single-wing offense and installed the Notre Dame box.

"With the Notre Dame box, he was a master of detail," says Don Salls, a fullback for Thomas, 1940–42. "He would tell you how to spin on the ball of your foot, and how you would place this step and that step, and hand the ball off this way. He treated every position like that, with specific detail."

Thomas played for legendary Notre Dame coach Knute Rockne, who accurately predicted that Thomas would make a fine coach someday.

THE COACH'S COACH

The legacy of Frank Thomas is not limited to Rose Bowl trips and national championships. That's just where it starts. The legacy ends with every accomplishment by Paul W. Bryant, who played for Thomas, coached for Thomas, and who became his dear friend.

"My father and Paul Bryant were as close as any two men. Even while my father was still coaching and Bryant was at Maryland, Bryant would call my father every week," Frank Jr. said. "They would talk for hours."

When Thomas's poor health forced him to resign after the 1946 season, he wanted Alabama to make a play for Bryant, who had just finished his first season at Kentucky.

"My father fought hard to get Bryant back," Frank Jr. said. "He considered him the best coach in the United States at the time. He tried desperately to get the athletic committee membership to select Bryant."

It would be twelve more years—and two more coaches—before Bryant returned to Alabama. Hootie Ingram, who had grown up around Thomas, and who had played for Alabama in the Red Drew Era, noticed that Bryant said and did things that seemed very familiar.

"I was coaching at a local high school in '58, and I'd hear Bryant say things, or read in the paper things he said, that I'd heard when I was in junior high from Coach Thomas," says Ingram. "I don't think people realize how much Coach Bryant received from his opportunity to play under Coach Thomas."

After Thomas died in 1954, Frank Jr. was going through his father's things when he came across an old playbook.

"I was looking at all his old notes as to what he thought made for a successful team, besides teaching techniques," Frank Jr. said. "Things like, 'let everybody play; it's good for morale.' I took that book with all of these notes to Bryant.

"He was joyous."

Jimmy Nelson (50) and Holt Rast (34) were two of Thomas' fine players, but another—Paul W. Bryant—applied what he had learned from Thomas, added to it, and became the best coach in Alabama's history.

He also was a gifted motivator, when the spirit moved him.

"He was a very intense person," recalls Hootie Ingram who, although he never played for Thomas, grew up around the Thomas family and spent a lot of time with the coach in retirement, when Ingram was an Alabama player. "He may have been as masterful at knowing what kids feel and what they're thinking as any coach around—even Coach Bryant."

Clem Gryska, who played for Thomas from 1946 to 1947 and later was an assistant under Bryant, says Thomas was like Bryant in that "He kept a distance; that was his personality."

Even his son, Frank, Jr., would say years later, "I never really felt that close to him, because it was very infrequent that we shared time together."

Thomas made time for various hobbies, however. In 1939, he won the state amateur golf championship. He went hunting and fishing.

When it came to recruiting, time was never a factor. He did whatever it took. He also was involved in various civic causes. In 1943, when Alabama and most other schools abandoned their football programs as would-be players went off to war, Thomas headed war bond drives.

Halfback Harry Gilmer, who played for Thomas from 1944 to 1946, and was one of his "War Babies," remembers the coach having a sixth sense about his players.

"He knew what I was thinking before I opened my mouth," says Gilmer, who now lives near St. Louis and is retired from coaching and scouting in the NFL. "He knew what all of us were thinking."

For example, Gilmer says Thomas once called him into his office to tell him, "I don't want to hear of anybody [sneaking] into 'Bama theater" without paying."

Says Gilmer: "Maybe it had been talked about, but it never happened. He stopped it before it took place."

Rockne's influence came to the fore when Thomas would give a pep talk.

"He had that ability to fire ya up before a game," Gilmer says. "Hugh Morrow [a quarterback on the team] and I

Halfback Harry Gilmer remembers Thomas as a gifted motivator.

would sit back and say, 'I don't care what he says today, we're not gonna let him get us excited.'

"And then he'd slap his hands together at the end of his talk, say, 'Let's go,' and we would jump to our feet and be the first ones out the door."

Like Bryant would many years later, Thomas won his first national championship in his fourth season. Alabama went 10-0 in 1934 and kept alive its undefeated streak in the Rose Bowl—3-0-1—with a 29–13 win over Stanford.

"We didn't want to be the team to spoil this record," said team captain Bill Lee.

Thomas's teams would keep right on winning and, in 1941, would claim another national championship with a 9-2 record and 29–21 Cotton Bowl victory over Texas A & M. Alabama was even better in 1945, going 10-0 and running over Southern Cal, 34–14, in the Rose Bowl.

The national championship eluded that Thomas team, but he delivered a championship-caliber pep talk right before kickoff.

"You've got to block, block, tackle!" Thomas yelled, something he rarely did.

"And then he walked over and started beating on, of all people, Vaughn Mancha," Gryska says, referring to the All-American center. "He was beating on his shoulders, screaming and hollering. We'd never seen him do that before. Remember, he was a distinguished guy."

That resounding Rose Bowl victory, when Thomas even put in a player with a broken leg near the end just so the young fellow could say he played in the Rose Bowl, would be the last big moment for Coach Tommy.

In 1946, his blood pressure high and his health laid low, Thomas coached sitting down from a homemade cart. Because his voice was so weak, he had to use a loudspeaker to be heard.

LEFT
In the 1941 national championship season, Alabama's largest victory was the 61–0 thumping it gave Howard University.

RIGHT
A 24–7 victory on November 30, 1946, marked the end of the Frank Thomas era.

By the time he resigned, after the '46 season, he had been heard plenty: a 115-24-7 record, two national championships, and four SEC titles. More important, he had taken the handoff from Wade and run on ahead, taking Alabama football with him.

"Anytime Alabama comes up, football is apt to be in the next sentence," says Gilmer, the halfback with the nifty jump pass.

"And if you mention football to me, it's Frank Thomas."

LOSING GROUND

If Frank Thomas had succeeded in following the legend that was Wallace Wade, then Harold "Red" Drew now had the challenge of following two coaching legends.

Drew had been an assistant to Thomas for most of his tenure, but left after the 1945 season to become head coach at Ole Miss. It perhaps took a bit of nerve to return to Alabama, but Drew had served his country in World War II by jumping out of blimps and into the Caribbean Sea as a naval paratrooper.

"Coach Thomas got sick and they asked Daddy to come back," says Bobby Drew, Coach Drew's son. "He was a good football coach—his players all loved him—but his only problem was he didn't handle the running of the athletic department, in my opinion."

There's no doubting how players felt about Drew. Vaughn Mancha, the great Alabama center, once said: "He was the kind of person I'd like my boy to play for."

Gilmer, who played one season under Drew after three for Thomas, went one better. He named his son after both his coaches: Thomas Drew Gilmer.

Drew compiled a 45-28-7 record from 1947 through 1954—Alabama had remained a winner in that sense—but every glory had been of the four quarters variety, not over an entire season.

When the Crimson Tide hammered Auburn 55–0 in Birmingham at the end of the 1948 season, in the first meeting between the rivals in forty-one years, it was a huge win and Drew was giddy in the aftermath, saying, "Boy, were we hot!"

In 1952 he probably had his best team, a 10-2 squad that put a 61–6 Orange Bowl crush on Syracuse.

"Finally, Coach Drew, trying to hold the score down, put the second and third offensive team on defense, and the second and third defensive team on offense," said Harry Lee, a guard and linebacker. "We were just making stuff up in the huddle. We just kept on scoring."

Unfortunately, there were not enough days like this. When Drew's 1951 team went 5-6, it was the first losing season at the Capstone since 1903.

Lineman Jim Davis played on that '51 team.

Coach Red Drew coached eight seasons at Alabama, his finest being the 1952 season which ended with 10 wins and a 61–6 win over Syracuse in the Orange Bowl.

"He was a good fella, nothing really wrong with him as a man," Davis says of Drew. "He was sort of a scatterbrain."

One of Drew's assistants was Hank Crisp, who had been assistant under Scott, Wade, and Thomas, and who had joined Drew's staff in 1950. Crisp was, by this time, a legendary Alabama coach in his own right, even though he had never been head coach.

However, the line between assistant coach and head coach apparently blurred come Saturday.

"Through the week, Monday through Friday, Drew was a great teacher," Davis says. "Sometimes he'd get lost on Saturday. Coach Crisp would take over for him."

Although the '52 season had been Drew's best, pressure already was mounting on Drew; he hadn't measured up to Wade and Thomas.

"They wanted to get rid of him before the '53 season started," Lee says. "I don't know why, because we'd had that good '52 season. But for whatever reason, a lot of alumni didn't want him in there. So, we signed a petition to keep him. Then the next year, '54, wasn't too good and they didn't keep him after that."

Technically, Drew resigned. He even stayed on the athletic staff as coach of another sport.

"They said my football teams were too slow, so they made me track coach," he quipped.

In his place, Alabama hired J. B. "Ears" Whitworth. He had played for both Wade and Thomas and had been an assistant at Alabama, Georgia, and LSU before becoming head coach at Oklahoma A & M. Whitworth's tenure lasted but three years. His teams went 4-24-2, his first team was 0-10, and he was 0-3 against Auburn as Alabama scored three points and gave up 100.

"He was an assistant coach who probably never should have been a head coach," says Baxter Booth, who played three years under Whitworth and one under Bear Bryant.

In fairness to Whitworth, he entered at an incredibly difficult time and under complicated circumstances. Because Drew had not picked up where Thomas left off, there was a growing unrest around the program.

More challenging, Hank Crisp remained as athletic director and assistant coach. He kept some of Drew's staff and limited Whitworth's hires.

"So, we had a mixed staff and I don't think they were ever in sync," says Dave Sington, a tackle on those teams.

"Coach Crisp was his assistant on the field, but off the field he was his boss," adds Booth. "They had conflicts in front of the players."

There was seldom much conflict on game days. The other team usually dominated. Not only did the 1955 team go 0-10, it was outscored 256–48. Only once in the Whitworth years did Alabama score more than 14 points in a game, and that was in Whitworth's next-to-last game, a meaningless 29–2 win over Mississipi Southern before the '57 season ended with a 40–0 humiliation at the hands of Auburn.

But it was no wonder, given the slipshod practices the team was having.

"He was not organized," Booth remembers. "We'd go out at three o'clock, not come in until seven or eight. We'd go to scrimmage and he'd have twenty-two scrimmaging and seventy watching. It was unbelievable. He and Coach Crisp would be fussing and arguing.

"It got to be miserable."

One wonders if it might have been just a little bit less miserable in 1955 had Whitworth made better use of his players, especially senior quarterback Bart Starr

Coach J. B. "Ears" Whitworth won only four games from 1955 to 1957.

In 1955, when 'Bama was 0–10, Whitworth mostly kept future Pro Football Hall-of-Fame quarterback and senior Bart Starr (10) on the bench.

"He had some pretty good players," Booth says. "Bart Starr, he put him on the bench."

Whitworth's three-year contract bought him exactly that—three years. Meanwhile, as the school waited on Whitworth's time to expire, the competition gained ground.

ONE TOUGH HOMBRE

HUSTLING HANK CRISP MAKES GOOD AT UNIVERSITY ON COACHING STAFF

That was a newspaper headline in 1922. It was meant only to describe Crisp as an important addition to head Coach Xen Scott's team. The story lauded Crisp for his in-the-trenches coaching style, for not just telling the lads how it should be done, but showing them by getting down in the dirt and scrimmaging with them.

What no one could have known then was that the headline would remain true for decades.

Hustling Hank Crisp arguably made a larger impact on Alabama football than any assistant coach in the program's history. After working for Scott, Crisp would coach under Wallace Wade, Frank Thomas, Red Drew, and J. B. "Ears" Whitworth, and serve as a sounding board for Bear Bryant.

Admittedly, there were conflicts in the 1950s when Crisp also was athletic director. It was not uncommon for Crisp and Whitworth to quarrel in front of the team. Crisp, however, was a perfect fit under Thomas, who preferred not to raise his voice. Bryant played under Thomas and Crisp, and it was evident that Bryant drew inspiration from both men. Thomas was "a brain when it came to football," said Young Boozer, a halfback and teammate of Bryant, and Crisp was "a doer."

As a boy, Crisp had lost his right hand in a cotton gin accident, which only served to make him tougher. Players feared a special invitation for one-on-one time with Crisp, particularly when he'd say, "I've got a few little problems I'd like to work out with you."

Said Boozer: "He had a leather kit that went over that nub and it had real sharp stitching around it. He was so quick with that nub. He could stick you every place you moved——stomach, chest, even in your face. That was the worst thing that could happen to you, for him to invite you out to practice."

Twenty years later, Crisp was no less the intimidator.

"Toughest hombre I've ever known in my life," says Tommy Lewis, an Alabama player in the 1950s. "He put some scars in my lip trying to teach me to be a linebacker."

Yet Crisp was beloved by his players. Beneath the raw exterior, he was a soft touch. In fact, he was generous to the point of his own detriment, once giving a player the new shoes off his own feet, and often handing out small sums of money he really couldn't afford to give away.

Doing whatever needed to be done was his habit. When he coached under Drew, Crisp often took over games on Saturdays. Before the 1952 game with defending national champion Maryland, Crisp did what Drew wouldn't or couldn't do.

"We went through our warmups, came in, and Coach Drew hadn't said anything," recalls Harry Lee. "The officials came by, knocked on the door and said it was time to got out, we all got up and walked to the door, and still Coach Drew had not said a word.

"So we just stopped. Something was missing. Coach Hank Crisp was standing pretty close so Bobby Wilson, who was the captain of the team, turned around and said, 'Coach, will you say something?'

"He always had that Pall Mall cigarette hanging from his mouth, and he only had that one hand and he had to blow the ashes off," Lee says. "Anyway, he says, 'I don't know why you want me to say anything, but the only thing I can tell you is you can beat those [SOBs] if you want to.'

"We about tore the door down getting out," Lee says, "and then we beat them pretty well [27—7]."

3

GRIDIRON
HEROES

NO matter how good the coaching is—and Wallace Wade and Frank Thomas were both good enough to be enshrined in the College Football Hall of Fame—it still takes players to build a program's reputation.

In the early days, newspapers popularized the reputation of the team and the reputations of the star players. The newspaper writer's word was gospel. What happened on the field was important, but no more so than what was printed in the paper afterward.

For instance, in 1905 when Albert Einstein proposed the theory of relativity, the *Crimson White* engaged in some relativity of its own: It lauded a 6–4 Alabama team for bringing "honor" to the school and gushed in a way that the press didn't even during the most glorious days under Bear Bryant.

"What is probably the best team that ever battled for the Crimson and White has doffed its

▲PREVIOUS PAGE
Holt Rast (45) was an
All-American end on
the 1941 national
championship team.

gridiron armor," the paper said after the 1905 season, "and the heroes of the pigskin have stepped down from their lofty pedestals to become again ordinary mortals."

And so it went year after year and so-called star after star. The college football hero was raised up and set apart.

Henry Burks, captain of the 1908 team, was said to have "no superior." Farley Moody, captain of the 1912 team, even received public praise for his role as master of ceremonies at an end-of-season banquet: "[He] handled the team as cleverly on this occasion as ever."

The early football heroes at the Capstone also were perceived to have endured a certain amount of self-sacrifice.

"Now that the hardships of the training season are at an end, the moleskin warriors are at their leisure," proclaimed the *Crimson White,* "and may openly indulge their fancies. Soft drinks, smokes and other items detrimental to training are no longer tabooed and the football hero has been forced to descend from his pedestal."

Yes, there was a lot of getting up and down from the pedestal in the old days—it took the place of running hills or stairs.

The *Corolla,* the school yearbook, was equally effusive about the boys of the gridiron and said of Tram Sessions, a center on the 1919 team, "Next to the circus, [he's] the biggest drawing card in Birmingham."

►RIGHT
In 1915, tackle W. T.
"Bully" VandeGraaff,
became Alabama's
first All-American. He
followed his brothers
Adrian and Hargrove
to the Capstone and
the gridiron.

ALWAYS ALABAMA

40

Just a few years earlier in Alabama's history, the family VandeGraaff had been a three-ring football act. In 1912, Adrian and Hargrove VandeGraaff had shared the same backfield with Captain Farley Moody. They were good players, but Brother Bully was better and, in 1915, became the school's first All-American.

When Alabama beat archrival Sewanee 23–10 in Birmingham during the 1915 season, it was its first victory over Sewanee in eighteen years. Bully scored 17 of the team's points and dominated the day. Not only did he return a punt 78 yards, but in the fourth quarter he tipped a pass in the air, caught the ball, and ran 65 yards for a touchdown. He also kicked three field goals.

Everyone, including Steely Dan, knows they call Alabama the Crimson Tide. But do you know why they're the Crimson Tide? Or why Alabama has an elephant for a mascot?

Or why the University of Alabama campus is commonly referred to as the Capstone? Or why the school band is the Million Dollar Band? Or why that big tower on campus is Denny Chimes?

Here are the stories behind the names:

Crimson Tide: In very early accounts, the football team was sometimes referred to as simply the Varsity. Around 1902, a sportswriter gave the football team the nickname the "Thin Red Line." His inspiration might well have come from a Rudyard Kipling poem about a British soldier that included the phrase "thin red line." In any case, the 1907 Alabama-Auburn game, supposedly played in a sea of reddish mud in Birmingham, moved another scribe to call that hard-charging Alabama squad the "Crimson Tide." The rest, as they say, is history.

The Elephant: In 1930, *Atlanta Journal* sportswriter Everett Strupper watched as Alabama crushed Mississippi, 64–0. Afterward, he gave an account that included this passage:

"The earth started to tremble, there was a distant rumble that continued to grow. Some excited fan in the stands bellowed, 'Hold your horses, the elephants are coming,' and out stamped this Alabama varsity.

"It was the first time that I had seen it and the size of the entire eleven nearly knocked me cold, men that I had seen play last year looking like they had nearly doubled in size."

After that, many writers of the day began referring to Alabama's linemen as "Red Elephants" because of the Crimson jerseys.

The Capstone: During an address on education, school President Dr. George H. Denny, who also fostered the growth in athletics starting with his arrival in 1912, called the university "the capstone of public education in the state of Alabama." According to the *Tuscaloosa News*, "It took little time for the word 'capstone' to earn a capital letter. Before long, our university became 'The Capstone.' "

Denny Chimes: The 115 foot tower is not only a campus landmark, but a tribute to Dr. Denny's passion for athletics. On A Day each spring, the previous season's football captains leave their hand and cleat prints at Denny Chimes in the Walk of Fame.

The Million Dollar Band: Again, a sportswriter gets credit for the name. As the story goes, Alabama was playing Georgia Tech in Atlanta and getting pounded severely. Alabama lost the 1928 game there, 33–13, so that's the likely time period. According to the Alabama media guide for the 1946 Rose Bowl, the writer is alleged to have written: "Although the Crimson Tide looked like two cents, Alabama's band looked like a million dollars."

"Bully is a natural star," proclaimed one sportswriter who covered the game.

Even after a 21–7 loss to Georgia Tech that season, Bully seemed to be the bigger story and owner of the larger reputation. "All hail VandeGraaff!" an Atlanta writer swooned. "Never has one man fought so hard to stave off defeat as this big bulwark of the Alabama defense."

It was the way of the day. There were no ESPN talking heads to set the agenda, no bright television lights to turn up the star power with a flip of a switch. There were only the men who covered the games and wrote what they saw, sometimes coloring their accounts with what they wanted to see or to simply make their stories better.

What little personal information there was to be gleaned about the players came from the newspapers, too. For instance, if fans wondered why center Tubby Barnett stopped playing during the 1915 season, the *Crimson White* was there to report that he had been a "victim of the malaria germs."

In 1920, when Alabama was christening Denny Field, named for school president Dr. George H. "Mike" Denny, the stars of the day included fullback Riggs Stephenson and halfback E. B. "Mully" Lenoir, who was from Marlin, Texas. When word got out that Lenoir was engaged to a girl attending the university, it was what today's editors would call a talking point.

Thus, one newspaper ran a picture of Mully in his football uniform under this headline: TEXAS JACK RABBIT TO TAKE PLUNGE INTO SEA OF MATRIMONY.

Presumably, Mully was to dive from his lofty pedestal.

THE STARS FALL ON ALABAMA

Alabama wouldn't have another All-American until quarterback Pooley Hubert in 1925. However, the 1922 team of Coach Xen Scott made heroes of all Alabama players—including Hubert, who came to the Capstone as a twenty-year-old freshman.

Hubert already had served in the Navy during World War I and had a brief, and apparently unhappy, stint at Princeton, then one of the top football schools in the country. Now, he would take part in Alabama's ascension into the college football elite, which began in earnest on November 4, 1922, at Franklin Field in Philadelphia. That was the day that Alabama beat Penn, 9–7, and it was more than a mere upset.

"A continent gasped," wrote the ever-breathless *Crimson White*.

Surely, Alabama fans were all aflutter. Shorty Propst was a hero for covering Hubert's fumble in Penn's end zone. So was Bull Wesley for kicking a field goal for the game's first score.

There was plenty of praise to go

A.T.S. "Pooley"
Hubert's play in the
1926 Rose Bowl had
the press raving about
him, the *Los Angeles
Times* saying he was
"a wow carrying the
ball."

around. Left end Al Clemens was said to have played the "greatest game of his career" after making many tackles of Penn players for lost yardage. Big Ben Compton "smeared Penn plays with disconcerting consistency." And Captain Shorty Cooper "bade his boys be of good cheer all the way."

Hubert would gain his greatest fame in 1925 when Alabama won its first national championship in the January 1, 1926, Rose Bowl, 20–19, over Washington.

"In addition to being a wow at carrying the ball," the *Los Angeles Times* wrote, "Hubert is a remarkable team general."

He had some pretty remarkable teammates, too. Among them: quarterback Grant Gillis and halfback Johnny

Mack Brown, "the gent with the sweet, elusive feet," the *L.A. Times* said.

Brown had been a second-team All-American in 1925, but his star was only

Johnny Mack Brown followed his Alabama football days with a career in Hollywood as a western star. His roles included Billy the Kid.

Two-time All-American
Fred Sington was said
to be the inspiration
for Rudy Vallee's song,
"Football Freddie."

beginning to rise. After his college football career was over, he took a Hollywood screen test and impressed MGM so much that the company signed him to a multiyear contract. He became a leading man of westerns and, when later Alabama teams came to California for Rose Bowls, Brown enjoyed playing Hollywood tour guide and providing scouting reports on opponents.

"Johnny Mack Brown had a big ranch out there," recalls Vaughn Mancha, an All-American center on the 1945 team, and later athletic director at Florida State. "He took us out to his place and we rode some horses."

As good as Alabama was in those days, it was not all championships and fun in the sun.

During the 1928 season, the Crimson Tide traveled to Madison to play the University of Wisconsin. While the home team won the game, 15–0, the visitors from the South managed a more personal victory.

As tackle Fred Sington recalled it, the day before the game, Alabama had watched Wisconsin practice and couldn't help but notice their foes had extra equipment: heavy jerseys, gloves, woolen stockings, and mufflers. Coach Wallace Wade sent a team manager into town to try and find the same for 'Bama's boys, but to no avail.

"So, Coach Wade did the best he could," Sington said. "He gave us a hot talk, which was pretty good, and we

went out on the field. Now, you have to get the picture of the Alabama team. We had those lightweight cotton jerseys, no stockings, no gloves, standing up there shivering.

"Finally, they blew the whistle and we kicked off and there was just a big pileup. Twenty-two guys. When they unpiled, the Alabama players were wearing the gloves."

A two-time All-American—in 1929 and 1930—Sington achieved even greater fame thanks to a song: "Football Freddie," supposedly written about him by Rudy Vallee.

Unfortunately for Sington, he heard the lyrics—"Football Freddie, rugged and tan; Football Freddie, collegiate man"—sung not by Rudy Vallee, but by teammate Frank Howard.

"Frank liked to get down beside me and at guard and sing that in my ear while I was trying to concentrate," Sington said. "And he couldn't sing, either."

A few years earlier, Hoyt "Wu" Winslett, who would become an All-American end in 1926, had come to Alabama with visions of being a rugged and tan collegiate man, surrounded by bathing beauties.

Recalling his recruiting trip, Winslett said, "[They] drove me by the country club, where all the pretty girls were out by the swimming pool. They indicated that, 'If you come over here, Winslett, all of this will be part of your life.' "

They just didn't say *when* it would be a part of his life.

"I didn't see the country club anymore," he said, "until I bought a membership in it when I moved back to Tuscaloosa."

THE HUMBLE BEGINNINGS OF THE LEGENDARY BEAR

Many of the young men who came to play football at the University of Alabama grew up in Alabama, rural and poor. Paul W. Bryant wasn't any different, except that he grew up in rural Arkansas instead of rural Alabama.

Home was Moro Bottom, where Bryant was born on September 11, 1913. He himself once said the place was "no more than what it sounds, a little piece of bottom land on the Moro Creek about seven miles south of Fordyce."

As a youth, Bryant would play in the first football game he ever saw, and had no reason to believe he would ever play football for the University of Alabama, or even travel much beyond Fordyce.

Life was day to day and hand to mouth.

"It was a burden on everybody back in that time to make a living," says Ray Bryant, a grandnephew of Paul Bryant, and still a resident of Fordyce.

Young Paul knew this too well. The eleventh of twelve children, he accompanied his mother, Ida Kilgore, on a mule

A young Paul Bryant (far left in foreground next to his father) was one of twelve children and grew up poor in Moro Bottom, Arkansas.

pulled wagon they rode into Fordyce to sell everything from milk and eggs to turnips and watermelon.

"It was six miles from the house over to Fordyce," Ray Bryant says. "In winter months, when it was real cold, Uncle Paul would heat bricks in the fireplace fire and they'd put them in the bed of the wagon to keep their feet warm."

Colder still were the taunts from those who had more.

"They had to ride by the high school," Ray says. "And that's where a lot of kids—they didn't mean anything by it—did make fun. But I think one of the things that hurt him the most was not that they made fun of him, but that they also made fun of his mama."

Truth is, little was expected of Paul W. Bryant. His father was a sickly man, the family was poor, and, years later, when Bryant left home to play football at Alabama, "nobody in Fordyce thought I'd stick it out," he once said.

An end for Coach Frank Thomas from 1933 to 1935, Bryant was a legitimately good player. However, his opposite, Don Hutson, was a great player.

Hutson, along with back Millard "Dixie" Howell and tackle Bill Lee, was an All-American in the 1934 national championship season. Bryant was commonly known as "the other end."

Bryant, however, almost left school before earning that distinction.

According to Young Boozer, a half-back during that time, Bryant often threatened to quit, telling assistant coach Hank Crisp, "I'm going back to Fordyce, Arkansas."

Crisp was the very man who had brought Bryant to Alabama. Bryant was Crisp's consolation prize after the coach failed to recruit twin brothers from Fordyce who chose the Arkansas Razorbacks over the Crimson Tide.

Finally, Boozer said, "Coach Hank had all of that [talk] he wanted. So one day, when [Bryant] went in, Coach Hank said, 'I'm so damn tired of hearing this. Go to the store room, get your trunk, and get all your stuff.' "

It scared Bryant into staying, Boozer said. So might have a certain telegram. Bryant's father had recently died and Bryant knew his mother was having a hard time. As he said years later, "If I was looking for an excuse [to quit], I had one."

Bryant wrote his cousin, Collins Kilgore, and told him of his plans to come home.

Cousin Collins wired Bryant back: "Go ahead and quit, just like everybody predicted you would."

Said Bryant: "I wasn't about to quit after that."

In the end, it was perhaps a case of a young man being true to his roots.

"Moro Bottom," Ray Bryant says with pride, "grows some of the best hardwood timber in the world."

BEAR VS. BEAR

When young Paul W. Bryant arrived at the University of Alabama to play football, he already carried the nickname that would become famous as he coached his alma mater to six national championships. And he had gotten his nickname the old-fashioned way: He earned it.

Although the tale has taken more than a few twists and turns over the years, the story has survived the test of time. Bryant offered many details in his autobiography, written with John Underwood more than thirty years ago.

As the story goes, one summer, young Paul and some friends walked in from the country to the town of Fordyce, Arkansas. Paul, then thirteen or fourteen years old, was a large lad and, by his own account, given to "big-dogging" it.

Bryant said he and his friends went to the movie theater in town and that outside the theater was a poster showing off a bear, and a fellow offering a dollar a minute to anyone who would wrestle the bear. The man who was supposed to wrestle the bear, if such person ever existed, never showed. So, with his friends urging him on, and a "good-looking little gal" standing nearby, Bryant agreed to wrestle the bear.

In recalling the circumstances of the day, Bryant almost makes the decision sound reasonable. The movie cost a dime, he said, and he was only getting fifty cents a day for chopping cotton. This was big money even if he only lasted one minute.

The theater, as Bryant described it, was a small room with a big stage. When the bear's owner brought the animal out, Bryant admitted that his friends thought the bear to be the "scrawniest" thing they had ever seen.

"To me," Bryant said, "it looked thirty feet tall."

What did or did not happen from this point forward is perhaps a little less certain.

"From what I understand, the muzzle came off the bear and the bear might have scratched Uncle Paul or bit him," says Ray Bryant, a grandnephew of Bear Bryant, and still a resident of Fordyce. "Anyway, it drew some blood.

"Uncle Paul got scared and jumped [off the stage]. Some say he almost choked the bear to death, but that's a crock. He was just a kid. Naturally, he got scared when the bear scratched or bit him.

"He went one way and the bear and the owner went another way. He never did get his money."

He did, however, get his nickname. Perhaps the more amazing part of the story is that the nickname stuck. Or as one of Bryant's great quarterbacks, Joe Namath, once asked: How many men could even carry the nickname Bear?

Chuck Allen, a tackle on the first Alabama team Bryant coached in 1958, knows some people still doubt the truth of the bear-wrestling story. He says he and other players had heard the story way back when. They also had lived with the man called Bear day to day, and survived under him, day to day.

"If he says he wrestled a bear," says Allen, "he wrestled a bear."

Paul W. Bryant already was known as "Bear" when he came to play football at Alabama, thanks to his bear-wrestling adventure as a young teenager in Fordyce, Arkansas.

RISE AND FALL

The stock market crash of 1929 had thrown America into the Great Depression.

And throughout much of the 1930s, prairie turned to dust.

The Lindbergh kidnapping was a 24-7 news story long before the term existed, and, across the big pond, over which Amelia Earhart had become the first woman to fly solo, Adolf Hitler and his National Socialist German Workers' Party were on the move.

At the University of Alabama, great players were advancing a great tradition. From 1931 to 1946, Frank Thomas's tenure as coach at the Capstone, seventeen players earned first-team All-American honors. It began with fullback

Johnny Cain, who was twice a first-team All-American (in 1931 and '32). By 1934, when Alabama was headed back to the Rose Bowl, the Crimson Tide for the first time had three All-Americans: Dixie Howell, Don Hutson, and Bill Lee.

Hutson also played baseball and ran track. As legend has it, he once wore his track suit under his baseball uniform when a ballgame and a meet were scheduled at the same time. Between innings, so the story goes, Hutson dashed over to the nearby track and ran a 9.8 100-yard dash.

Bryant's recollections of his fellow end, who was one of the first receivers to make pass catching high art, were a bit more sedate. Hutson, Bryant once said, was so relaxed he could "go to sleep on the bench before the Rose Bowl."

ALWAYS ALABAMA

48

Lee, apparently, was even better at relaxing.

Coach Thomas's son, Frank Jr., years later told the story of the day his dad didn't believe Lee was giving a good effort in practice and sent a team manager to fetch a rocking chair for the star tackle.

"Bill, I know you're tired," Coach Thomas said. "You just go over there and sit down while the rest of us work."

As for Howell and Hutson, they proved a formidable passing combination in the 29–13 Rose Bowl win over Stanford after the '34 season, but Howell had not always been so accurate.

Before the game, Coach Frank Thomas told famed sportswriter Grantland Rice that there was a time when Howell "couldn't hit a barn with a pass. So last spring I told him the difference it would make if only he would add passing to his equipment. That was all I had to say. He went out and learned it."

A decade later, after the 1944 season, Grantland Rice was quite impressed with halfback Harry Gilmer's performance in a 29–26 Sugar Bowl loss to Duke. Rice wrote that Gilmer was "better than Baugh," referring to the Washington Redskins' star quarterback Sammy Baugh.

"Grantland Rice kind of went overboard," says Gilmer, who went on to coach and scout in the NFL. "I'm sure there were many times he wished he wouldn't have said that."

Thomas himself tended to go overboard about the players on that team. He couldn't help it. Because of World War II, there had been no team in 1943. He called the players on his 1944 team his "War Babies," and they were young, feisty, overachievers.

Gilmer, a 157-pound tailback from Birmingham's Woodlawn High School, was the embodiment of the team. He showed his skill in his first game, returning a kickoff 95 yards for a touchdown against LSU.

It was his jump passing that made him famous. And, because Gilmer played as a freshman, he had four years to amass numbers that still have him among Alabama's career leaders in several categories, including touchdown passes (29).

"I had an advantage," Gilmer says. "I walk in as a freshman right before the war ends, and all the boys hadn't come back out of the service yet. I had a chance to be a starting player right off the bat."

He was a very good starting player and his jump passes had boys all over the South running and jumping in fields, trying to be Harry Gilmer.

"I was in high school when Harry Gilmer was playing," says Tommy Lewis, who lettered from 1951 to 1953 for the Crimson Tide. "He'd take that direct snap from center and run to his

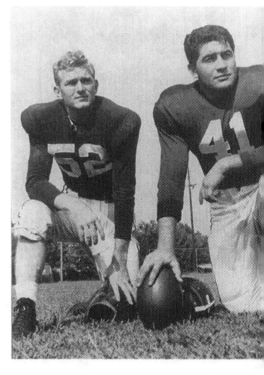

right and then jump a mile high and throw the ball forever.

"I worked at a camp one summer and Gilmer was the drawing card. I'd say, 'Throw me a Harry Gilmer pass,' and I'd go out and cut left, cut right, and he'd go over there and jump and *whoooosh*, sting that ball in there."

Says Gilmer: "It was a natural thing for me to get my hips turned around, so I could throw overhand same as if I was standing on the ground. The other thing was I didn't have to stop to throw it. I played as a single-wing tailback. I was a running back as much as a passer. Now, I'm quick to say I wasn't sure the coach liked it, but he wouldn't mess with it because it seemed to work."

THE GOOD OLD DAYS (MOSTLY)

If it is not quite right to say they were always the "good old days," it is fair to say that there was much good in them.

Don Salls played fullback on offense from 1940 to 1942, but also played on the other side of the ball. In his view, this was the best of both worlds.

"It was great to be on defense," Salls says, "because you wanted to save what you made on offense. I loved to play defense and I was only 169 pounds soaking wet. I loved tackling. I loved to hit."

Vaughn Mancha, an All-American in 1945, perhaps loved the contact even more.

"I was a mean SOB," says Mancha, who as a child lost an eye while playing with a bow and arrow. "And I could outrun anybody."

Says Gilmer: "Mancha was our finest player—a center and linebacker, a leader and an entertainer."

Other players were just happy to be a part of it. Clem Gryska was recruited out of Ohio by Frank Thomas despite the fact that as a boy Gryska had lost most of his right hand in a meat grinder.

"I wasn't that good of a football player," says Gryska, who was a long-time assistant under Bear Bryant. "But I was a warm body during World War II."

The highlight of the 1950s was Alabama's 61–6 thrashing of Syracuse in the Orange Bowl after the 1952 season.

Jim Davis was an Alabama lineman from 1951 to 1953.

"Bobby Marlow was an All-American running back; he was tough," recalls Davis, whose son-in-law, Hoss Johnson, played offensive line in the 1980s. "Herb Hannah—he was the father of [John, Charles, and David Hannah], was a tremendous football player. Tommy Lewis was a good runner and Bud Willis, my roommate, was a good end.

"But I wasn't that outstanding of a player. I just gave them what I had."

It's what they all did, from the first Alabama football team in 1892 right on through the last, and sad, excuse for a team in 1957 under Coach J. B. "Ears" Whitworth, the last year before Bryant's return to Alabama.

Naturally, some of these young men had more to give than others. And some were fortunate enough to hear how much their gridiron glory meant even to people that they probably had not thought about in years. Such was the power of Alabama football and the men who played it.

Holt Rast, for example, was in 1941 an All-American end for Alabama. Teachers from Barrett School in Birmingham did not wait for that honor to let Rast know how they felt about his exploits on the football field.

In a letter dated November 20, 1939, they wrote:

ONE OF A KIND

Charley Compton.

Just say his name to teammates Harry Gilmer and Clem Gryska and the stories begin to flow. Start with the 1947 game against Georgia at Athens. Compton comes off the field and onto the sideline yelling for a manager to get him a pair of pliers.

"We thought he had a bad cleat," recalls Gryska. "Back then we had those screw-on cleats. I wasn't too far from him, and I kept watching. He knelt down and pulled that tooth out, spit a bunch of blood, walked over to the coach, and said he was ready to go."

The best part about that story: Compton was only armed with pliers. Gilmer and Gryska also have double-barreled stories, if you will, about tackle Charley Compton.

"He used to get on the top of the building we lived in, on the roof, and strip down to his shorts and he would sunbathe," says Gilmer, the team's star halfback. "Well, when we found him doing that it was kind of funny to walk by and pick up a piece of gravel and throw it up on the roof and disturb him a little bit.

"What he did, he didn't say anything to anybody, but he went down to his room and got his gun out of his closet and took it back up there with him. Next time anybody threw a rock up there, he walked over to the edge, leveled the gun out, and fired.

"He didn't really shoot at anybody, he was just teaching them a lesson," Gilmer says. "And that was Charley. The way he thought, 'If you mess with me, you're gonna have to pay a price.' "

Gryska remembers good old Charley living in a corner of the dormitory and cherishing his study time.

"We'd start out talking or something, and the hallway was long, and noise would kind of echo down," Gryska says. "So he'd stick his head out and say, 'Better get quiet down there.'

"A day or two later we started up again, same thing, and he came out and he had a shotgun. He aimed that thing out and he shot. Didn't get any of us, but he was serious. He gave us a warning, and then he shot that thing.

"Next time we came in the [dormitory], we got real quiet."

Charley Compton also was afraid to fly. This presented a problem near the end of the 1946 season, when the football team was to take its first plane trip to play at Boston College. Compton told Coach Frank Thomas that he didn't fly. He said he would need to take the train. Thomas, Gilmer recalls, didn't understand this because Compton was a decorated veteran of World War II.

As Gilmer remembers it: "Coach Thomas says, 'As brave a man as you are, if we were to get a parachute and put in on the plane with you—in case the plane runs into any trouble—we could give you that parachute and you'd be brave enough to jump out and save your life.'

"Well," Gilmer says, "Charley thought about that and he said, 'No, I'm not gonna do that because I know good and well as soon as that plane got in trouble, you'd come to me and say, 'Charley, give that parachute to Harry.' "

But the faith that Compton didn't have in his coach or airplanes, he apparently did have elsewhere.

"He ended up becoming a minister," says Gryska.

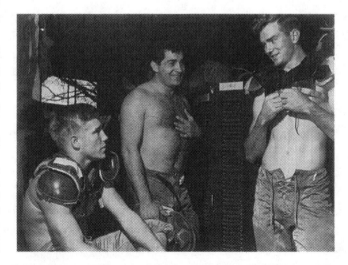

Every team needs a character. Alabama had one in Charley Compton, a teammate of, from left to right, Lowell Tew, Mancha, and Gilmer.

Dear Holt,

We the undersigned, some of your elementary school teachers, want to congratulate you on the fine showing you are making in football. Knowing you as we do, we are not in the least surprised. We are looking forward to your continued success in all of your endeavors and wish for you a very happy and fruitful life.

They, too, just wanted to be a part of it.

4

THE BEAR

JANUARY 26, 2006——twenty-three years ago, to the day, Paul W. Bryant died.

Two men who knew Bryant better than most, worked for him, loved him, and, if possible, love him even more now, are on their way to Birmingham. They are on their way to Elmwood Cemetery, where the great coach is buried.

Jack Rutledge played for Bryant, and was a freshman in 1958 when Bryant arrived from Texas A & M, bringing with him the so-called Junction Boys mindset. Rutledge then worked as a coach on Bryant's staff from 1966 to 1982.

In the 1940s Clem Gryska played for Frank Thomas, who was Bryant's coach when he played at Alabama in the 1930s. Gryska served as an assistant coach to Bryant from 1960 to 1976, and remained part of the athletic department afterward.

All of that was a long time ago. It also seems just like yesterday, which is the double-edged

▲ PREVIOUS PAGE
During his twenty-five
seasons at Alabama,
Bear Bryant was the
National Coach of the
Year three times
(1961, 1971, and
1973). He was SEC
Coach of the Year ten
times, once at
Kentucky and nine
times at Alabama.

ALWAYS ALABAMA

56

sword that forever keeps Bryant's memory alive and sharp, but sometimes cuts—and hurts—those who love him still.

As the men leave the University of Alabama campus in Tuscaloosa—Rutledge at the wheel of his pickup truck—they roll by Druid City Hospital, where Bryant died of a heart attack. But in this moment, Gryska and Rutledge are not hurting, and not really thinking about his death. Rather, they are again marveling at the reaction when Bryant's white hearse passed by on the day of his funeral.

"Doctors, nurses, and patients were standing outside the hospital," Rutledge says, which kicks off other memories: the schoolchildren who lined the streets and held homemade cards for the Coach, all the people—black and white—who waved from porches and lawns, and the mourners who waited on overpasses above Interstate 59 just to pay their respects.

"Every overpass," Gryska says, sounding more proud of that than Bryant's six national championships.

They drive on, and there seem to be three hours of stories packed into what is about a one hour's journey. There's the story about the time in the 1960s when Alabama hit a rough patch, by its standards, and Bryant seriously entertained an offer from the Miami Dolphins. As the story goes, he signed a contract that he needed help getting out of.

The details don't matter so much now, because the story is in the larger, almost mind-boggling, what-ifs. Bryant, at that point, had won only three national championships, if you can put the word *only* before three national championships, 1961, 1964, and 1965.

What if he *had* gone to the pros for a bag of Miami money? The legend of Bear Bryant, as we know it, effectively would have ended at halftime.

Next comes one of those stories about Bryant noticing everything, including the time he looked out a window one day in the late 1970s, and saw his quarterback, Steadman Shealy, playing tennis.

Rutledge, who loves to throw his voice into low gear, down where Bryant sounded like he was driving over gravel with every syllable he spoke, says, "Steadman, we don't play tennis during football season."

And then there's a story about another funeral, that of assistant coach Ken Donahue, who had played at Tennessee and had been a coach at Alabama from 1964 to 1984. This mixed lineage naturally led to a division of mourners: some from Alabama, some from Tennessee.

Gryska happened to be standing near Tennessee coach Phil Fulmer when a man said to Fulmer, "That's a good-looking ring you got on. What is it?"

Fulmer said, "That's a national championship ring."

"From when?" asked the man.

"Fiesta Bowl, 1998," Fulmer said.

Then the man noticed the ring with a red gem stone on Gryska's finger.

"Is that a national championship ring?" the man asked.

"Sure is," Gryska answered.

"What year?" the man said.

"I'll have to check," said Gryska. "I've got seven of them and I don't know which one I wore."

No doubt Coach Bryant would have loved that story. And yes, all these years later, Rutledge in his sixties and Gryska in his late seventies, they still call him Coach Bryant.

On the Alabama campus, of course, *Bryant* is everywhere: the Bryant Museum, the Bryant Conference Center, Bryant Hall, Bryant Drive and, naturally, Bryant-Denny Stadium.

Even in death, he's larger than life—everywhere, that is, but at his grave.

Here, there is a simple marker with the barest of facts about the man they called Bear.

PAUL WILLIAM BRYANT, SR.,
SEPT. 11, 1913
JAN. 26, 1983

That's all.

No mention of his teams' championships. None of his famous quotes engraved onto his tombstone.

His beloved wife, Mary Harmon, is buried next to him. She died the year after his passing. They had two children: a daughter, Mae Martin, and a son, Paul Jr.

"She represented him real well," Gryska says. "Sweet lady, got along with the assistant coaches' wives, never met a stranger. She was never Mary Harmon Bryant, she was just Mary Harmon. It didn't go to her head."

Sometimes, visitors will leave things at Bryant's grave: flowers, of course, but also Alabama caps, A-shaped wreaths,

Bryant and his wife, Mary Harmon, had two children: daughter Mae Martin, and son Paul Jr.

and pictures. On this day, there is only one small framed photograph of the coach—he's wearing his trademark houndstooth hat and jacket—and the glass covering the picture is cracked.

The wind puts a chill in the air and, suddenly, his death is all too real to these men who loved and respected him, and who, just moments ago, were laughing and telling stories.

There is silence now, save the sound of the wind and a few chattering crows in the trees. Each man looks at the grave marker, at the name of the man who changed his life for the better, then each walks away to his own space, his own thoughts.

They're tough old birds in their own right, these two, but this is more than they can take. They sniff a little, clear their throats . . . and then one of them says what just about every man who ever played or coached for Bear Bryant might say:

He was more than a coach, says Rutledge, "He was like a father figure."

CHANGE AGENT

Bear Bryant's influence as the head coach at Alabama would span twenty-five years, from 1958 to 1982. It might have begun even sooner.

When Bryant finished his playing career at Alabama, he coached at Union College in Tennessee, then returned to

Alabama as an assistant to Coach Frank Thomas from 1936 to 1939. Bryant then worked as an assistant for two seasons at Vanderbilt and served in the Navy during World War II, Japan's bombing of Pearl Harbor effectively ending Bryant's intentions to become head coach at Arkansas.

While in the Navy, Bryant coached the football team at the North Carolina Pre-Flight School. After his discharge from the service, Bryant became head coach at Maryland and in 1945 posted a 6-2-1 record. He then left Maryland for Kentucky, and, in 1946, turned in a 7-3 mark his first season.

Bryant's coaching acumen was now plainly evident. Thus, when Thomas stepped down as Alabama's head coach

While serving in the Navy during World War II, Bryant coached a military football team.

after the 1946 season because of poor health, he wanted to bring Bryant in from Kentucky. But Bryant and the Alabama administration couldn't come to terms. Bryant stayed at Kentucky for eight seasons, finally leaving for the Texas A & M job, after he became fed up with basketball coach Adolph Rupp's status as Kentucky's king.

In 1957, Bryant was preparing to take his Aggies to the Gator Bowl when word leaked out that he might come to Alabama. At least one Alabama player already had an idea Bryant might be the school's next coach. Dave Sington was a junior tackle on the J. B. "Ears" Whitworth 1957 team, which was in the midst of its third straight losing season. Sington remembers that, with about four games left, school president Dr. Frank Rose paid the players a visit. "Dr. Rose came down to the locker room and said, 'Just hang in there. We're going to get a real good coach.' "

Sington's father, Fred Sington, was an All-American tackle under Wallace Wade, and played on Alabama's 1930 national championship team. Now, he was on the search committee for the next coach.

"My father wouldn't tell me who," Dave Sington remembers, "but I had an inkling. Of course, it all broke loose because they caught them out in Houston. It was real funny, my father and Dr. Rose were going under false names on the airplane and the stewardess knows them—their real names and their real [mission]."

Bryant's reputation preceded him to Tuscaloosa. Even so, he made quite a first impression.

"The first meeting was in the bottom of the football dorm," says Chuck Allen, who had played two years under Whitworth and would survive two more under Bryant. "The meeting was scheduled for one-fifteen, the first time we ever saw him. We're packed in there, must have been like 120 players in that room. He walked in and he had the biggest pair of alligator shoes on and I thought, 'Wow, that [SOB's] something.'

"At one-fifteen, they closed the door," says Allen. "At one-sixteen, the door opened and one guy came in. And Bryant never looked at him. He didn't know who he was from Adam. He just turned to one of the coaches and said, 'Pack him out.' He could have been an All-American. He could have been anything. But when that door closed, that was it."

It proved to be a moment of foreshadowing. Over the years, and especially in his first few seasons at Alabama, Bryant never hesitated to run off talented players he believed had failed to measure up in some way.

"He always took pride in running somebody off that everybody else thought was indispensable," says Harry Lee, who played at Alabama in the 1950s and is president of the A Club.

If this sometimes looked like madness, and years later even Bryant would admit he chased away too many good players, Bryant also knew it would be foolish to deviate from what had worked for him in the past. Bryant's starting point was always to find out who wanted to play badly enough to suffer for the privilege. As a plan, it was as simple as it was brutal: If a player could survive Bryant's practices, then he'd never be tempted to quit in the fourth quarter of a game.

The coach carried this strategy to a new height, or a new low, depending on one's perspective, during his first season at Texas A & M in 1954. Bryant took his team into the middle of nowhere for a ten-day training camp. As Junction Boys survivor Gene Stallings famously said, "We went out there in two buses and came back in one."

Although there was not an exact replication of this in Tuscaloosa, Bryant's players from the 1958 season believe what they suffered was as bad as the ten-day boot camp that inspired a book and a movie, *The Junction Boys*, if only because it was longer. Stallings, who was a young and feisty assistant coach on Bryant's first Alabama staff, disagrees.

"The thing about Junction is it was basically twenty-four hours a day," says Stallings, "In Tuscaloosa, it was sort of hard practices, but they had dorms to go to. When Coach Bryant took us to Junction, there was nothing there. You couldn't even go to town. It was all-encompassing.

"The other thing that made Junction hard was the lines were so short (because of all the guys who had quit). So, you never did get any rest. It was always your turn."

Stallings, however, will allow this much regarding that first camp at Alabama: "It wasn't a cakewalk."

Under Whitworth, discipline was said to be lacking; Tommy Brooker recalls that, as freshmen in 1958, football players still suffered from the reputation that preceded them; other students and even teachers referred to the team's housing as the "ape dorm."

Bryant made his players pay a steep price for the right to wear the red jersey, but from the start it was all about changing the collective mindset. Whitworth's teams won four games in three years.

In some respects, it was the last thing in the world Bear Bryant needed: The coach already was larger than life. Yet the tower, which was the most visible symbol of his stature, his command, and his absolute control while coaching at Alabama, seemed to fit him, too. Watching practices from the tower, which afforded Bryant a view of every drill, made him officially omnipresent and omniscient.

Although he often had a loudspeaker in the tower with him, he usually didn't need it. Players and coaches alike could feel his eyes on them. The tower, then, was as much about motivation as the view it offered.

"You know that SOB's up there watching you," 1961 All-American Billy Neighbors says, recalling his sentiments during that time.

Players and coaches also tuned into the sound of the small chain across the top step of the tower hitting the metal railing—a sign that Bryant had seen something he didn't like and was now descending from on high.

"I was there when he built the very first one," says Jack Rutledge, a player from 1958 to 1961 and an assistant through much of Bryant's tenure. "You thought it was a tower, but it wasn't but ten or twelve feet tall.

"We'd be going through things Junction-style [a reference to Bryant's Junction Boys at Texas A & M], and at that time, he was hands-on coaching. That chain would hit that metal bar and you're gonna turn to see if he's coming for you or not.

"He had a little hop as he started coming across the [field]," Rutledge says. "His favorite thing was to stand right in front of you. He'd hit that face mask and knock your helmet back."

In 1971, Sylvester Croom and the other freshmen were practicing on a field opposite the Tower. They would hear the megaphone first, and then they'd see Bryant rumbling down the steps and onto the field for a "little verbal interchange with one of the players," Croom says. "It was something to behold. It put fear in you. You watch it from 100 yards away and it got your attention."

Dude Hennessey, an assistant from 1960 to 1976, recalls that drills were timed to the minute, with players expected to flow seamlessly from station to station. Bryant had no patience for lateness—not ever—and, one day, a player didn't know where to go next. So he approached Hennessey.

"Coach," the player said, innocently enough, "where am I supposed to go?"

"I don't know," Hennessey said frantically, "but get the hell away from me!"

To be sure, it was a Tower of Power—an almost holy place that accepted few visitors.

In the early 1960s, a young quarterback recruit named Joe Namath went up in the tower. And President Gerald Ford visited the tower during the 1970s. By 1982, Bryant's last season, passage to the tower became easier to obtain. Don McNeal, a cornerback from the '78 and '79 national title teams, and who then played for the Miami Dolphins, was visiting practice one day when he heard his name called.

(continued on next page)

"Don McNeal, come on up," this voice from above commanded.

"You want me to come up there?" McNeal answered.

A little wary, McNeal started up the steps. The coach and player talked for a long time, Bryant inviting McNeal over for dinner that night and McNeal, once he got over the shock, accepting.

"It was a precious time," McNeal says. "I'll never forget that."

An even more precious time was to come on the last day of practice in Tuscaloosa in December of 1982, before the team left for the Liberty Bowl. John Pruett, sports editor of the *Huntsville Times*, was at that practice and had brought along his twelve-year-old daughter, Afton.

"Coach," Pruett asked, "do you ever let girls on the practice field?"

"Well, not usually," Bryant said with a laugh, "but she can come on today."

"So, we stood there on the sideline watching practice," Pruett says, "and he invited her up in the tower. I didn't go up there, but she did and what she remembers about that day is he kept feeding her peanuts and they stood up there in that tower for about thirty minutes."

Finally, the old coach came down the steps one last time.

"He was very relaxed," Pruett says. "We walked off the field together. And, I remember, he never looked back."

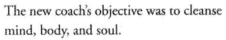

Bryant's coaching tower was, on most occasions, a Tower of Power.

The new coach's objective was to cleanse mind, body, and soul.

"Once you start losing, it's very easy to expect to lose," says Baxter Booth, who suffered through all the Whitworth years, and was a senior in 1958. "Coach Bryant, it took him a while to get us out of that losing mind. But, once he did, you didn't want to disappoint him.

"Out of fear or whatever, you played harder than you did for Whitworth," Booth admits. "It's not right, but it's how people's minds work."

"AIN'T NOTHING BUT A WINNER"

Paul W. Bryant knew his Xs and Os, of course, but his genius wasn't something that could be captured on a chalkboard.

He held advanced degrees in coachology.

More than that . . .

"Bear had a mystique about him," says former University of Arkansas coach and current athletic director Frank Broyles. "He had the ability to get peak performances more often than any coach of the last fifty years.

"General [Robert] Neyland [former Tennessee coach] used to say that in a regular season, you'll get four peak performances, four about average, and two not so good," Broyles continues. "Bear would get seven, eight, or nine peak performances.

"That was Bear's strength. His players would do things and you'd look back and say, 'That's a miracle.' "

It is a lost art today, at least at the stratospheric levels that Bryant reached as a motivator.

"The thing that Coach Bryant had, that I don't know if any guys have today, is he got you to a point where everything you do is about pleasing him," says Sylvester Croom, a team captain for Bryant in 1974, and now coach at Mississippi State.

Bryant joked—but he was dead serious, too—that the first thing a coach needed to be successful was "a wife willing to put up with a whole lot of neglect" and a five-year contract. While there's truth in all of that, neither will save the coach who can't change with the game while simultaneously remaining true to his own core beliefs. College football's scrap heap—not to mention a certain network television studio—is littered with coaches who failed in one or both of those areas.

This is why John Croyle, an Alabama defensive end in the early 1970s, maintains "Coach Bryant's great gifts were his adaptability and flexibility" on football matters, and his "absolutes" on matters of honesty and integrity.

It's true that Texas A & M was put on probation during Bryant's tenure there in the 1950s but, in the 1960s, when Bryant and John Underwood

Sylvester Croom, an All-American center for Bryant, says no coach today is in Bryant's class as a motivator.

wrote the five-part series, "I'll Tell You About Football," for *Sports Illustrated,* Bryant said: "I don't know any sure way of motivating a boy. You talk about paying players. That's a form of motivation. Very popular after the war, too. Well, I've done that, or at least let some of my alumni do it, and if I was a young coach 28 or 30 years old and just starting out I might do it again, if the competition was paying boys and I felt I had to meet the competition. Wouldn't do it now, of course. Don't have to and wouldn't anyway. I'd resign first. That's the one thing I told them when I came to Alabama. I wouldn't cheat."

All of which isn't to say that Bryant didn't possess multiple legal, but seemingly unfair, advantages.

The Bear was that rare man who could move easily from intimidating to charming and back again.

"Coach Bryant lived his life at different levels," says long-time assistant coach Jack Rutledge. "He lived with presidents (several visited Alabama practices) and he lived down here where you were working for him. And whatever category you were in, that's where you'd better stay."

Tommy Brooker, who had been an end and a kicker for Bryant, later coached Alabama's kickers as a volunteer: "I learned really early to say, 'Don't you think,' because I'd heard others in coaching meetings say, 'Coach, I think,' and he'd come back and say, 'You think? Hell,

I don't pay you to think. I pay you to coach.' So it was like, 'Thinking's mine.' "

Bryant's players and coaches always had one thing in common: They feared him. Even the great ones, even the toughest ones, would tread lightly. Billy Neighbors was an All-American tackle on Bryant's first national championship team in 1961 and he says, "If I saw him coming, I'd go the other way."

Had the fear Bryant instilled been his only note, he would have driven players, coaches, and everyone else away. But his mystique was linked with a magnetic attraction. It drew players from every nook and cranny within the state and from points far beyond. The latter was especially true after Bryant had won his three national titles in the 1960s and added a fourth in 1973.

John Mauro was a defensive end (1978-80) from northwest Indiana. He was Catholic. He had a girlfriend in his hometown. In sum, he had many reasons to play for the neighborhood football factory that was Notre Dame.

Mauro took his visit to Alabama, anyway. He liked what he saw, but was torn. It would be difficult to tell people he was forsaking the golden dome. His brother, Jay, had a different view.

"Think about it, John," Jay said. "Some day, this man will be a legend. Twenty or thirty years from now you can say you played for Bear Bryant just like people say they played for Knute Rockne."

John Mauro considered all of this and later, when coming back home and doing a radio interview, he essentially repeated what his brother had told him.

"I had people call me up and tell me I didn't know what I was talking about because Bear Bryant would never reach the plateau of Knute Rockne," Mauro says. "I guess history proved them wrong."

Within Alabama, Bryant's pulpit was his weekly Sunday afternoon television show. In a way, it was television's first reality show as the coach munched the sponsor's potato chips (Golden Flake), sipped the sponsor's soda (Coca-Cola), while mumbling, bumbling, and rumbling through Saturday's missed blocks and made tackles.

Always, he played to the only audience that mattered: the good mamas and papas of future Alabama football players.

Says All-American running back Johnny Musso: "That's what Coach Bryant's show was about—I saw So-and-So's mama and papa over in Fairhope,' and all those parents of kids who were thinking of going to school there were saying, 'Maybe he'll be saying our names one day.' "

That's not to imply Bryant wasn't picky about the players he would take and the ones he wouldn't.

"For a person that grew up like he

The Bear's Sunday afternoon TV show held the state spellbound and was also a great recruiting tool.

did [poor in rural Arkansas], he had more awareness," says former player Jackie Sherill, who later had several college head coaching jobs. "He could tell in two minutes everything about you. He just had that innate ability. The coaches hated for him to go with them on recruiting trips because he may just walk in and say, 'We're not taking the kid.' And those coaches had worked on the guy for two or three years."

Gryska, who was Bryant's recruiting coordinator for many seasons, recalls that Bryant also was quick to realize mistakes. Once, they had recruited an All-State, much-hyped offensive lineman. When Bryant got a good look at him in practice the coach noticed something that told him all he needed to know: The player had trouble bending his ankles.

"That doesn't sound like much," Gryska says, "but if you're gonna be an offensive lineman you've got to bend those ankles. He said he'd never play and he never did."

Bryant also had the ability to realize whether a player, any player, was giving all he had. He could live with marginally talented players who got the most out of their ability, meager though it might be. A supremely talented player who tried to get by on talent alone was another matter.

"He loved overachievement and he hated underachievement," says All-American receiver Ozzie Newsome.

Although gracious in defeat, Bryant sometimes had contentious moments with the press.

ALWAYS ALABAMA

This may explain why Bryant, as intense as he was, always seemed to find his composure after a loss. He understood that, in many cases, the other team had overachieved. He respected that, even as he loathed what he surely must have seen as his own team's underachievement. He always directed the responsibility for these failures at himself and his coaches.

"He was as gracious a loser as I've ever seen," says *Huntsville Times* sports editor John Pruett, who covered Bryant through most of his time coaching at Alabama. "He always took the blame."

He did, however, have his contentious moments with the sporting press.

Clyde Bolton, a retired writer and columnist for the *Birmingham News,* covered Bryant from 1961 through 1982. He says Bryant mostly didn't want to be bothered with the sportswriters covering the team, an attitude Bolton found strange, given the coverage the coach was getting.

"I thought it was unusual because he really had a kiss-ass press, and you're welcome to use that term," Bolton says. "Nobody was critical of him at that time."

And yet, Bolton says, Bryant always knew how to *use* the press, too, and enjoyed a friendly relationship with Bolton's boss, Benny Marshall.

"Bryant knew it was politic to be on good terms with the sports editor of the biggest paper in the state," says Bolton.

In the 1960s, Bryant would play host to select sportswriters and editors in the state at an annual "cabin retreat."

"He wasn't the only one doing that," says Pruett. "Auburn and some others did the same thing. You'd come down to Lake Martin and spend two or three days, play golf, and he'd have a steak cookout. He cooked a good steak, too. It was an informal kind of thing."

One year, a bunch of the writers and Bryant were sitting around at night, and one guy asked a question that set Bryant off.

"An old-time Birmingham sportswriter named Bob Phillips," Pruett remembers. "Bryant was kind of holding court and Mr. Phillips asked a question. I don't remember what it was, but Bryant said something like, 'That's a stupid question, Bob, I'm not even going to answer it.'

"And Phillips, who was a distinguished old gentleman and a graduate of Sewanee [an old Alabama rival], stood up and kind of slammed his notebook closed and said, 'Who do you think you are, Paul? I don't have to take that from you,' and stormed out of the room.

"And Bryant immediately got up and went after him, took him by the arm and said, 'Look, Bob, I didn't mean that. C'mon back. Let's talk about that question you had.'

"I was a young, impressionable sportswriter," Pruett says, "and I thought that was an amazing thing because this was the late '60s and Bryant was still a pretty imposing, crusty old guy. And here this sportswriter [stood up to him]. I never forgot that."

Bryant's sheer size—6-foot-3—made him imposing even when he wasn't trying to be.

Linda Knowles, his secretary in the football office for most of his time at Alabama, recalls meeting him the first time and being taken aback. "Very handsome, strapping, tall, broad-shouldered, a commanding presence," she says.

Even what could have been a flaw—Bryant chewed his words like he was eating taffy soaked in molasses—seemed to work for his greater good.

"Coach Bryant's mumbling was very effective in getting people to concentrate on what he said," says Sylvester Croom. "He was such a dynamic figure he didn't have to talk loud. Anytime he spoke, there was absolute quiet out of respect."

Wes Neighbors, a son of Billy Neighbors, had grown up around Bryant. In 1982, Bryant's last season as coach, Wes was a freshman, albeit a medical redshirt freshman, but still in team meetings. "When he walked in the room, you could feel the air pressure change," Neighbors says. "You could feel it right before he walked in the room. It was really weird. He had this aura about him."

And if Bryant could have that much impact in a mere meeting on those who knew him and played for him, how much effect might his aura have had on opponents who would see him leaning against the goal post before games, rolled-up roster sheet in hand, houndstooth hat perched atop his wise old head?

"You've got to think having Coach Bryant on your sideline was worth, what, a touchdown? Ten points?" asks Marty Lyons, a defensive lineman on the '78 national title team. "They could think they were ready to play and then they'd look over and think, 'When's Coach Bryant going to do something?'"

If opponents looked at Bryant and figured he was bound to win, there was a flip side for all who played, coached, and

Bryant's friendship with New York Yankees owner George Steinbrenner brought Reggie Jackson and friends to Tuscaloosa for an exhibition game.

worked under him. A man who bills himself as "nothing but a winner" does not take kindly to losing.

"After losses," says secretary Linda Knowles, "you sat in your office at your desk Mondays and Tuesdays. By Wednesdays, things kind of eased up, because they were looking to the next game."

There was nothing worse, however, than in the moments immediately following a lost game. Alabama athletic director Mal Moore played and coached for Bryant. He still gets a sick feeling when recalling those rare times when a Bryant team finished on the short end of the score. "The toughest thing you had to do was face him after a loss," Moore says. "Because you knew when you looked at him, he is not supposed to lose."

A SONG IN HIS HEART

"If Coach Bryant ever walked down the hall singing 'Jesus Loves Me,' you knew you were going to win," says Knowles. "You could count on it."

It seems like a contradiction: the man who oversaw Junction and a brutal first training camp in Tuscaloosa, walking along singing "Jesus Loves Me."

Bryant, after all, was a man's man. "Coach Bryant would drink a little bit, he'd go hunting a little bit, and he'd get involved with business," Rutledge says.

When not coaching, Bryant liked to fish, hunt, and play golf.

When John Underwood and Bryant teamed up to write his biography, *Bear*, in the 1970s, the subtitle, *The Hard Life and Good Times of Alabama's Coach Bryant*, spoke to more than a rugged upbringing in Fordyce, Arkansas. Bryant was known to enjoy life to the fullest.

Mary Harmon, being the good football wife that she was, did put up with a whole lot of neglect. Knowles recalls her stopping by Bryant's office only "a couple of times" during the nearly twenty years Knowles worked for him.

Retired Birmingham sportswriter Clyde Bolton, who wrote the 1972 book *The Crimson Tide*, says Bryant, during his first championship run at Alabama, was driven to the point of obsession. Bryant's opposite at Auburn, Shug Jordan, had more varied interests.

"He'd go to New York every summer and go to Broadway plays," Bolton says. "I can't imagine Bryant at a Broadway play."

Bryant's upbringing had been simple, spare. His mother, Ida Kilgore, was an ordained minister and had a huge hand in starting a church where she became a full-time preacher. "He gained his principles from his mother and father," says Ray Bryant, who is Bear Bryant's grand-nephew, and who still resides in Fordyce. "The foundation was laid for him when he was a little bitty fellow. They believed in hard work, they believed in discipline, and they believed in church.

"People would come from all over the southern part of Arkansas to have his mother put her hands on and pray and heal," Ray Bryant says. "She just had a special way with the Lord. Some people brush that off nowadays, as though there's no such thing, but I'm here to tell you there is such a thing."

AN INFLUENTIAL FRIEND

Bert Jones was one of the Alabama football team's managers in 1958, Bryant's first year. Now, it was 1962 (Bryant had won his first national title in 1961) and Jones was taking his sick mother to a Birmingham hospital. The hospital, however, was overcrowded, with officials telling Jones that they didn't have a room for his mother. The best they could do was to put in her in a fifteen-bed ward.

"So I had to leave my mother there," Jones says. "When I came back the next day, to visit my mama, she's got a private room on the same floor and there's a spray of flowers from Coach Bryant.

"He sent her those flowers with a card on it and they saw who it was from—and I don't know that he did anything more than that—but that was enough.

"From then on, she was *somebody*."

There seems little question that Paul W. Bryant's life left behind a record of generosity, though he generally tried to cover those tracks. Ray Bryant says the coach quietly helped many people in and around Fordyce.

"He liked to help people," says Ray, "but he didn't like it to be advertised. Our little church that his mother helped found, there wasn't a year that passed that he didn't send money."

Back at the University of Alabama, Knowles recalls Bryant providing for an elderly black janitor who worked in the athletic building during the 1960s, known as Hooch Man. She also remembers Bryant performing kindnesses large and small. Two examples of the small: making sure the girls in the office got to meet comedian Bob Hope when he was in town and playing errand boy for Knowles and the other women.

"In our old office building, we had a Coke machine," Knowles says. "But it was down by the coaches' dressing room, so the ladies couldn't go by the door. A lot of afternoons he'd come through and say, 'You ladies need a Coke?' And he'd go down there and bring us a Coke."

Then there was the day a man from Memphis, Tennessee, called. The man said his son only had a couple of days to live and his son's dying wish was to meet Coach Bryant.

"And Coach Bryant got on a plane and met the young man," Knowles says.

It wasn't a prayer tower, but Bryant did once tell quarterback Steadman Shealy, who is a devout Christian, "I betcha I pray more than you do."

"And the young man passed on either the next day or the following day."

Steadman Shealy, who played quarterback in the late 1970s and was very upfront about his own Christianity, says, "Coach Bryant was Coach Bryant. He was a very tough individual. But I remember one time I was in his office and he looked across at me and said, 'Steadman, I bet you won't agree with me on this, but I betcha I pray more than you do.' And he said there was never a time he didn't pray for somebody less fortunate.

"There was a lot of things with Coach Bryant spiritually that your 'typical' Christian wouldn't necessarily agree with," Shealy says. "But that was the best he knew and how he understood, because he was such a tough individual and he demanded that you give your all. And Coach Bryant was just the best at taking guys like Steadman Shealy and making them into something more than they ever thought they could be."

Cornerback Jeremiah Castille played for Bryant during his last four years as Alabama's coach. Today, Castille is the Crimson Tide's team chaplain. "There was a freedom of ministry within our team," Castille recalls of his playing days. "A gentleman from Campus Crusade discipled me, and Coach Bryant was open to that."

In the Bible Belt that is Alabama, there has long been a great, mostly unspoken, question that matters very much to many people: Was Bear Bryant a Christian? Ultimately, it was a question no one could answer. But Knowles recalls a telegram arriving after Bryant's death.

"From Robert H. Schuller, the Crystal Cathedral founder," she says. "In Dr. Schuller's telegram he said he sat next to Coach Bryant on an airplane just a year and a half before that, and said he asked him if he was a Christian and he assured him that he was. So, that's comforting."

John Croyle, a defensive end from 1971 to 1973, says he saw Bryant about a week before the coach died and as they talked Croyle became convinced that at some point in time "Coach Bryant had accepted Jesus Christ into his heart."

Castille is inclined to agree.

"This is what I tell people," he says, "you had to have a spiritual base to love people the way Coach Bryant loved people."

BLACK, WHITE, AND CRIMSON

In the midst of the 1978 football season, the *Washington Post* published a story on the integration of the Alabama football team. They were a few years late with the news, of course, because, in 1970, Wilbur Jackson had become the first black player to sign with Alabama, and in the first game of 1971, against Southern Cal, John Mitchell became the first African-American to play in a game for the Crimson Tide.

The *Post*'s story, however, revisited the recruitment of another black player: halfback Ralph Stokes of Montgomery, who would go on to earn varsity letters at Alabama from 1972 to 1974.

Specifically, the story recounted Stokes's mother grilling Bryant during a recruiting visit: "I recall vividly seeing you on television saying you don't want any black boys on your teams, and now you say you do. Why do you now? Why do you want my son?"

Bryant's answer, Stokes told the *Post:* "At that time, that was the way I felt. But times change and I've matured and changed . . . I don't see any white players or black players . . . it's just ballplayers. People are people and they can't be treated by the color of their skin."

So, why didn't Bryant come to this conclusion sooner?

Actually, he might have.

In a 2004 interview with the *Pittsburgh Post-Gazette*, Mitchell, an assistant coach for the Pittsburgh Steelers, said he believed Bryant would have integrated the team earlier had the tensions in the state of Alabama during the 1960s not been what they were.

There's an oft-told story that what really changed Bryant's mind was losing the season-opening game in 1970 in Birmingham to Southern Cal, when Sam "The Bam" Cunningham, an African-American, ran over the Crimson Tide in a 42–21 Trojans win. As the legend goes, Bryant brought Cunningham into the Alabama locker room after the game and said something to the effect of, "This is what a football player looks like."

Only problem is, plenty of people who were in the Alabama locker room that night refute the story. Assistant coaches Jack Rutledge and Clem Gryska insist the story is untrue. And Terry Rowell, a noseguard on that Alabama team, calls the story a "myth" in Kirk McNair's book, *What It Means to Be Crimson Tide.*

"It never happened. I don't know why anyone would say it did," Rowell wrote. "I can imagine that Coach Bryant went to Southern Cal's dressing room and congratulated them, and he may have said something to Cunningham there because Cunningham had a great game. But can you imagine Bryant bringing another player into our dressing room and telling John Hannah and Johnny Musso, 'This is what a football player looks like'?"

Meanwhile, another African-American running back, Birmingham's Tony Nathan, remembers watching the 1970 USC-Alabama game on television.

"That's all they were talking about, 'Sam the Bam,' " recalls Nathan, who played at Alabama from 1975 to 1978. "Growing up, hearing about all the controversy during that time, and being

Offensive guard John Hannah (1970–72) was a great commodity to have as Bryant switched to the wishbone in 1971, but Hannah much preferred blocking in pro-set offenses.

black, you thought [Alabama] was the last place you could go and play."

Bolton believes people who say Bryant could have integrated the football team much sooner either do not remember the times in which Bryant was living or give the coach too much credit for having the ability to, in effect, overrule a governor who literally stood in the schoolhouse door in the name of segregation.

"Bryant was a powerful man," says Bolton, "but Bryant, like everybody in Alabama, was standing in the middle of hundreds of years of tradition. I don't know that he was powerful enough to just snap his fingers and all of a sudden the state of Alabama would be integrated.

"He probably would have liked to have done it sooner; he probably did it on a timetable that was best for him to do it. But I don't know, there are a million angles to that."

Once the decision was made to integrate, Bryant turned to 1971 team captain Johnny Musso and asked him to head off any potential problems.

"He encouraged me to reach out and be a leader as far as how the black players were treated," Musso says. "It went remarkably well. He recruited some wonderful people who just happened to have black skin. They were leaders, they were liked, and they were 100 percent teammates, and that had more to do with their character."

Mitchell, an All-American defensive end, roomed with offensive lineman Bobby Stanford, who was white and from Albany, Georgia.

"I'm still friends with him," Mitchell said in that 2004 interview with Pittsburgh sportswriter Gene Collier. "His parents, this was amazing, they had a mobile home they'd drive in from Georgia for home games. Whatever they brought for Bobby, they brought for me. When they left, his mom would give me a kiss and his dad would hug me."

It's also worth noting that Bryant and Alabama were ahead of several other Southeastern Conference schools.

"When I played for Alabama, we played LSU, which had no African-Americans," Mitchell said. "Ole Miss had none. Mississippi State had none. But I didn't have any problems. It was probably out of respect for Coach Bryant more than out of respect for me."

In 1980, Walter Lewis became Alabama's first black quarterback. "Coach Bryant did all I could ask for, especially me being the first black quarterback to start at Alabama," Lewis says. "He was fair in how he dealt with me and other players."

Not that Walter Lewis only thinks about this historic first, because he doesn't. Lewis started for Bryant in his last season in 1982, including Bryant's final game at the Liberty Bowl in Memphis.

Says Lewis: "I was his *last* quarterback."

MAKE A WISH

The men who played for Bryant and later became college head coaches themselves always see him in a little brighter light.

They haven't walked in his shoes—no one can fill those shoes—but they have covered some of the same ground, fought some of the same battles, and wrestled some of the same questions. They know how he did it, they know how they did it, and they know how coaches are currently trying to do it.

"Coach Bryant had forgotten more about winning than all the coaches today will ever learn," Jackie Sherrill says.

Another former Bryant player-turned-head-coach, Danny Ford, who led Clemson to the 1981 national championship, says, "I wish I'd took

more notes and learned more under him. I'd have been a whole lot better coach. I just didn't want to bother him, you know? I was only there as an assistant [in the early 1970s] for two or three years.

"I was respectfully afraid of him," Ford continues. "Why would I pick up the phone and worry a man like that?"

The answer is in another question: What did Bear Bryant do after successive poor seasons in 1969 and 1970?

He picked up the phone and called Texas coach Darrell Royal, who had just won back-to-back national titles running the wishbone offense.

"He called me up and said, 'Could we look at some film?' " recalls Royal. "He had put in good words for me which helped me advance in the profession. We had a good rapport before the wishbone days."

◀ LEFT
Walter Lewis, Alabama's first African-American quarterback, was also quarterback for Bryant's final game.

▼ BOTTOM
Bryant changed to the wishbone offense because he didn't have a passer like Ken Stabler, who was an All-American in 1967.

TO CATCH A THIEF

Every king needs a crown.

Bear Bryant's was that houndstooth hat.

It was only natural, perhaps, that after another Alabama win over Auburn, a rival fan would try to steal the crown. After all, maybe the hat had magic powers.

Bryant himself admitted that he had made a mistake wearing a baseball cap instead of his houndstooth at the 1972 Orange Bowl because it rained; Nebraska throttled Alabama that night, 38–6.

"I don't know whether I'm superstitious or not," Bryant later told the *Atlanta Journal.* "But I wouldn't want to stop wearing a houndstooth hat now. I wouldn't want to take a chance. Even if it was raining."

Bryant took his chances later in the decade when Alabama played in the new Louisiana Superdome, but that was a matter of manners: Bryant said his mama told him never to wear a hat indoors. Otherwise, the houndstooth could be found resting comfortably atop the coach's head every game day.

"That was a part of him," says Tommy Wilcox, a safety on Bryant's last national title team. "Just like Tom Landry used to wear that little hat."

Well, not exactly. Landry's staid hat matched his staid personality.

Bryant usually wore a black-and-white houndstooth, but also had red and blue patterns. Whatever the color, the houndstooth hat was his, or at least it was until after a victory over Auburn at Birmingham's Legion Field when a young, long-haired fan snatched the hat right off the coach's head as he was walking to the dressing room.

Assistant coach Jack Rutledge ran down a young man who stole Bryant's houndstooth hat; looks like Jack could use a hat himself.

"A college student, probably," says Jack Rutledge, then an Alabama assistant coach. "And he took the hat and put it on his head and that made it worse."

That made it sacrilegious.

The thief began running across the field, darting here and there between all the people, until he made his way to Auburn's sideline. Once there, he hopped over the team bench and began to scale the fence separating the field from the stands.

"I was right behind him," says Rutledge. "And, by that time, he knew I was chasing him."

Soon enough, Rutledge was catching him. An offensive lineman when he played for Bryant in the late 1950s and early '60s, Rutledge was still stout. He knocked the hat off, grabbed the guy "by the hair of the head" and sent him flying, feet first, onto the ground. A fan picked the hat up off the ground and handed it to Rutledge, who carried it back to Bryant in the Alabama dressing room.

"Thank you, Jack," Bryant said.

They were three little words that, coming from him, said so much more.

The next Monday in their team staff meeting, Bryant told Rutledge to go down to a certain store in Tuscaloosa where a gift would be waiting for him.

"He had bought me a hat exactly like his," Rutledge says with a smile. "And I still have it at my house today."

As Royal remembers it, Bryant didn't enter into this venture sure he would switch to the wishbone offense. Although Bryant was firm in the belief he didn't have the kind of passer he had enjoyed in previous seasons—no one like Scott Hunter, Steve Sloan, Kenny Stabler, Joe Namath, or Pat Trammell—to play quarterback in a more traditional offensive system, Bryant didn't know enough about the wishbone to just automatically commit to it.

When they got together to watch film Bryant was amazed by what he saw in the passing game in the wishbone, which was very much a run-first offense.

"How much time do you spend in pass protection?" Bryant asked.

"Very little," Royal said.

"Why is that?"

"Because everything starts with a rollout," Royal said. "We don't throw anything from the pocket."

Now, the wheels were turning.

"You don't spend any time on pass protection? That's unbelievable," Bryant said. "We spend 75 percent of our time on pass protection. Turn that damn thing off. That convinces me. We're going to do it."

Says Royal: "He liked that. That was the thing that really sold him on it."

To what extent Bryant was ready for

change—just proving his football flexibility, as John Croyle called it—and to what extent he believed he had to do something different is debatable.

The 1969 team went 6-5 and the 1970 team was 6-5-1. Alabama lost to rivals Tennessee and Auburn in each season, and neither of the games against the Vols had been close. Although Bryant had had an undefeated team as recently as 1966, such perfection had only served to spoil the program's biggest backers that much more.

"A number of fans were beginning to get pretty disgruntled," says *Huntsville Times* sports editor John Pruett. "I remember going to The Masters and talking to Charlie Land, sports editor of the *Tuscaloosa News* at that time, and Charlie said, 'I tell you what, he better turn it around this year or he's going to be in trouble.' "

Pruett found this impossible to believe, telling Land, "You gotta be kidding."

"I'm not kidding," Land replied. "There's a lot of big-money guys who are getting unhappy."

Says Pruett: "Along about that same time, he flirted with the notion of going to the Miami Dolphins. Bryant got it in his mind that he was slipping. After having built the Alabama program to the heights it had reached, and having lost the fire in his belly for it, he didn't just want to hang on.

"So, that's why he entertained the Dolphins' offer."

At some level, even Bear Bryant was susceptible to human nature's most ordinary flaws. All that success had bred multilayered rewards.

"He said himself he got sidetracked with making appearances and enjoying the celebrity role," recalls former sportswriter Clyde Bolton.

"There were a lot of things going on in the program," says Johnny Musso, a running back from 1969 to 1971. "Coach Bryant had been toying with the Miami job and I think that hurt recruiting. The program kind of went sideways for a while."

All of this intersected with changing times in America at large. Just about every college campus in the country was home to Vietnam War protests. It sometimes seemed life was upside down, as evidenced by the popular saying: Boys were wearing their hair long, and girls were wearing their skirts short. Alcohol also had a new doubles partner in marijuana and other illegal drugs.

Musso was the guy Bryant relied on to get an accurate read on what was happening within the team. Bryant was concerned enough about possible drug use that he dispatched assistant coaches to the dorms to go on a search-and-destroy mission.

"It was really a fairly comical affair," Musso recalls. "They didn't know what they were looking for. They wouldn't have known a drug if it had been right there in front of them."

In a sense, Bryant looked upon the wishbone as an elixir. He also was determined to keep this change top secret.

When the *skywriters* came through Tuscaloosa in the preseason—sportswriters touring the conference to write their preview stories—Alabama showed its old offense and everyone connected with the program was under strict orders to say nothing of the wishbone. Bryant wanted Southern Cal coach John McKay to be as surprised as anyone when the Crimson Tide unveiled the new offense on the night of September 10, 1971, in Los Angeles.

"I think one lineman slipped in one interview," recalls John Croyle, a defensive end on the '71 team. "And he just hinted at it."

It didn't take long to realize Alabama had succeeded in keeping this grand secret. Alabama lined up in the wishbone formation and Southern Cal's defenders immediately looked to the sideline with hands raised and eyes wide as if to say, "What do we do now?"

"They finally adjusted and shut us down," says then-assistant coach Mal Moore. "But we scored the first three times we had the ball. I didn't think we'd make a first down . . . but, like in war, it was the element of surprise. They did not have a clue and we won [17–10]."

More important, the implementation of the wishbone had reset Alabama's long-term course. The Crimson Tide went 11-1 in 1971 and, two years later, Bryant's team had another national championship. Two more national titles came at the end of the decade, in 1978 and 1979, and the Crimson Tide easily could have won national championships in '75 and '77, too.

The wishbone further turned the focus to the defense, which was perfect for Bryant's teams. Assistant coach Bobby Marks says Bryant went to the wishbone not to merely win more than he had in recent years, but because "he wanted to dominate people."

Says Musso: "The heart of our line was Jim Krapf, Buddy Brown, and John Hannah—three All-American players. And that's where it starts with the wishbone. I suffered as far as number of carries, but it was a good offense for our team. The best part was we had a chance to win."

They had much more than a chance. The 1970s became a decade of excellence bordering on a dynasty as Alabama won three national championships and eight SEC titles. It was Bryant at his best, as he made the wishbone offense more diversified than it had been at Texas and Oklahoma.

"With the wishbone, you either had to overload one side or the other to stop the option," says Ozzie Newsome, an All-American receiver in 1977. "If they overloaded away from me, it left me in one-on-one coverage. I didn't catch a lot of balls in the game, but I would catch balls for 30-, 40-, and 50-yard gains."

Former Arkansas coach Frank Broyles says, "Coach Bryant had never been an innovator offensively, but he'd be the first to tell you he could take the best of what other teams were doing and coach 'em better than you could."

Not that Bryant took anything for granted. The more he learned about the wishbone, the more he wanted to learn about how other coaches would try to stop it.

"When we were both running the wishbone we talked every Sunday after we'd studied film," Royal remembers. "We talked about what kind of defense we saw and what we'd do if we met it again."

Bear Bryant was back—all the way

back—with a fire in his belly and a song in his heart.

FOREVER

Year after year, the wins piled up. Until, finally, on November 28, 1981, in a 28–17 win over Auburn, Bryant surpassed Amos Alonzo Stagg as college football's all-time wins leader with victory number three hundred fifteen.

Sportswriter Clyde Bolton better remembers October 4, 1980, in Birmingham. "Bryant was going to win his three hundredth game—that was back when you could assume Alabama was going to beat Kentucky—and my assignment was to just shadow Bryant," Bolton says. "So, I was down on the sidelines

The Bear scored his 315th career win, breaking Amos Alonzo Stagg's record, with a victory over Auburn in 1981.

early. Bryant had a tradition of walking around the playing surface before the crowd got there. They had let the students into their section and so Bryant started to take his walk and he said, 'C'mon, take my walk with me.'

"Well, I thought he was the best college coach that ever lived and I was honored to be asked. So, we got over there in front of the student section and they gave him a standing ovation. He looked over at me and said, 'Damn, you got a lot of fans.'

"He and I had some moments that weren't real pleasant," Bolton says, "but that's one I always cherish."

Wes Neighbors would have cherished playing for Bryant, but that never happened. Wes's father Billy had been an All-American and a member of the '61 national title team; Wes was redshirted as a freshman in 1982. He remembers well, though, what Bryant told that team.

"Coach Bryant felt like he was letting us down, that the wishbone wasn't cutting it anymore and we needed to go to a pro-style offense and he was too old to change," Wes says. "That's basically what he told us."

It had been a great career. When Bryant announced he would retire after the Liberty Bowl in Memphis, it was cause for sadness, but not regret. Bryant had devoted his life to football, much of it at the University of Alabama as a player, an assistant coach, and as the best

head coach college football had ever known.

If he was ready to slow down a little, well, that was his right.

Few, however, knew just how much Bryant's health had deteriorated. And even in his last season, at age sixty-eight, he had done some hands-on coaching during spring practice.

"He was so strong," says Jeremiah Castille, a senior cornerback. "He still did things with us on the field at that age."

But, by the fall, Bryant's secretary, Linda Knowles, was seeing a marked change.

"He would lie down for an hour, hour and a half, before practice,"

In 1982, Bryant, fighting failing health, announced he would retire after the Liberty Bowl in Memphis.

Knowles says. "The last few months I was very concerned about him, so I kept his doctor's number by the telephone. I was afraid to go wake him up. I didn't know what I would find."

On January 25, 1983, after Bryant had coached his last game and one of his former players, Ray Perkins, had been installed as his successor, Bryant became ill and was taken to Druid City Hospital by the Alabama campus.

Knowles learned of this on that night's ten o'clock news. She immediately called Billy Varner, who was Bryant's personal driver. Varner told Knowles that Bryant had a badly upset stomach.

The next morning, January 26, Perkins was leaving for Greensboro, North Carolina. He stopped by to see Bryant on the way.

"It was about eight or eight-thirty in the morning and, it seemed to me, he was doing fine," Perkins says. "The last thing he said to me had something to do with recruiting."

Early that afternoon, Knowles received the call from the hospital saying that Paul W. Bryant, age sixty-nine, had died.

"The first person I called was Coach Stallings," Knowles says. "He was working for the Dallas Cowboys. I just didn't want him to hear it on the radio or television."

Even though Stallings knew more about Bryant's ill health than most, he was still surprised.

"I just couldn't imagine anything happening to Coach Bryant," he says. "I couldn't think in those terms. I thought he'd just keep on living."

Hoss Johnson was a freshman offensive lineman who had been red-shirted in 1982. He and several other players were in the dorm's game room when they learned of Bryant's death.

"It felt like everything just stopped, was in slow motion," he says.

Jay Barker, who would play quarterback on Stallings's 1992 national championship team, was in the fifth grade. His first clue that something was wrong came from his teacher.

"Mrs. Prescott came back into the room crying," Barker recalls.

The boy figured his teacher had had a death in her family. In a way, she had.

"Mrs. Prescott was a huge Alabama fan, actually had a motor home and went to all the games—still goes to the games with her husband," Barker says. "They made an announcement over the intercom that Coach Bryant had passed away. All the kids started crying. Even all the Auburn-fan kids started crying.

"It's like when a president passes; I'll never forget that."

Bryant's funeral was presidential in scope and emotion. It's generally considered to be one of the largest funerals ever held in the South, along with those of Martin Luther King, Jr., and Elvis Presley.

Eight players from the '82 Alabama team, including Castille, Walter Lewis, Eddie Lowe, and Tommy Wilcox, served as pallbearers.

Bryant's death left rough-and-tough football players from the past and present defenseless.

"I don't think I've ever cried as hard, except when my dad died," says Marty Lyons, who played on Bryant's '78 national championship team.

"I tell people he was my second father," says Lee Roy Jordan, a linebacker on Bryant's first national championship team in 1961. "He cared about me that way."

President Ronald Reagan made plans to attend the funeral but, when he couldn't make the trip, Washington Redskins coach George Allen represented the president. A crowd of more than two thousand gathered outside the First United Methodist Church of Tuscaloosa.

Coverage of the service and burial was broadcast live throughout the state.

"I remember sitting there, and I could hear him call my name," says Knowles. "He never pronounced it 'Linda.' It was always more like 'Lynna.' Just sitting there in that service, I could hear how he pronounced my name."

No, even the best coach of them all couldn't just go on living.

Hoss Johnson was the last player Bryant signed to a scholarship. That's as close as he got to playing for Bryant. But he hangs onto that connection.

"Having any part in the life of a legend is better than having no part at all," he says.

Bryant's players always held on to one truth after their Alabama careers were done. Perhaps they have held it closer since January 26, 1983.

"As long as you lived," says Jordan, "you were one of his."

Less than a month after winning his last game, Bryant died of heart failure.

5

GOAL-LINE STAND CAN'T STAND ALONE: THE 1978 NATIONAL CHAMPIONSHIP

That was a better play than the goal-line stand. That was the play of the game, to be honest with you. By all rights, he should have scored.

—Penn State running back Mike Guman
on Alabama defensive back Don McNeal's hit at the
1-yard line that kept receiver Scott Fitzkee out of the
end zone in the 1979 Sugar Bowl.

▲ PREVIOUS PAGE
Alabama's goal-line
stand in the 1979
Sugar Bowl, to win the
'78 national
championship, is one
of the most vivid
images in the football
program's illustrious
history.

EVERY coach knows this truth: No one play determines the success or failure of a season—unless it's one of those seasons determined by the success or failure of one play.

In the 1979 Sugar Bowl between Alabama and Penn State, with the national championship at stake, that one play seemed to be everywhere.

It could have been when 'Bama running back Major Ogilvie chased down Rich Milot after he intercepted a first-half Jeff Rutledge pass, perhaps saving a touchdown.

It could have been the fourth-quarter third-down play inside the Alabama 1-yard line, when the Crimson Tide stopped running back Matt Suhey with nary a carpet fiber to spare.

It could have been the fourth-and-goal play when Guman was turned back as he tried to dive into the end zone, but hit a red wall.

Or, maybe, it wasn't a play at all. Maybe it was the two timeouts Penn State coach Joe Paterno called late in the second quarter, timeouts that ultimately left the Crimson Tide just enough time to score a touchdown and take a 7–0 lead into the half.

Or, it might have been, with a different and depressing outcome, the moment in the fourth quarter when Alabama quarterback Jeff Rutledge pitched the ball onto the Louisiana Superdome turf and Penn State recovered, 19 yards away from Alabama's end zone, and needing only 7 points to tie the score.

It even might have been when Penn State, about to the get the ball back with plenty of time on the clock and good field position after a short 'Bama punt, was caught with too many men on the field and the penalty gave the Crimson Tide a first down.

The Nittany Lion faithful still roar over that foolishness, and Penn State offensive lineman Keith Dorney still sighs when recalling "the 12-men-on-the-field debacle."

Or, maybe, Guman is right. The play that most determined the winner of the 1979 Sugar Bowl—Alabama 14, Penn State 7—and which team would lay claim to a share of the 1978 national championship, occurred when McNeal broke from the man he was covering in the end zone and forced Fitzkee out of bounds.

"The Don McNeal play?" says Bobby Marks, a Crimson Tide assistant coach. "He blew that guy up on the sideline."

Happy New Year, Scott Fitzkee.

"He got under his numbers and made the perfect hit," says Allen Crumbley, a defensive back on that Alabama team. "Don's a great athlete and he kept his feet driving, driving, driving.

"How many times when you're a kid do they say, 'Keep your feet moving'?

In defensive back Don McNeal's great career, no play was bigger than his touchdown-saving tackle on second-and-goal in the '79 Sugar Bowl.

Well, a lot of people just hit and drag. If he'd have done that, that guy would have scored no problem."

For his part, McNeal says what he did on that one play is what he tried to do on every play: follow his fundamentals, execute his assignment, and, once that's done, look to see if he can help make a play somewhere else.

"Just do what you're supposed to do," McNeal says of the credo of that team and that defense. "And if you have to do more, then do that. And that's what happened with the play I made.

"I had my man covered, I saw the ball being thrown, and I just reacted."

And he made, if not the game's single most important play, certainly the game's most overlooked play as everyone focuses on the freeze frame of linebacker Barry Krauss meeting Mike Guman high in the air outside Alabama's end zone.

"Krauss's play was certainly a big play," Coach Bear Bryant told reporters that night in the Superdome. "But he'd never had the chance to make the play if McNeal hadn't made the great play on the pass receiver or had not David Hannah made a great play on [third] down. There were other big plays in the game.

"The way it turned out, those were three big plays and Alabama made all of them."

Of course, the season did not come down to even just those three big plays. To say that is to suggest that nothing that came before mattered.

In fact, the season's story had started long before the Crimson Tide arrived in New Orleans for the 1979 Sugar Bowl. It started as they were leaving New Orleans after winning the '78 Sugar Bowl, 35–6 over Ohio State, and believing they had done more than enough to be voted the best college football team in the land.

WAIT 'TIL NEXT YEAR

In the new math that only poll voters understand, number-5 Notre Dame's win over top-ranked Texas in the Cotton Bowl vaulted the Irish over number-3 Alabama after the Crimson Tide had thumped number-9 Ohio State in the Sugar Bowl.

While Notre Dame's fans would argue that the Irish deserved to be number 1, and Alabama number 2, because Notre Dame defeated the previously unbeaten Longhorns, this conveniently ignores the circumstances of Notre Dame's

one defeat: an early-season meltdown against unranked Mississippi in which the Irish lost 20–13, as they made five turnovers and had a punt blocked.

Meantime, Alabama's only loss came at Nebraska, by a touchdown, and the Cornhuskers finished twelfth in the final poll while Ole Miss was nowhere to be seen.

"That was the saddest day for me, when we were coming back from New Orleans and found out," says Rich Wingo, a linebacker from 1976 to 1978. "We just dominated Ohio State and Coach Bryant had basically called off the dogs at halftime.

"We had gone from number 3 to number 2. Not because it was us, just because it was Notre Dame. I still feel that way to this day."

Steadman Shealy, who would be the starting quarterback on the 1979 national championship team, felt the pain, too.

"I cried like a baby," Shealy says.

"We should have gotten a share of it," says Marty Lyons, a defensive tackle on the '77 and '78 teams. "It really showed the popularity of Notre Dame."

It also showed how thin the margin for error had become. In 1973, Alabama had gone through the regular season undefeated and, because the UPI held its final poll before the bowl games, Alabama was voted a national championship. Notre Dame then beat Alabama

24–23 in the Sugar Bowl, and there were some observers who felt Alabama's national title was now tainted.

What's certain is that in 1977 Alabama had left room for debate, or even bias, by losing in the season's second week at Nebraska, 31–24.

"A heartbreaker," remembers running back Tony Nathan.

"Any time you lose, you're outplayed," Lyons says all these years later. "And we were outplayed. They took the game to us."

The chance for redemption would come right away: Alabama opened the 1978 season at Birmingham's Legion Field against the Cornhuskers.

This was just the first game of a col-lege football murderer's row. Next came a game at Missouri, then a solid program with Phil Bradley at quarterback and Kellen Winslow as a favorite target; then a date at Legion Field with Southern Cal and running back Charles White; and, after a visit from Vanderbilt in Tuscaloosa, a trip to Seattle to play a University of Washington team quarter-backed by Warren Moon.

And still to come, the teeth of the Southeastern Conference schedule, in-cluding the always tough rivalry games with Tennessee and Auburn.

"Have you ever seen anybody that had stiffer competition than our schedule?" asks defensive back Allen Crumbley.

Poll voters didn't reward running back Tony Nathan and the Crimson Tide after their 35–6 defeat of Ohio State in the '78 Sugar Bowl, setting the stage for a national title run the following year.

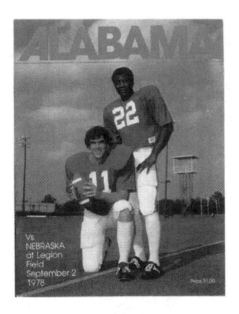

A 20–3 win over Nebraska in the first game of the '78 season got the Tide rolling.

"Then the clouds parted, the sun came out, and you can imagine how hot and humid it was. I was playing cornerback and special teams and that was the most tired I've ever been in a football game."

By halftime, Bryant was tired, too—sick and tired.

"He walks into the dressing room and he says, 'Oh, this must be the women's restroom,'" recalls Clem Gryska, an assistant coach. "'I don't see any men in here.' And then he walks outside and lights his Chesterfield. Just that little thing hacked them off real good."

Bryant apparently spent some more time in the locker room because Lyons remembers the coach finding the people he believed could make the most difference.

"Coach Bryant came over and stood in front of the defense," Lyons says, "and looked down at Barry Krauss and myself like, 'OK, [hot shots], show me how good you really are.' I believe we shut them out in the second half."

They did and Alabama, the preseason number-1 team in the AP poll, escaped with a 38-20 win.

The key play in the game was probably when big E. J. Junior blocked a punt in the third quarter, and Rickey Gilliland picked up the ball and ran it back for a touchdown.

"It seems like I always come up with a big play when we need it," Junior told the *Tuscaloosa News.* "I didn't want to

Alabama passed the first test, shucking the Cornhuskers 20–3.

The next week at Missouri started well, too, Alabama racing to a 17–0 lead early in the second quarter.

Then, the unexpected: Missouri scored 20 points and led 20–17 at the half, one touchdown coming on a 69-yard run by Bradley and another on a 30-yard interception return.

Alabama quarterback Jeff Rutledge, who had not thrown an interception in his previous 100 passes, threw two in the first half. Losing to Missouri would send them tumbling in the polls, possibly to the point of no return.

"I thought the half would never end," Bryant said, recalling the hail of points in the second quarter.

"Right before kickoff, it was raining and overcast," Crumbley remembers.

run with the ball, but I sure wanted somebody on our team to get it."

LOSS AND RECOVERY

In 1977, Alabama had gone out to Los Angeles to play Southern Cal and returned home with a 21–20 victory. When the teams met in Birmingham, in the third week of the '78 season, the Trojans had a score to settle.

They also had a plan of attack geared just for Alabama's defense.

"What they did, because we were such a fast, flowing defense with the linebackers, was they designed all their plays to cut back, go wide, cut back, go wide," says defensive back Allen Crumbley. "That's how they beat us."

The final score was USC 24, Alabama 14. The Trojans rolled up 309 yards rushing, often starting plays behind the left side of a line that included future Pro Football Hall-of-Famer Anthony Munoz. Frequently, the ball was in the hands of Charles White, who finished with 199 yards rushing and ripped off a 40-yard touchdown run.

"Coach Bryant took out his starting defense," Lyons remembers. "Charles White ran that student body right for a touchdown. Coach Bryant looked at me—and I want to say that was one of the few plays I missed my senior year—like, 'what are you doing here on the sidelines?' And I wanted to go, 'Well,

that was the same question I was asking you.'

"It was his way of telling everybody that's how you build a tradition—put some of the younger players in there in a situation where he's looking for them to make a big play.

"Did it cost us the game? No."

But it was a huge play. Crumbley remembers two others.

"Don McNeal went up for an interception and the ball slipped through his hands and was caught by the receiver and he went in for a score," Crumbley says. "And then the offense fumbled and they got a field goal. The difference in the game was those two mistakes—the almost interception and the fumble."

Afterward, McNeal had to answer the hard question: How did you not catch that ball?

"I guess it was a lack of concentration," he said. "I have no excuse. It was one of many mistakes we made."

Bryant said the team went "backward" and added, "Most of the afternoon, it looked like a bunch of fine young men from Alabama playing against a football team."

They were now 2-1, same as they had been after three weeks in 1977. Their national championship hopes had not been eliminated because USC was a formidable opponent, same as Nebraska the previous season.

There was now no room for a slip—

not just on the field, but off the field and in the locker room, and in attitude and commitment.

The defense on that '78 team was a tight-knit group.

"We really enjoyed playing together," Lyons says. "We had fun working together and being happy for one another's accomplishments."

Lyons recalls the seniors coming in as freshmen and most of them staying in Tuscaloosa over the summer between their freshman and sophomore seasons.

"We stayed right there on campus and worked out together," he says. "And as you build friendship, you also build accountability—'this is what we have to do to win. And I'm gonna hold you accountable and you're gonna hold me accountable, and let's just get it done for one another.' "

There was still time to be accountable for achieving the dream. Eight games still remained.

"When you lose early," Lyons says, "you can always recover."

Although the players on that Alabama team probably never thought of it in these terms during the regular season, 1978 was a year for special champions in all sports.

America's team, the Dallas Cowboys, won the Super Bowl in January. Affirmed won the Triple Crown. And Mr. October, Reggie Jackson, and the New York Yankees won the World Series.

Why shouldn't the most tradition-rich team in college football enjoy a national championship season, too? By the time the team left for New Orleans and the Sugar Bowl, players realized a national title could be within their grasp.

"We all wanted to be what Alabama used to be," says Mike Clements, a sophomore defensive back on the '78 team whose interception in the Sugar Bowl ended Penn State's last, dim, hope.

However, getting back to the Big Easy was going to be hard.

Alabama beat Vanderbilt 51–28 in week four, but led only 24–21 after three quarters.

"We're not as good now as I thought we'd be at this time," Bryant said.

Safety Murray Legg agreed, saying, "Maybe we took too much for granted."

Alabama fans took nothing for granted. Several thousand fans watched the Washington game on closed circuit television inside Memorial Coliseum.

Crumbley remembers the game as a near miss, Alabama being somewhat fortunate to win 20–17.

"If Spider Gaines [a world-class sprinter] would have caught the ball as many times as he was open, I don't think we would have won," Crumbley says.

The next week against Florida, the defense flexed its muscles in a 23–12 win. The Gators started five drives at or inside Alabama's 40-yard line and came away with only two field goals.

Then, at Knoxville, on the third Saturday in October, the Crimson Tide

pounded Tennessee, with a 30–3 lead after three quarters, ending in a 30–17 victory.

"We have talked our heads off this season about how good we are going to be," linebacker Rich Wingo said after the Tennessee game. "But now we have changed. We have shut our mouths and gone to work."

The Crimson Tide had no trouble with Virginia Tech, blanking the visitors 35–0. The day was perhaps more notable for George Wallace holding the hand of a University of Alabama homecoming queen for the last time as the state's governor.

Meanwhile, Bryant lamented his team's continued failure to hold onto the football. After five more fumbles brought the season's total to thirty-two, Bryant said: "I'm open to any sugges-

tions. I'll take suggestions from preachers, the alumni, opponents, and anybody else."

After a 35–14 win over Mississippi State, the Tide disposed of LSU, 31–10. Talk about the ultimate goal could not be avoided. Only the Auburn game remained and Alabama was up to number 2 in both polls, Penn State sitting in the top spot.

"We don't really care what bowl we end up in," running back Tony Nathan said, "as long as we're playing for the national championship."

As Auburn games go, this one was relatively easy: a 34–16 'Bama victory in which Jeff Rutledge threw three touchdown passes.

Penn State and Alabama accepted Sugar Bowl bids in a game that would pit number 1 against number 2, and the

Fullback Steve Whitman and Alabama had their hands full with Washington, beating the Huskies 20–17 in week five.

ALABAMA

vs. VIRGINIA TECH at Bryant-Denny Stadium October 28 1978

Bryant's team scored its only shutout of the 1978 season by whipping Virginia Tech, 35–0.

growing reputation of Joe Paterno against the established legend of Bear Bryant.

Winning the game and the national championship would be the only acceptable outcome for either team.

Or as Lyons said then: "We weren't brought here to play football for the fun of it."

A STRANGE TIME AND TWO OLD-FASHIONED TEAMS

Bookshelves were lined with Richard Nixon's memoirs and John Irving's *The World According to Garp*, Sony introduced a funky little portable stereo called a Walkman, and moviegoers laughed at *Heaven Can Wait* and gritted their teeth through the tense *Midnight Express*.

And, in college football, a coaching legend named Woody Hayes embarrassed himself, his team, his school, and the game by throwing a punch at an opposing player.

On December 29, 1978, Ohio State was playing Clemson in the Gator Bowl. Hayes's Buckeyes were trailing by two points, but driving into field-goal range. And then Chris Bauman intercepted freshman quarterback Art Schlichter's pass and was run out of bounds on the Ohio State sideline.

Hayes, then sixty-five years old, took a swing at the Clemson player and had

to be restrained. Ohio State fired him the next morning.

With this as a backdrop, Alabama and Penn State would meet to determine college football's best team.

"We related to Penn State more than any other team," Crumbley says. "They were coached like us. They acted like us.

"They had class. They were blue-collar guys from the North and we're blue-collar guys from the South. We had a lot of respect for them."

The feeling was mutual.

"The whole week their fans were classy," remembers Penn State running back Mike Guman, who now works for Oppenheimer Funds in Allentown, Pennsylvania. "There was no trash talking, like you see so much today. It was all good-natured stuff—fun and what college football should be about.

"They had the white uniforms with no names on their jerseys, and same thing with us. Two storied coaches, Joe a little bit earlier in his career and Bryant toward the end of his.

"We were two teams that got there by playing good, hard-nosed football."

Comments from newspapers in the days before the game also showed the respect each team had for the other.

Alabama safety Murray Legg called Penn State quarterback Chuck Fusina "by far, the best we've played."

Penn State defensive tackle Matt Millen—one half of the famed salt-and-pepper tandem he formed with Bruce

Clark—said it wasn't the wishbone that concerned him, *per se,* but the guys who would be wearing those red helmets.

"The formation doesn't scare you," Millen told *The States-Item* of New Orleans. "It's the people they have making it work."

And Alabama guard Mike Brock, when questioned about taking on Millen and Clark, said: "What we've got to do is hit them, hit them for four quarters."

That's exactly what both teams did—hit, hit, and then hit some more.

"Everybody just let it all hang out," Guman says. "It was a very rough, tough, physical football game."

And, thus, a thing of beauty to former Arkansas football coach Frank Broyles, who was up in ABC's broadcast booth calling the game with Keith Jackson.

"It was a terrific football game," says Broyles, who's still athletic director at Arkansas.

HELMET TO HELMET, TOE TO TOE

Penn State had the number-1 defense in the country and allowed a mere 54½ yards rushing a game.

Alabama running back Major Ogilvie rushed 14 times for 40 yards, and scored Alabama's second touchdown; it doesn't begin to describe what it felt like to play in the game. Making

matters worse was that Ogilvie and several other players had gotten a flu bug a couple of days before the game and did not get much sleep. Every hit Ogilvie took echoed through his joints, muscles, and bones.

"They had those two tackles—Matt Millen and Bruce Clark—that could read the fullback and quarterback," Ogilvie says, referring to Alabama's wishbone offense. "If the fullback got it, Clark and Millen seemed to be quick enough to get it, and if the quarterback kept it, they were quick enough to fend off the fullback and get back to the quarterback.

Running back Major Ogilvie says the '79 Sugar Bowl was the most physical football game in which he ever played.

THE HURT THAT KEEPS ON GIVING

They wore white jerseys instead of red, but the hearts beneath those jerseys were filled with the same hopes and aspirations the Alabama boys had.

"Disappointment is inadequate to describe the feeling," Penn State running back Mike Guman says of what he felt that night in the Louisiana Superdome when Alabama had beaten the Nittany Lions 14—7 in the Sugar Bowl.

"Winning a national championship is what we came to Penn State for," says Guman. "To have it slip through your grasp, it was very hard. It affected a lot of us in a lot of different ways and it was tough to try and put it behind you and move forward, to be honest."

Put it behind you?

If games such as the 1979 Sugar Bowl die, they also rise from the dead on ESPN Classic and elsewhere, forever haunting those on the low end of the score and the high end of the pain.

For Nittany Lion offensive lineman Keith Dorney, the instant replay came almost immediately: The morning after the Sugar Bowl, he was on the same airplane as Alabama's Barry Krauss and Marty Lyons—all of them headed to the East-West Shrine Game.

"I'll never forget that," Dorney says. "It was obvious they had been out all night partying. I was so jealous."

Krauss now spends some of his time autographing prints of his famous head-on stop of Guman on fourth-and-goal.

"I'm one of the reasons that play happened," Guman cracks, "and I didn't even get a copy."

Guman, who works for Oppenheimer Funds in Allentown, Pennsylvania, has learned to laugh through the pain.

Dorney wrote a memoir of his college and pro football career—*Black and Honolulu Blue,* and he sounds like his football soul still aches from that game.

"For that to be my last Penn State football experience, I don't know that I'm over it still," he says. "I hate Alabama."

Guman knows there's no getting over it in the sense that it'll never be over. Every so often the game shows up on television again, or at least his desperate and ill-fated leap for the end zone does, and then it's only a matter of time until his phone rings.

By now, Guman has developed the perfect answer:

"Call me," he says, "when I score."

"It was the hardest-hitting football game I ever participated in. There's not even a close second."

So hard was the hitting that, after the game, while teammates celebrated the victory, Ogilvie eased his battered body into his parents' car, rode back to Birmingham, and went to bed.

Yet by yardage, Alabama had some success: 208 yards rushing, 127 of them by Tony Nathan, whose 30-yard scamper was the longest run from scrimmage all game.

"You're trying to make every play you run a big play," says Nathan, who's now running backs coach for the Baltimore Ravens. "But, as long as our offense was on the field, theirs couldn't be."

Alabama had a six-minute advantage in time of possession: thirty-three minutes to twenty-seven. And Alabama's less-heralded defense stuffed the Penn State running game, holding it to 19 yards on 38 attempts.

Most of the first half played out in slow motion, the offenses being ground to a halt or taking themselves out with a turnover or penalty. The struggle was evident, too, in the teams' failures throughout the game in converting third downs: Alabama was 6-for-21 and Penn State was 4-for-17.

"We never were able to get any rhythm offensively," says Guman, the Penn State running back. "When we did make a good play, there was something we did that offset it. The character of the game, that's how it went. They did some things with packages we had trouble picking up."

Penn State tried dumping passes to Guman, who had five receptions for 59 yards—the most offense any Penn State player produced.

"Some of those were swings and screen passes," Guman says. "Those were ways we could at least try to simulate a running game."

The game's first score came with just eight seconds left in the half, the second quarter essentially extended because Penn State coach Joe Paterno called two timeouts in hopes of forcing an Alabama punt and getting the ball back.

When Nathan made his 30-yard sweep to the right, Alabama called time-out. And then, with eight seconds left, quarterback Jeff Rutledge tossed a 30-yard touchdown pass to receiver Bruce Bolton, who made a half-diving, half-sliding catch in the front of the end zone.

"The safety kind of bit on the play action and we beat the corner," says Mal Moore, then the offensive coordinator and now Alabama's athletic director. "That was a big play in the game."

It wasn't even the first option. Rutledge said afterward that he was going to pass to one of his backs—Bolton was to be a decoy used to clear out one side of the field—but then Rutledge saw Bolton breaking free and threw to him.

Momentum was clearly clad in crim-

son but, when Bryant walked off the field at halftime and stopped for a brief interview with ABC's Jim Lampley, the coach led with his chief concern.

"Their line's whipping our offensive line," Bryant said, chewing his words for the national television audience. "We gotta do something about that. The defense is doing great."

The defense, however, could not shut them out.

Before the third quarter would end, Penn State would tie the score at 7–7. The drive started after Pete Harris made a leaping interception. A Chuck Fusina sideline pass to Guman gained 25 yards and pushed Penn State inside Alabama's 20-yard line. The touchdown came as Fusina found receiver Scott Fitzkee at the back of the end zone, just able to get one foot down for the score.

There was now 4:25 left in the third quarter. Although most of the game had been played on Penn State's half of the field, the competition was even. By score, Alabama was as close to defeat as it was to victory. That was about to change.

The next time Penn State had the ball, it had to punt. Normally, Ogilvie would have been the return man, but he had been shaken up on the previous series. Lou Ikner, who had returned one punt all season, replaced him and found a lane on the left side of the field and returned the punt 62 yards; Ogilvie later said he would have called for a fair catch.

Ogilvie got his moment, however, when he took a pitch and ran eight yards around left end for a touchdown. With twenty-one seconds left in the third quarter, Alabama owned a 14–7 lead. If Alabama could hang for another fifteen minutes and twenty-one seconds, it also would own a fifth national championship under Bryant, and the tenth in school history.

"We knew we were underdogs in the public's eyes, in Penn State's eyes, in the media's eyes," says Don McNeal, recalling the tenor of the times. "But we weren't underdogs in our eyes."

SWEET AS SUGAR

Fumbling had been an issue all season for Alabama, and it would be once more as quarterback Jeff Rutledge made a wild pitch to his left just before being tackled. He pitched the ball toward running back Tony Nathan, but the pitch came so late that Nathan never even saw it.

"Where a pitch is involved, there's a certain point in time when you think the quarterback is going to keep the ball," says Nathan. "When you've got people following you, taking away the pitch, you don't expect the ball."

Penn State's Joe Lally covered the ball at the Alabama 19. Moments later, the ball was resting on the Alabama 8 after an 11-yard burst from fullback Matt Suhey.

◀ FACING PAGE Alabama scored a late first-half touchdown for a 7–0 lead on a play-action pass. "That was a big play," says then offensive coordinator Mal Moore.

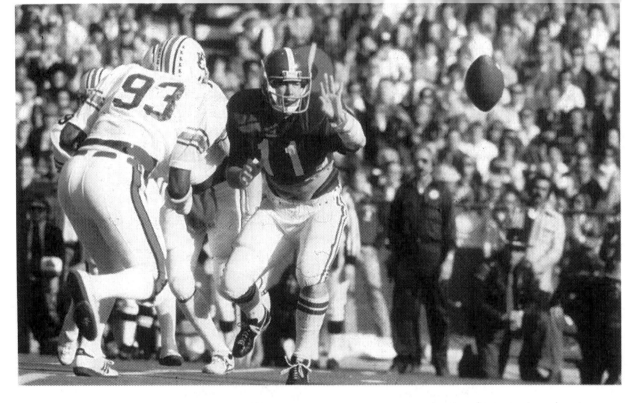

Guman says the Nittany Lions were confident the moment they got the ball back with a short field.

"We didn't need to win the game, we probably just needed to tie the game to win the national title," says Guman. "And we thought, 'Here it is, here we go.'"

Nathan was worried. "When you put your defense's back against the wall, it's always a concern," he says.

At this point, first-and-goal from the 8, there was still a little wiggle room. It was reduced to 2 feet when quarterback Chuck Fusina hit receiver Scott Fitzkee on a square-out pattern. Fitzkee was wide open after defensive back Murray Legg fell. If Fusina's pass had hit Fitzkee in perfect stride, he surely would have

scored. But Fitzkee had to slow his steps a bit and wait for the ball to reach him; that small hesitation gave McNeal just enough time to leave his man in the end zone and knock Fitzkee out of bounds inside the 1-yard line. Fitzkee was stunned, saying after the game that he didn't know where McNeal had come from. On the Alabama sideline, Nathan had the same reaction.

"OK, we get to live another day," says Nathan, recalling the breathless moment.

It was now third-and-goal. Alabama assistant head coach Ken Donahue was the mastermind of the defense. Alabama had frustrated Penn State with its blitzing and would sack Fusina five times in the Sugar Bowl.

It's best to demand perfection from a defensive back from day one. That way, he understands the nature of the position: that no one has his back. A receiver runs by him, a ballcarrier runs over him, the next stop is probably the end zone.

In time, Don McNeal came to understand this, but he didn't as a freshman, when it seemed Alabama's defensive backs coach, Bill Oliver, lived each day to make McNeal miserable.

"I thought he didn't like me at all," says McNeal. "I asked him one day, 'Do you like black people?' And he said, 'Mac, I saw something in you. I saw that you were raw and I wanted to get it all out of you.'

"He taught me so much," McNeal continues. "I came back my sophomore year and he said, 'McNeal, I'll get off your butt now because I know you can make it.'"

McNeal was a junior when he made a touchdown-saving stop of Penn State receiver Scott Fitzkee inside the Alabama 1-yard line in the fourth quarter of the 1979 Sugar Bowl. He also intercepted a pass in the end zone in that game.

In retrospect, it might even look like that Sugar Bowl was an easy day's work for the defensive backs. After all, the score was Alabama 14, Penn State 7.

However, going into the game, the press had written much about Alabama's so-called vulnerable secondary. Injuries meant that freshman Jim Bob Harris and sophomore Mike Clements would play more. And, with the fleet McNeal starting at one corner, senior Allen Crumbley looked to be an appealing target at the other.

"I think they took me deep four times that game," Crumbley says, recalling that none of the passes was completed; Penn State's long passing play of the day was a 25-yarder to a running back.

"On one play, I was a little late and I was running for my life," Crumbley adds. "When he jumped up to catch the ball, I went right through him" and he dropped it.

Remember, too, that after Alabama's famous goal-line stand, Penn State got the ball back. The game was not over.

Clements had come in to play at the end of the Vanderbilt game earlier in the season——a game Alabama already had won——and been burned for a deep pass and a touchdown at game's end. He had spent the rest of the season building his confidence back. Now, he was in a position where just that type of play would be an unmitigated disaster.

Even the team trainer remembered that Vanderbilt play.

"[Jim] Goostree came up to me on the sideline and tugged on my shirt, 'Now, you gotta watch that deep pass,'" Clements says.

"Marty [Lyons] and them are having a fun time at the end of the game, running around chasing the quarterback," Crumbley says of the linemen. "We're back there going, 'We can't make a mistake.' They've got these 6-2 receivers out there that can run like the wind. The game is very much alive.

(continued on next page)

"We're the last resort," continues Crumbley. "We're out there on our own."

Fittingly, the game effectively ended with Clements making Alabama's fourth interception of quarterback Chuck Fusina with just seconds left on the clock. He returned the ball 42 yards.

"I remember thinking, 'What is he doing throwing the ball straight at me?'" Clements says. "I remember seeing the laces roll over in kind of an uneven fashion and saying, 'I better not drop this.'"

He caught the ball and, for a while, he kept the ball——getting it autographed by other players.

"It had 'Penn State' stamped across the side of it," Clements says. "I don't think I've stolen too many things in my life, but I was keeping that thing. I had a house fire [years later] and it destroyed the ball."

But not the memory. After all, better to lose that ball than the receiver for whom it was intended.

Now, though, was the time to play it by the book. Penn State's tendencies, defensive tackle Marty Lyons recalls, were "drilled into us. And they were not going to go away from their tendencies."

Keith Dorney, one of the Penn State offensive linemen, remembers the confidence in his team's huddle: "We all thought we were going to score. There was no question."

The fullback, Suhey, carried on third down out of a tight I-formation, and tried to dive into the end zone. He needed 2 feet and came up about 6 inches short, David Hannah and Rich Wingo in on the hit. Wingo had just come into the game because Rickey Gilliland had been injured.

"Before he even got off the field, I was in the huddle," Wingo says. "That's

how I got a chance to play on that goal-line stand. I just wanted to get on that field so bad and hit something."

Wingo explains how each player did his job on the third-down stop: "We had practiced to where if the fullback came to your side—Barry [Krauss] was on one side, I was on the other as an inside linebacker—take him head on and hit him back into the hole. And if the fullback goes to the other side, the other linebacker would take him head on and your job was to make the tackle.

"So on third down, Barry took the lead blocker on and David Hannah up-rooted [the ballcarrier] and I was able to make the [finishing] hit."

Now, it was fourth-and-goal. Penn State called a timeout. Fusina checked the spot of the ball.

"Fusina came over, and we'd just done the Bob Hope show, the All-American show," Lyons says. "And he looked at me and said, 'Well, what do you think?' I said, 'I think you better throw the ball.' Half-jokingly said that to him and ran back to the huddle."

In that Alabama huddle, players held hands and Legg shouted, "It's a gut check, it's a gut check," recalls corner-back Mike Clements.

"Gut check" was a phrase Bryant had used often, two words that said more than a thousand others ever could have.

As the teams approached the line of scrimmage, noise rocked the Super-dome.

"I remember the crowd going berserk," says Dorney, who now laughs at the thought of him waving his arms to

LEFT
Defensive tackle Marty Lyons believed Penn State would run on fourth down but told quarterback Chuck Fusina that he better pass.

RIGHT
Bryant often spoke of "gut checks," and that's what the goal-line stand was: a gut check.

try to quiet the fans. "I briefly, and kind of stupidly, thought I was playing at home. But I was concerned about hearing Chuck Fusina's signals."

As Guman lined up, knowing he would carry the ball and his team's hopes, he reminded himself, "Get acceleration, and get off the ground."

Donahue, staying true to the idea that a team does not break from its tendencies in such situations, called a defense designed to stop yet another dive-over-the-middle play.

It was a risk, a calculated one, but still a risk.

"E. J. Junior was on my side and he was a pretty good athlete," Clements says. "He might have been able to cover somebody [on a pass play]. But if they'd gone against their own percentages, I think they could have scored on the outside."

Of course, they didn't go against their own percentages. They went straight up the middle, or up the gut. Wrong choice. The defensive line made

Alabama stopped Penn State running plays from inside the 1-yard line on third and fourth downs.

a strong submarine surge and the cornerbacks pinched, with Clements making a mad dash around the right side of the Alabama line and diving at Guman's legs.

"He came in pretty hard and sort of clipped me," Guman says. "I really wasn't able to get off the ground."

Hannah led the defensive line's charge and Krauss dove from the Alabama side of the line and caught Guman in midair—"just a wall," Guman says—and the force of the collision knocked the rivets from Krauss's helmet and left him lying on the ground in a daze.

On the turf inside the Superdome there was now a pile of exhausted football players. Some were in red jerseys, some were in white, and many players didn't even know the result of the play.

"The crowd noise just kept getting louder and louder," Dorney says. "There were people lying on top of me. I didn't know if we'd scored or not."

"When I heard the yell, I thought it was Penn State," Hannah told the *States-Item* of New Orleans. "When you're pinned to the ground and you look over and see the blue and white shakers everywhere, you think, 'My gosh, they've done it.' "

Says Clements: "I knew I'd made contact [with Guman], but I had no idea what was going on because I was on the bottom of the pile."

Lyons knew. He picked up his good buddy Barry Krauss—the two of them had taken a trip to California in Krauss's Buick Skylark the previous summer—and said, "Barry, you stopped him, man."

Says Lyons: "I remember running off the field putting up the number-1 sign and thinking this is a heck of a way to go out."

Although Lyons and Krauss were All-Americans that season, this team's defense was not the most talented Bryant had at Alabama.

"Defensively, we just played over our heads—just played superhuman football," Bryant said. "That goal-line stand is something I'll never forget."

Penn State got the ball back, but never seriously threatened again, the last gasp coming when Clements made Alabama's fourth interception of the game with just a few seconds remaining.

As for Krauss, he was so happy that he was also just a little sad. His Alabama football career was now over.

"I wish I had four more years," he said.

6

MISSION POSSIBLE

THE Crimson Tide had just finished a spring scrimmage on an unseasonably warm day. The sweat was running down players' faces.

It was only a few weeks after a beautiful wounded duck of a Cotton Bowl kick had given Alabama a 13–10 victory over Texas Tech, a 10-2 record, and a number-eight national ranking to end the 2005 season.

But there was little time to rest. Although still months before the first game of the 2006 season, the journey to the promised land had begun once again.

Now, people can say a particular season is a re-building year or that expectations aren't as high, but it is just so much howling at the dark side of the moon.

Here, the goal never changes. Alabama *always* aims to win college football's national championship.

"That's our mission statement every year,"

▲ PREVIOUS PAGE
Of Alabama's
twelve national
championships, six
came under Bryant
(1961, 1964, 1965,
1973, 1978,
and 1979).

The third of Coach
Wallace Wade's three
national titles, in 1930,
seemed unlikely, given
his announcement
before the season that
after the season
he would leave
to become coach and
athletic director
at Duke.

says Kyle Tatum, a senior offensive line-man on the 2006 team.

So there it is, out in the open, whether other people like it or not. Win twelve national championships and come within a whisker of winning five others, and your mission statement just about writes itself.

However, that is not to say the mission statement or the person in charge of executing it are never up for inspection.

Alabama won three national championships in a six-year span during the Wallace Wade era—1925, 1926, and 1930. Yet, in between the 1926 and 1930 titles, were three ordinary years, too ordinary for school president George H. Denny and a fan base that, even then, showed a clear and present preference for perfection.

This escalating criticism chafed at the coach. So much so, that on April 1, 1930, Wade announced his resignation, effective after the next season, to become football coach and athletic director at Duke. This proved something of a delicious April Fool's joke as Wade's last team marched through its schedule undefeated and yielded but 13 points all season, finishing with a fantastic 24–0 win over Washington State in the Rose Bowl.

Alabama's school yearbook, the *Corolla*, was just about delirious in its description of the accomplishment:

"Wallace Wade and his peerless 1930 team have made the word 'Alabama' a household phrase throughout the world, from England's foggy Thames, to Mother India's sacred Ganges, from

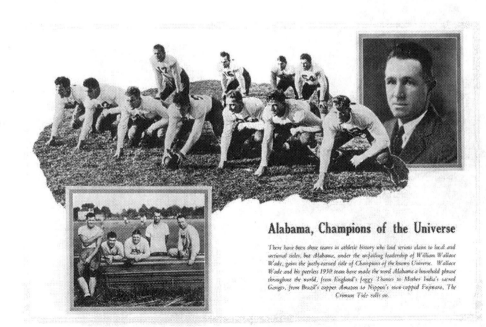

Alabama, Champions of the Universe

There have been those teams in athletic history who laid serious claim to local and sectional titles, but Alabama, under the unfailing leadership of William Wallace Wade, gains the justly-earned title of Champions of the known Universe. Wallace Wade and his peerless 1930 team have made the word Alabama a household phrase throughout the world, from England's foggy Thames to Mother India's sacred Ganges, from Brazil's copper Amazon to Nippon's snow-capped Fujiwara, The Crimson Tide rolls on.

Brazil's copper Amazon to Nippon's snow-capped Fujiwara, The Crimson Tide rolls on."

However far the word spread, the national-championship tradition continued when Frank Thomas succeeded Wade. Four years later, in 1934, Alabama had its fourth national title. Another came in 1941. And the 10-0 season of 1945 was worthy of another, but instead became the first of what Alabama fans commonly refer to as the "other five"—national championship seasons in spirit and in the NCAA football record book, though not formally recognized by the game's major selectors.

The '45 team featured a colorful cast of characters, led by All-American center Vaughn Mancha and halfback Harry Gilmer. The *Corolla* described the 238-pound Mancha as "causing more havoc than a young tornado," and aptly described Gilmer as a "leap-and-toss artist" for his splendid jump passes.

The national championship trophy case wouldn't gain another member until 1961. The 1950s not only had been devoid of this most grand glory, it had seen the program fall into complete disrepair in the three years, 1955 through 1957, that former Crimson Tide player J. B. "Ears" Whitworth coached the team to a miserable 4-24-2 record.

When Bear Bryant replaced Whitworth, he delivered his mission statement in his first team meeting.

"He said, 'If y'all stay here, we'll win the national championship,'" recalls Billy Neighbors, who did stay for the title Alabama won in 1961. "I didn't even know what a national championship was, to tell you the truth."

A lot of players at a lot of places didn't know, and still don't know. But they know at Alabama. They know because of coaches such as Wallace Wade, Frank Thomas, Bear Bryant, and Gene Stallings.

They know because of great players, because of good players who played great, and because of average players who became so much more because they were playing for so much more than their own ego.

Now, of course, the challenge is to get an up-close and personal look at another national championship trophy.

"It's gonna happen sooner than people think," says Shannon Brown, a defensive lineman on the last national title team, in 1992, under Stallings. "Because those guys Coach [Mike] Shula is getting in here understand the tradition of putting on the red jersey."

Roger Shultz, a center from 1987 to 1990, and a graduate assistant on the '92 national title team, goes even further.

"There's no reason Alabama can't do what USC has done and what it looks like Texas might be braced to do the next couple of years," Shultz says. "All you've got to do is throw two or three years together."

He makes it sound easier than it is, yet any Alabama fan would understand what Shultz means.

Wade's teams won back-to-back titles. Bryant's teams turned the trick twice—in 1964–65 and 1978–79. Each time, the Crimson Tide might have had a threepeat before the word even had been coined.

The 1966 team went 11-0. The 1977 team went 11-1 and finished with a resounding Sugar Bowl victory; Notre Dame still jumped from number 5, and over Alabama, to number 1 in the final polls.

Of course, before any team can throw together two or three championship years, it first must survive the grind at season's end. Alabama was 9-0 and had risen to number 3 in the country during the 2005 season only to lose, 16–13, in overtime to LSU. Then, Auburn defeated Alabama before Shula's team rebounded for an upbeat finish with the victory in the Cotton Bowl.

"They had it," says Brown, who's now the football coach at Bob Jones High School near Huntsville, Alabama. "But when Tyrone Prothro went down in the Florida game [he broke his left leg], he was like David Palmer was for us in 1992—the spark, that guy that could score any time he touched the freaking football. Nobody knows what kind of emotional toll that took on that team."

Nobody knows what might have

happened, which is the way it always is. After Alabama's first national championship in 1925, the *Corolla* said in a review of the year: "Who could have told us last September, at the beginning of the season, how it would all end?"

No one. Same as no one knows about this season, and the next and the next . . .

Only the objective is certain.

"You gotta go win 'em all," Shula says, giving his mission statement.

WORK TO WIN

For the players who now wear the red jersey, the first national championship under Bryant in 1961 is about as remote as the first under Wade in 1925.

It's all so much history captured in black-and-white photographs, the players in funny-looking helmets, the goal posts looking like oversized capital H's.

But the 1992 national championship, they can *feel*.

"Who can forget '92?" asks Wallace Gilberry, a defensive lineman on the 2006 team. "I grew up watching John Copeland and Eric Curry. "To me, Alabama has always been about defense."

Go back to the first national championship team in 1925. Although it had an offense prolific enough to score 297 points in ten games—almost 30 points per game—the defense shut out eight

To keep Coach Gene Stallings's 1992 team's national title hopes alive, cornerback Antonio Langham had to make a big play in the '92 SEC title game against Florida.

opponents and allowed only 26 points, with 19 of them coming in the 20–19 Rose Bowl win over Washington.

So, defense always was in style, and always will be in style, even if the offensive guys get all the style points.

"We're the fighters," Gilberry says, "and they're the lovers."

Defense was the strength of the 2005 Alabama team, which stayed in the national title hunt until late in the season. And it has been the runaway strength of most national championship teams at Alabama, and all of them under Bryant and Stallings.

Even in years when the defense allowed more points, such as in 1973 and 1978, the defense held when it mattered most. The 1978 team's goal-line stand in the 1979 Sugar Bowl win over Penn State is the single most memorable defensive image of Alabama football.

Such hard defensive work doesn't just happen in the most important game of the season. Rather, it starts in spring practice and goes right on through the last play of the season.

Before Bryant's first national title in 1961, he was grousing in spring practice about everything in general, and his defense in particular.

"I remember in the preseason he called that team a bunch of sissies," says Clyde Bolton, a retired columnist from the *Birmingham News*. "Billy Neighbors, Lee Roy Jordan, and all those other sissies. Somehow, they pulled their skirts up and got through the season."

That same spring, Bryant said: "We have very few people who have the correct mental picture of hitting through people."

At its most basic level, that's all defense is: hitting through people, making tackles sure and true. The best example of this in a Bryant national championship season also comes from the 1979 Sugar Bowl win over the Nittany Lions. Before those two goal-line-stand plays, cornerback Don McNeal saved a touchdown by hitting through a receiver and carrying him out of bounds inside the 1-yard line.

McNeal was practicing what had been preached.

"There's no such thing as having a perfect practice," McNeal says, "but we tried."

By the time McNeal came to the Capstone in the late 1970s, the national championship tradition had been solidified by three titles under Bryant in the

'60s and a fourth in 1973. The tradition of aiming for a perfect practice had started long before then.

"Everything we did was organized to the damn second," says Billy Neighbors. "Every drill, the way we did exercises, warmups, everything. Blow the whistle, do this for 10 minutes, this for 15 minutes, this for 30 minutes. Every now and then [Bryant] would get mad and show out a little bit, but I think now that was just his way of motivating you."

It was the ideal blend of precision and emotion, elements that a championship-caliber team would need on game day. Decades earlier, when some players referred to Wallace Wade as "The Bear," he was just as resolute about the way he prepared his teams for competition.

"Wade believed in isolation," said Fred Sington, a tackle on the 1930 team.

Sington, who later played professional baseball for the Washington Senators, recalled that the night before Saturday games in Birmingham, the team would "go to a picture show, but other than that we were always in skull [sessions]. We never had any contact with people."

Bryant relied on repetition in practices as a means for breeding instinctive reaction.

"We had athletes that would be walking around campus, and if you yelled real loud or clapped your hands, they'd break down in a football

Johnny Mack Brown and Pooley Hubert were star players on the first national title team in 1925.

position—literally," says Tommy Brooker, an end on the '61 team.

Such attention to detail was all part of the master plan. And, at least under Bryant, it went toward the idea that the head coach never wanted to hear of luck playing a role in the outcome of a game.

"There is no such thing as the bad bounce of the ball in football," Bryant said before he'd ever won a national championship. "The good team makes the bad bounces."

Defense, in particular, can make bad bounces. Sack the quarterback. Pop the receiver who dares to come across the middle. Pound the running back who strains for an extra yard.

Stallings's 1992 team, which went 13-0, gave up more than 13 points only twice: in a 30–21 win at Mississippi State and in the 28–21 victory over Florida in the first Southeastern Conference title game.

The calling card of this defense was its hard hitting, often led by All-American defensive ends John Copeland and Eric Curry.

Although Louisiana Tech hung tough, before losing 13–0 in the fourth week of the season, Tech quarterback Sam Hughes was happy just to have survived.

"It's hard," he said after the game, "to prepare yourself for getting knocked down every play and getting up feeling like you're going to die."

Shannon Brown, a backup defensive lineman as a freshman on the '92 team, says: "I played side by side with [Curry and Copeland]. When you got on the field with them, you stepped your level of play up because you didn't want to

The '62 Sugar Bowl victory over Arkansas, 10–3, was sweet for fullback Mike Fracchia, trainer Jim Goostree, and linebacker Lee Roy Jordan.

look like you didn't belong. Those guys were tremendously talented."

But even the best of players, and none was better than linebacker Lee Roy Jordan, credits coaches for putting defenders in the right place at the right time.

"We played some defenses that gave me and Darwin [Holt] a chance to run to the football," says Jordan, a member of the '61 national title team and an All-American in 1962, a season he capped with an incredible 31-tackle performance in an Orange Bowl win over Oklahoma.

"We had certain responsibilities," Jordan continues, "but they gave us a chance to move instead of taking on guys straight on. We were able to move from left to right and go through the holes and get some opportunities where we wouldn't have to knock down a big offensive lineman to make the tackle."

Bryant preferred his players lean, mean, and quick. He'd sacrifice size for speed just about every time. After the team integrated in 1971, Bryant's defenses only got better, and faster, at running to the football.

"When you talk about what we had across the defensive line in 1979 with Warren Lyles, and E. J. Junior and Wayne Hamilton at ends, I mean, they could fly," says Tommy Wilcox, a safety on that team. "They could outrun a lot of the defensive backs.

"And then we had Thomas Boyd and Randy Scott at linebacker—they'd backed up [Rich] Wingo and [Barry] Krauss the previous year—and both of those guys could fly. We were tough enough to stop people when they tried to run north and south. And if they tried to go east and west on us, one of those guys up front would just run 'em down before they had a chance."

While no one would suggest that a team from the 1920s could run with one from the 1970s, there was precedent for running people down in an awe-inspiring way.

The kicking game was a much bigger part of football in 1925, and Alabama excelled at defending returns. So much so that, when the *Corolla* wrote of that first national championship season, and recapped the all-important shutout of archrival Sewanee, it said: "Sports writers agreed that the most noticeable thing on Rickwood Field was the way Alabama tacklers went down under punts like racing wolves."

More than fifty years later, Alabama players, especially those on defense, were expected to maintain that same frothing-at-the-mouth intensity. And not just if they were playing up front. At Alabama, there would be no such thing as a "cover corner."

"If you're going to play in that secondary, you have to be able to cover and be physical," says Jeremiah Castille, a cornerback on the '79 team. "You had to be a hoss. The responsibility of the defense, the expectation of the defense, was high."

Just like it is today, when everyone understands the mission statement never changes at Alabama and that fulfilling it begins on the defensive side of the ball.

"Not taking anything away from the offensive guys," says Gilberry, a defensive end on the 2006 team, "but it's really our duty to take pressure away from those guys.

"That's our job, and we take pride in it."

HAPPY ENDINGS AND CLOSE CALLS

Don Salls played on the 1941 national championship team. He also was the long-time head football coach at Jacksonville State University in Alabama.

A few years ago, his former players had made for him a ring commemorating the '41 national championship.

"It's the only one," Salls says.

Some critics would say it's one more than there should be, that the '41 national championship is questionable. And perhaps it is. Other national championship selectors picked Minnesota (8-0) or Texas (8-1-1) over that 9-2 Alabama team.

But the process of picking a national

champion has never been perfect, or anything close to it. Over the years, the process has both helped and hurt Alabama. Six times, Alabama has gone undefeated and untied and won the national championship: 1925, 1930, 1934, 1961, 1979, and 1992. Another time, in 1926, the Crimson Tide was undefeated but had one tie. Four times—in 1964, 1965, 1973, and 1978—it won with one loss; the '65 team also tied one game. The 1941 team, after a 9-2 season, was awarded the national title by the old Houlgate Index System, which was used in *The Football Thesaurus.*

Paul Crane, a center/linebacker on the '64 and '65 teams, says, "We were fortunate in that one year they picked the championship before the bowl, and the next year they picked after the bowls. We were able to catch it both ways."

He's right. In 1964, Alabama was 10-0 heading into an Orange Bowl

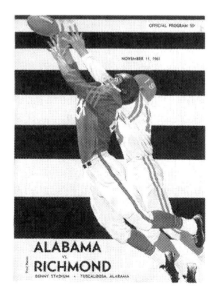

ALABAMA vs RICHMOND

Voted national champions in 1964 before playing Texas in the Orange Bowl, quarterback Joe Namath called the news "simply wonderful."

showdown with Texas. The major wire service polls—the Associated Press (made up of sportswriters and broadcasters) and United Press International (a poll of college coaches)—voted before the bowl games.

Although Alabama still had a game to play, players were giddy over the news they had been proclaimed national champs.

"Simply wonderful," said quarterback Joe Namath.

Unfortunately, Texas then beat Alabama, 21–17, the victory preserved by a fourth-quarter goal-line stand and some questionable officiating. With the ball inside the Texas 1-yard line on fourth down, Namath tried to sneak the ball over. Alabama players were so sure they had scored that they started jumping up and down to celebrate certain victory. But after one official had signaled it was a touchdown, another overturned the call.

Texas was now 10-1, same as Alabama. And the Longhorns' lone loss had been by one point to Arkansas, which finished 11-0 and was awarded a national title by various other, lesser, selectors. Notre Dame, at 9-1, also got a small piece, but Texas was left out.

"They close the polls after the tenth game," Longhorns coach Darrell Royal said. "We won it last year, Alabama won it this year. I wasn't going to be mailing back our trophy if we got beat last year, and I don't believe Alabama is going to be mailing us theirs this year."

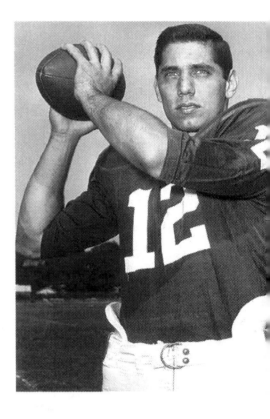

The timing changed in 1965, with the final poll votes being taken after the bowls. Alabama was 8-1-1 going into an Orange Bowl date with Nebraska. The Crimson Tide had started that season, in defense of their 1964 title, with an opening-week 18–17 loss at Georgia on a day so hot that one writer referred to it as the "heat between the hedges."

Afterward, Bulldogs coach Vince Dooley was tepid in his assessment of the Crimson Tide: "It's not a great team, like some of the Alabama teams of the last four or five years. It could be a great team later on. I wouldn't say it wouldn't be, but today it wasn't."

Then, on the third Saturday in October, Alabama got stung in the form of a 7–7 tie with Tennessee that didn't have to happen. Alabama had driven deep into Vols territory and was in position to kick a game-winning field goal. Bryant had been switching out senior Steve Sloan and sophomore Ken "Snake" Stabler at quarterback. After a busted pitch play resulted in a 10-yard loss, Bryant inserted Stabler, and the Snake faked a pass and ran for a 14-yard gain, but failed to get out of bounds.

It was now fourth down, but Stabler did not realize that. Needing to stop the clock, he threw the ball away. Tennessee took over on downs. Bryant said afterward: "It's my job to have things organized on the sideline and they weren't."

"He always took the blame and gave the players the credit when we won," recalls Stabler, who handles the color commentary on Crimson Tide radio broadcasts. "After the [Tennessee] game, he kicked the door [to the locker room] off the hinges, came in and raised hell with the coaching staff and said, 'We didn't have you guys prepared to play.' He took all the heat. He didn't have to do that very much: we were 28-3-2 and we won two SEC championships and one national championship."

This national championship appeared a long shot, although, by January 1, Alabama had won six straight and had pushed itself into the fringes of the national title picture. An Associated Press story presented the odds this way: "Alabama could grab off a second straight national crown if it convincingly beats Nebraska and both Michigan State and Arkansas are convincingly upset. These last two are highly unlikely taken separately and barely inside the realm of possibility taken together."

Gamblers perhaps wanted to make sure those odds would hold. The days leading up to the Orange Bowl were rife with wild rumors. Among them: Steve Sloan had been in an auto accident, Sloan had been declared ineligible for signing a contract with the National Football League's new Atlanta franchise, and Bryant had suffered a stroke.

Bryant was most troubled by his quarterback receiving unwanted middle-of-the-night phone calls. Finally, Bryant cut off all calls to Sloan's hotel room.

Once New Year's arrived and the game started, all the problems went away. It was great football weather: seventy-one degrees with a soft breeze. There was the usual star-gazing, with Michael Landon, alias Little Joe from Television's *Bonanza,* in the house.

Alabama easily built a 24–7 halftime lead en route to a 39–28 victory as Bryant began the game with some trickery: a tackle-eligible pass to Jerry Duncan (a play soon to be outlawed). The Crimson Tide scarcely resembled the team that had lost to Georgia on the season's first day.

Because Arkansas and Michigan

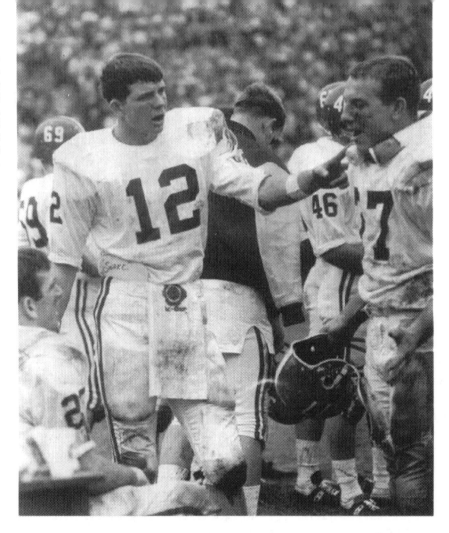

Quarterback Ken Stabler and tackle Jerry Duncan were teammates on the '65 national title team. Bryant began the 1966 Orange Bowl with a tackle-eligible pass to Duncan.

State both lost, Alabama was able to overtake them in the A.P. poll and win the national title.

"I'm so proud and happy," Bryant told the *Miami News*. "I wish I didn't have such a limited vocabulary to say how I feel about them."

Bryant perhaps had an easier time finding words before the 1966 season as his team began pursuit of glory previously unimaginable.

"Our seniors can become the first group in the history of football to play on three straight national championship teams," he said. "I get fired up just thinking about it."

Alabama started the '66 season 3–0, then escaped with an 11–10 win over Tennessee in Knoxville as Steve Davis kicked a game-winning 17-yard field goal with 3:23 to play.

Afterward, Bryant described himself as feeling "lucky, thankful, prayerful, and tired."

Alabama Nation was now consumed with the pursuit of their third straight national title. So much so that, on Saturday, November 26, 1966, the front page of the *Mobile Press* featured team rosters for Alabama and Southern Mississippi, and pictures of Stabler and Southern Miss defender Tommy Rousel just below a headline that read: 27 DIE IN SAIGON TRANSPORT CRASH.

The Crimson Tide, despite being two-time defending national champ, was only number 3 in the A.P. poll. So, after putting a 34–0 hurt on Southern Miss, Bryant made his plea.

"If the voters want something besides winning, we'll try and do it," Bryant told Benny Marshall, sports editor of the *Birmingham News*. "If they want it, we'll try triple reverses, forward laterals, lateral forwards and dipsy-doodles."

When Alabama thumped Auburn, 31–0, it was the team's fourth straight shutout. Banners in the student section that day in Birmingham were pointed at poll voters:

" 'Bama plays football," read one sign. "Notre Dame plays politics. In your heart you know we're No. 1."

The Tide's 34–7 win over Nebraska in the Sugar Bowl did not convince a columnist from New Orleans' *States-Item* that Alabama wasn't number 3, but it did change his mind about who were now one and two: the Green Bay Packers and Kansas City Chiefs, who were to meet in the first Super Bowl the following weekend.

Bryant learned of the final poll vote in a phone call from Benny Marshall. Notre Dame had been voted number 1 despite a 9-0-1 record.

"I hadn't heard," Bryant said for publication when the sports editor gave him the bad news. "I don't agree, but that's that."

What Bryant might have said privately, we don't know.

But he had to wonder: How much did football really have to do with the final vote? Had some national voters perhaps penalized the Alabama football team for other recent events in the state, such as the Selma civil rights march, Rosa Parks taking a stand by refusing to give up her bus seat in Montgomery, and Governor George Wallace's grandstand plays in promotion of segregation?

What's certain is that the 1966 season joined the 1945 and 1962 seasons as near-misses. With the 1975 and 1977 seasons, they all became part of the "other five."

"I've still got a craw, and it's still sticking in there a little bit," says Ray Perkins, an end on the '64-66 teams and the first Alabama coach after Bryant. "I just think it was the mere fact they didn't want to give it to somebody three times in a row."

The 1962 season was another heartbreaker. Had Alabama been voted champs that year and in 1966, they

The '61 team went undefeated and allowed just 25 points all season.

would have had a run of four titles in five years. The '62 team went 10-1, and its only blemish was a late-season 7–6 loss in Atlanta to Georgia Tech. Bryant blamed himself for not at least coming out of the game with a tie. A fourth-quarter touchdown brought the Tide to within a point but, instead of kicking the extra point, Bryant went for the two-point conversion, which failed, costing them a victory that would have extended their 19-game winning streak.

The '73 national championship was something of a reprise of the 1964 title: UPI again voted after the regular season and before the bowls. Alabama, at 11-0, was voted number 1. It had been a season of decisive victories, the Crimson Tide dominating on offense and defense, scoring 477 points, more than any team in school history, while giving up only 113.

Only Kentucky, which Bryant was coaching against for the first time since he left the Wildcats for Texas A & M, gave Alabama a true scare. "Kentucky's been waiting twenty-one years to get even with me," Bryant said.

For a half, it looked like Kentucky would get even. The Wildcats led 14–0 before Alabama scored three touchdowns in the third quarter, and another in the fourth, for a 28–14 win.

When 'Bama blitzed Miami, 43–13, to run its record to 9-0, the stars aligned for an Alabama-Notre Dame Sugar Bowl, the first-ever meeting between the two schools. It made the college football world seem like a smaller place, given that Frank Thomas, who had coached Alabama to two national championships (in 1934 and 1941), had played at Notre Dame for Knute Rockne.

After Alabama ended the '73 regular season with a 35–0 win over Auburn, UPI voters, in their final poll, placed Alabama number 1, and the school had its ninth national championship, its fourth under Bryant.

There was still a game to play, however, and it didn't disappoint. Two legendary coaches—Bryant and Ara Parseghian—and two elite programs produced a college football instant classic.

Even when Notre Dame went ahead, 24–23, by kicking a field goal with 4:26 left in the game, the matter was not set-tled. Alabama appeared primed to get the ball back one last time, when it had the Irish backed up against their goal line facing third and eight. Quarterback Tom Clements, standing in his end zone, connected on a 35-yard pass to tight end Robin Weber. That killed the clock, and secured the Irish's one-point victory.

"The long pass beat us," Bryant said, adding, "Notre Dame is a great football team, but I wouldn't mind playing them again tomorrow. In fact, I'd like it."

Quarterback Richard Todd, a sophomore on that Alabama team, doesn't point to that late Notre Dame passing play or even the Irish's 93-yard kick return for a touchdown as the backbreakers, but rather the substitution patterns.

"They kept their first teams in the whole time," Todd remembers. "We were substituting left and right after the second series. That's the only game I can tell you, where, if we'd kept our substitutions down a little bit, we would have won quite handily.

"But that's just the way Coach Bryant did it. He played a lot of people in those days."

Sylvester Croom, a center on that team, offers a different perspective: "Coach thought going into the season—and we felt it, we sensed it—that we wanted to be proclaimed the greatest team that he ever had," says Croom, now head coach at Mississippi State. "And we just didn't finish."

Yet it's hard to find too much fault with any Bryant team in the decade once you get past the 1970 team's 6-5-1 mark. Consider the record for the '70s: 103 wins, eight SEC titles, three national championships, and two near misses in '75 and '77. The decade ended with Alabama on a twenty-one-game winning streak, with three straight SEC titles and back-to-back national championships.

The 1979 team went 12-0 and outscored opponents 383–67. Only once that year did Alabama beat a team by fewer than 7 points and that came on a nasty November night in Baton Rouge, when Alabama held off LSU, 3–0.

"A torrential downpour," recalls Alabama safety Tommy Wilcox. "The raindrops were about as big around as quarters."

Rain, mud, wind . . . the defense knew what had to be done.

"We just kept saying we had to hold them," defensive end E. J. Junior said.

The teams were tied 0–0 at halftime. Alabama had had it chances, but kicker Alan McElroy missed two field-goal tries. Then, in a third-quarter drive, halfback Major Ogilvie made a 19-yard run and quarterback Steadman Shealy a 16-yard run that moved the ball inside LSU's 10-yard line. Two penalties pushed 'Bama back, but, when McElroy attempted a 27-yarder with 8:43 left in the third, his kick was on target.

"The good Lord was just looking after us," Bryant said.

Defensive back Jeremiah Castille was a member of the '79 team that finished 12-0 and outscored opponents 383–67.

Auburn fans had to wonder if Alabama had used divine intervention to escape with a 25–18 win over their Tigers that season: Alabama survived losing four fumbles.

The last step to the last national championship of the Bryant Era proved easier: The Crimson Tide beat Arkansas, 24–9, in the Sugar Bowl and the AP and UPI both voted Alabama number 1.

Offensive coordinator Mal Moore had tweaked the wishbone for the Sugar Bowl and, three times, Alabama scored touchdowns off a double-wing formation.

"Mal Moore probably did the best

coaching job of his career when he put in the double-wing," says Shealy. "It kept them in a base defense. If anybody ever stayed in a base defense against us, they were history."

Stallings turned in the coaching job of his career during 1992, which was the one hundredth anniversary of football at Alabama, when the Crimson Tide went 13–0. *Sport* magazine picked Alabama number 1 in the preseason and Stallings embraced the pressure, saying, "I'd rather be ranked high than low."

From the start, there were distractions. Receiver and return man David Palmer, who would be named All-American in 1993, didn't play in the season opener on September 5 because of a drunken-driving charge over the summer. In the early morning hours of Sep-

Shannon Brown was a defensive lineman on the '92 national title team, and says he felt pressure to play well whenever he got a chance to be on the field with All-American ends John Copeland and Eric Curry.

THE LAST WORD

Steve Webb had to go to the 1993 Sugar Bowl game against Miami. Not just because Alabama was undefeated and playing for the national championship, but because he'd heard all the hot wind out of the Hurricanes he could stand.

Webb, a linebacker and defensive end from 1988 to 1991, now a city councilman in Northport, Alabama, near Tuscaloosa, wanted to be there for the revenge. He was still angry about what Miami players had said at the Sugar Bowl three years earlier, following the 1989 season.

"The Miami guys, when we first got down to New Orleans, you know what they had the nerve to say to us?" Webb asks. "They said, 'Y'all messed up the game. Y'all was supposed to come down here undefeated and it automatically would have been a national championship game.'"

The reference, of course, was to Alabama taking a 9-0 record into Auburn, then getting beat. Miami then defeated Alabama in the Sugar Bowl and, for the record, won that national championship anyway.

So, three years later, with Miami woofing as much as ever, and Alabama an 8-point underdog, Webb wanted to be there, "to make sure," he says, "we showed the world Alabama was better."

Leading up to the '93 Sugar Bowl, Miami had shown more nerve than ever. Linebacker Rohan Marley, son of the renowned Jamaican reggae singer Bob Marley, seemed to have appointed himself team spokesman. He talked trash in general, ridiculing Alabama's offense by saying, "How can it be football without a passing game?"

Miami talked a good game before the '93 Sugar Bowl, but David Palmer and the Crimson Tide played it.

But he got personal, too. When Marley and a group of Miami players encountered 6-4, 290-pound offensive lineman Roosevelt Patterson and some Alabama players, Marley called Patterson a "big, fat, sloppy, so-and-so" and said, "there's no way you're going to block me," recounted Alabama running Derrick Lassic, who then told reporters, "I like Bob Marley. I can't say the same for his son."

Meanwhile, Miami quarterback Gino Torretta, the 1992 Heisman Trophy winner, was saying he wasn't scared of All-American defensive ends and quarterback eaters Eric Curry and John Copeland. When Curry heard that, he had a message of his own: "I'll put fear in him."

When game day finally arrived, Lynyrd Skynyrd's "Sweet Home Alabama" played on at the Hyatt Regency. It proved a bit of foreshadowing. Alabama stomped Miami 34—13. Things got so bad for Torretta that, at one point, Curry gave him a sympathetic pat on the helmet.

Afterward, Miami coach Dennis Erickson needed but four words to describe what had happened to the defending national champions.

"It was just domination," the coach said.

"They did their talking off the field," Alabama quarterback Jay Barker said. "We let our actions on the field speak for us."

And, ever since, Steve Webb has had the right to say "I told you so."

tember 6, Palmer was arrested again for driving under the influence. Stallings suspended Palmer indefinitely.

Without Palmer, Alabama struggled to get by Southern Miss, 17–10, the following week. Its biggest play of the day came when punter Bryne Diehl passed to cornerback Tommy Johnson, lined up as a flanker in punt formation, for a 73-yard touchdown. Quarterback Jay Barker's longest pass had gained a mere 17 yards.

ALABAMA HAS EARNED BORING TAG, complained one newspaper headline.

Although the Crimson Tide crushed Arkansas the next week, they managed only 167 yards of total offense the following week at Legion Field against Louisiana Tech, and were fortunate to

win 13–0. Palmer had been reinstated and he scored the game's only touchdown on a 63-yard punt return.

"The best defense we played that year, other than the one we played every day in practice, was La Tech," says Barker, who now has a sports talk radio show in Birmingham. "Everybody thought that was crazy, but it was true."

Meantime, Stallings took heat over the Palmer situation from both sides. When the coach didn't play Palmer in the season opener, he was criticized for putting the first game of the season at risk. He took such criticism again when he suspended Palmer indefinitely. Some outside observers ridiculed Stallings for reinstating Palmer.

Whatever Stallings did, there were

those who were going to second-guess him.

"You handle every player a little different," says Stallings, who is retired and living with his family on a ranch near Paris, Texas. "I felt like David had a hard time in his growing up, didn't have some of the privileges other people did. I felt like he needed to be involved with our program.

"And though I did not dismiss him from the team, I didn't let him play in a few games. I think it all had a way of working out."

With or without Palmer, there was going to be unrest.

Fans continued to fret about an offense they just didn't quite trust. Or like.

"People were complaining, complaining, complaining," remembers Roger Shultz, a graduate assistant on Stallings's staff that year. "We were getting drilled every week about how bad the offense was. But when you run a dominating defense, it's not going to be pretty."

Alabama carried a number-two ranking and 9-0 record into the November 14 game against Mississippi State at Starkville. The Crimson Tide built a 20–3 halftime lead. And then the Bulldogs intercepted two passes and recovered a fumble on the way to scoring 18 points in the third quarter for a 21–20 lead that pushed Alabama's national title aspirations to the edge.

"It was the first time as a defensive

unit that we were ever rattled," recalls Chris Donnelly, a starting safety on that team. "I remember being in the huddle and we were trying to compose ourselves. It was a shock."

Barker, who was then just a sophomore, led Alabama on two scoring drives in the fourth quarter. A George Teague interception halted MSU's last drive, and Alabama walked away with a scary 30–21 win.

"The thing I remember most about it is, 'Okay, it's not all about us,' " Donnelly says. "The offense stepped up for the first time [in a close game] and took over for us. At that point, I knew we could [win the national championship.]"

Sophomore quarterback Jay Barker wasn't flashy, but he was an effective leader in 1992.

After a 17–0 win over Auburn, Alabama was set to meet Florida in the first Southeastern Conference title game. In the second game of the 1991 season at The Swamp in Gainesville, the Gators had beaten 'Bama 35–0, the only loss the Crimson Tide suffered that year. Now, Alabama was on a twenty-one-game winning streak and looking to go back to the future.

"It's a game we've been looking forward to for a long time," Barker said. "It's revenge time."

The score was tied 21–21 when Antonio Langham picked off a Shane Matthews pass and ran it back for a touchdown with 3:16 to play. Alabama had a 28–21 win and a Sugar Bowl date with Miami that would prove anything but sweet for the trash-talking 'Canes: Alabama 34, Miami 13.

Before the game, some Miami players had mocked Alabama for its conservative, run-oriented offense. Afterward, when the defense had shut Miami down, and running back Derrick Lassic had run for 135 yards on 28 carries with 2 touchdowns to win the game's MVP award, Hurricanes linebacker Micheal Barrow told the *New Orleans Times-Picayune:* "I can see why they don't need to pass."

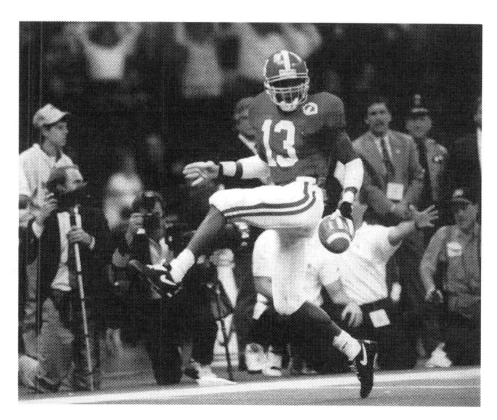

Alabama's George Teague picked off a Gino Torretta pass in the '93 Sugar Bowl and ran it back for a touchdown.

Stallings, looking back on that national championship season, says simply, "We had some close calls."

Retired sportswriter Clyde Bolton puts it a little stronger: "That '92 team was fun to cover because you kept thinking they were bound to lose, but they never did."

Instead, they made mission impossible into mission possible.

And although it has been more than a decade since the last national title, there will be another.

Lemanski Hall, a linebacker on that '92 team, gives voice to the mindset that still reigns.

"At Alabama," he says, "we *expect* to win national championships."

◄ FACING PAGE
Times change, but expectations don't. Fans and former players are waiting for Coach Mike Shula and his team to bring Alabama a thirteenth national championship.

7

TOUGH GUYS

IN his mind's eye, Johnny Musso could see every crushing hit.

Radio by his side, he listened for the details, for how Crimson Tide linebacker Lee Roy Jordan read the play, reacted to the play, then pursued until the man carrying the ball had nowhere to turn.

This, as Musso recounts it, wasn't just listening to the Alabama football game on a Saturday afternoon. Rather, this was "listening to the descriptive play of Lee Roy Jordan ripping heads off, and roaming from sideline to sideline and looking for somebody to devour," Musso says decades later, after his own career as a two-time (1970-71) All-American halfback at Alabama. "He was bigger than life."

As Musso transports himself all the way back to 1961 and Birmingham's Legion Field, he relives those innocent, or at least mostly innocent, days. Musso is just a kid, not yet the Italian Stallion.

On this Saturday, Musso and a cousin arrived at the stadium early. They watched in awe as Coach Bryant, also bigger than life, stepped from the team bus. It was Iron Bowl Day: Alabama vs. Auburn. The anticipation in the air was as sticky and sweet as cotton candy.

Musso had never seen an Alabama game in person. And so this figured to be a glorious day, except for one little problem: Musso and his cousin didn't have tickets.

"I was eleven years old," he says. "Back then, they didn't have turnstiles. It was right about kickoff and nobody was going in the gate and the ticket takers were not paying attention.

"We just ran for it."

It was like crossing a threshold, or coming of age.

"We ran up the ramp and into the stadium and got to see the magic of college football for the first time—the sights, the sounds and the colors," Musso says. "It was very captivating."

The irony, of course—and old Lee Roy could have explained this to young Johnny—was that to be captivated by Alabama football during the Bryant Era was to eventually follow a path that would make you a captive *of* Alabama football.

Yet what kid could imagine that? To a kid, the stars that fell on Alabama all wore crimson and white.

Billy Neighbors had been raised on Alabama football, too. His father even drove out to California for the Crimson Tide's first Rose Bowl after the 1925 season. Neighbors grew up in Northport, Alabama, which is little more than a long pass from Tuscaloosa. He used to sell soft drinks and peanuts at Alabama football games.

"You wanna go there all your life," says Neighbors, a freshman on Bear Bryant's first team in 1958 and an All-American defensive tackle on his first national title team in 1961.

Bryant's players, tough guys one and all no matter how much or how little talent they had, almost universally had one thing in common: They had been dreaming of playing for Alabama and/or for Coach Bryant for as long as they could remember. They were loyal to and protective of Alabama tradition before it ever became their responsibility to uphold and their job to defend.

As far as any eleven-year-old knew, Alabama football was just the pomp and circumstance of Saturday's game and the cozy comfort of Coach Bryant's Sunday statewide rehash of the big event.

"If you grew up in Alabama," says Sylvester Croom, an All-American center in 1974, and now head coach at Mississippi State, "you watched the game and the television show."

You did not watch practice or wrestling room workouts, which means you did not witness the literal blood, sweat, and tears the players gave just to run onto that sun-splashed field on Sat-

urday afternoons. If you had, you might have had second, and third, and even fourth, thoughts.

Or maybe, you would have better understood why Lee Roy Jordan so wanted to rip someone's head off.

JUNCTION REPRISE

Without question, 1954 was a year of historic significance in America. That's when the Supreme Court unanimously banned segregation in public schools (*Brown* vs. *Board of Education of Topeka*).

But, four years later, when players began workouts for Bear Bryant's first team at Alabama, the year 1954 represented something else: Bryant's first sea-

son as coach at Texas A & M and the infamous training camp he held in Junction, Texas, a camp so savage that, by the mid-1960s, Bryant himself was publicly saying he had gone too far and that, "I believe if I had been one of those players, I'd have quit, too."

That, however, was not his attitude in 1958 at the start of his first training camp in Tuscaloosa. Players, some of whom had prayed that Bryant would not be hired, wondered just what awaited them.

"We'd heard about Junction and we feared it," says Tommy Brooker, a freshman that season. "We feared it the whole time we were there."

What ensued was a Junction encore.

Bryant put his first Texas A & M team through ten days of two-a-days in the heat and isolation of West Texas. Fewer than half the players who started this training camp finished it and played on a team that would go 1-9—the only losing season Bryant ever had as a head coach.

Alabama players don't discount what those Texas A & M players suffered, but they make this point and they make it over and over. Their torture lasted longer. "Junction lasted 10 days," says Jack Rutledge, an offensive lineman and later a long-time assistant coach under Bryant. "He put us through three months of the same stuff."

It started in January, soon after Bryant had been hired to replace J. B.

Center Sylvester Croom was a team captain in 1974, and one of Bryant's favorite players.

"Ears" Whitworth, who, by comparison, had been running a camp for Boy Scouts.

Chuck Allen had played under Whitworth and, as the 1957 season played out to a 2-7-1 finish, Whitworth's third straight season of two or fewer wins, players knew change was coming.

"The one we didn't want [as coach] was Bryant," Allen says. "All we knew about him was, man, he's one tough sucker."

They found out firsthand with the initial wrestling room workout. Players went into the room by position. The centers and ends went first. Baxter Booth, Allen's good friend from their mutual hometown of Athens, Alabama, was in that first group. Allen arrived for his workout and, with other players, waited on the stairs.

"We've all got on our sweats and we're sitting out there and nobody knows what's going to happen," Allen says. "Finally the door opens and Booth comes out. And he is bleeding from his nose and his ear, and he's got vomit all down the front of his sweatshirt. And he says, 'Don't go! Don't go in there! They'll kill your ass! Don't go in that room!'

Allen and the others went inside anyway. They left in the same sorry state: covered in their own blood and vomit.

"It was brutal," Allen says.

It remained brutal. Indoors, outdoors, it really didn't matter.

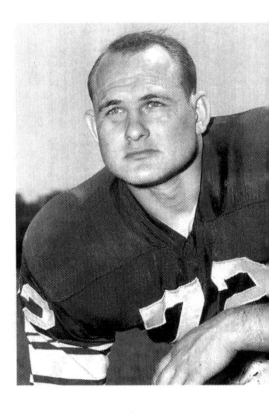

"You quit every day [in your mind]," Rutledge says. "You said you were never gonna go back. When you were through with a workout and you went home or wherever you were going, you would have to lean against the wall and slide down to sit down, and you'd probably stay there thirty or forty minutes without moving—totally exhausted."

Booth and Allen almost did quit.

While Bryant was testing all of them, he made broad assumptions about the players who had been part of Whitworth's teams, often shuffling players from the top of the depth chart to the bottom.

"The seniors, he just automatically put on the last team," says Booth, who was one of those seniors. The manhood of the holdover players was especially in question, because they had been front and center in the humiliating 40–0 loss to Auburn at season's end. "His point was the guys that started in that Auburn game, which I did, we'd already proven we were losers," says Allen, who was a junior in Bryant's first year.

So, between the life-sapping practices and the discouragement of seeing so many names ahead of them on the depth chart, Chuck Allen and Baxter Booth came to believe they had plenty of good reasons for quitting when one weekend they went home to Athens. After a while, Booth worked up his courage and told his mom and dad, "I'm giving it up."

"They said, 'You ain't giving it up,' " Booth remembers. "Get your ass back down there."

They both went back.

"I didn't want to pump gas in Athens," Allen says. "I was the first one in my family to go to college, so it was kind of important. But probably the best players quit."

One of those "best" players was Billy Neighbors's older brother, Sid, a tackle who had played under Whitworth. "Big Sid was 6-3 and ran like a 4.6 [40-yard dash]," says Wes Neighbors, Sid's nephew and Billy's son, and an Alabama player during the 1980s. "Uncle Sid was the best athlete out of all of us."

He wasn't the most disciplined. Playing for Whitworth, Billy says, had allowed Sid to get away with giving less than his absolute best. When Bryant came in, he established strict weights for players—he wanted his players lean and fast—and Sid Neighbors didn't make weight. He came close, but close wasn't good enough.

"He wouldn't lose the five pounds," says Billy, still annoyed all these years later. "He was hard-headed as hell. In July, in Tuscaloosa, Alabama, you can lose five pounds walking around the block."

Staying wasn't easy for anyone. The temptation to quit was always there.

Allen's mental trick, if you want to call it that, was to tell himself over and over, "I just wanna make it through this day." He adds, "I wasn't even trying to make first team again. I just wanted to live through this day."

Baxter Booth was a senior in '58, and was so discouraged at one point he went home and told his parents he was quitting; they ordered him back to Tuscaloosa.

Many players left under cover of darkness, which was less humiliating, but their soon-to-be-former teammates knew. Everyone came to recognize the *thump, thump, thump* of trunks and suitcases being dragged down the hallway.

In some respects, it was amazing they waited until night to quit because they were going through hell during the heat of the day.

There were no water breaks back then. Water, according to the conventional thinking of the time, meant weakness. The players' bodies didn't get the message. In fact, a body pushed to its limits will persuade the mind to make concessions that would be unthinkable under normal conditions.

"The kind of jerseys they had for us you could have worn in Siberia," says Brooker, an end who played on the '61 national championship team as a senior. "We'd ball them up just so we could get a little breathing room down there. The sweat would collect there and we'd suck on it."

That wasn't the worst of it. There was the time in two-a-days when Booth felt a tug from behind. "[Another player] was sucking the sweat out of *my* jersey," he says.

It all pointed to Bryant believing one thing: "He didn't think he could kill us," Billy Neighbors says.

Players weren't so sure.

"The great thing that could happen to you during spring training was to get hurt real bad," Allen says. "I got whacked out pretty good one day [suffered a concussion], and the first thing I remember is I was in the back of a station wagon behind the dressing room, by myself, with full gear on, and I had a lot of blood coming out of my mouth because I'd cut it. In a few minutes, they opened the door and they put another guy in there. And they waited until they got a full load, and when they got five of us, they took us to the hospital.

"They kept me overnight. That was one of the best nights I had in the spring," he says. "I can't tell you how happy I was to be in that hospital.

"The big guy couldn't get me in there."

ALWAYS ANOTHER TEST

Years rolled by, championships stacked up—the Bryant Museum doesn't have enough room to display all the trophies—and playing for Bryant remained essentially the same.

He changed with the times enough to eventually grant water breaks, but a little cup of water merely made a man thirsty for more. By the time Tony Nathan was a running back at 'Bama (1975-78) players were not desperate enough to suck the sweat from each other's jerseys.

"But you'd take an ice bag off somebody's arm or leg and put a hole in it, if you got a chance," Nathan says.

What players toward the end of Bryant's tenure discovered was that they were part of a great continuum.

The practices, the so-called lower gym workouts, and the motivational speeches had worked before and they were going to work again, if only they were tough enough to take it, and to live up to the tradition of it.

Tommy Wilcox was a safety on Bryant's last four teams, from 1979 to 1982, after being red-shirted in 1978. He remembered well the goal-line stand from the 1979 Sugar Bowl. He played on a national champion as a freshman

the next season, and was part of another goal-line stand at Penn State as a junior in 1981, when Bryant was going for his 314th career win, the one that would tie Amos Alonzo Stagg's record.

In the second half of that game, Penn State drove to inside Alabama's 10-yard line. Because of an Alabama penalty, the Nittany Lions ended up getting seven plays from inside the 10, four of them from inside the five.

Maybe they could hold them off for two plays, or three, or even four. But seven? Yet Wilcox says they had been prepared for exactly this type of situation.

"We had the lower gym workout

The dreaded lower-gym workouts, Tommy Wilcox says, steeled players for the toughest moments they faced on the field.

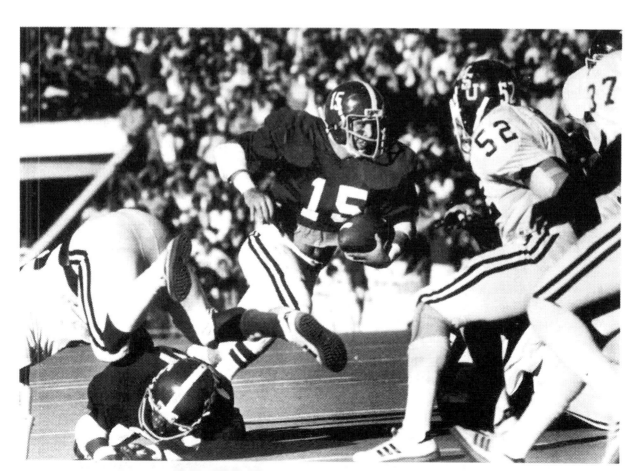

once a week and they called it the gut-check day," he says. "One hour, you were constantly moving, people barfing in garbage cans, coaches mentally pushing you when you didn't think you could take another step, always screaming, 'Fourth quarter, what ya gonna do? Your back's to the wall, they're on the goal line, they're fixin' to score. Give me that extra wind sprint!'

"So it was just one of those things, 'Been there and done that,' and they're not getting in the end zone," Wilcox says. "We held them. And as we were running off the field in jubilation, Coach Bryant took his hat off and tipped it at us, as if to say, 'A job well done, men.' And man, that just sent goosebumps."

Alabama won, 31–16 and, with a victory the next week against Auburn, Bryant broke Stagg's record.

Baxter Booth remembers a far more desperate goal-line stand from the 1958 season. Alabama was coming off a loss at Tulane, a loss that resulted in some of the roughest practices of the season. Now, they were in Atlanta playing Georgia Tech.

"They had the ball inside the five and it was first-and-goal and he sent another player in there with a message: 'Have y'all forgotten about last week?' We were fighting for our lives. We ended up holding them and winning the game. And the next week we were practicing in sweat clothes, so he could make it as good or as bad as he wanted."

To play for Bryant was also to take one or more personal tests.

In 1963, Paul Crane was a sophomore center-linebacker. Lee Roy Jordan had just finished his All-American career at Alabama in 1962; he would now wear number 54 for the Dallas Cowboys. Crane tells what happened when he showed up for team picture day in 1963.

"The equipment manager gave me Lee Roy's old number, 54," Crane says. "I was going out on the field [wearing the jersey], and I was proud of it. But it wasn't my choice or anything like that."

So, Crane walks onto the field and naturally crosses the coach's path.

Bryant: "What are you doing with that jersey on?"

Crane: "Coach, they just gave it to me."

Bryant: "You go take that jersey off."

Crane: "Yes, sir."

And then there was a pause, a pause that Crane still wonders about more than forty years later. He already had started toward the locker room.

"Wait a minute," Bryant called after him. "Just leave it on."

And that was that. Crane wore number 54 and, in 1965, was an All-American at center.

"I don't know if he used that as motivation for me or if he sincerely was not going to let anybody have the jersey,"

says Crane. "It was a stunning thing, almost like he accused me of getting the jersey that they just gave to me.

"But it was a real motivating factor. I was proud to wear it. I was proud to wear it the first time I thought I was going to wear it, and I was even prouder the second time I was going to wear it."

Marty Lyons recalls the challenge Bryant gave him in 1976, his sophomore season. The team was having a controlled scrimmage. Lyons, a defensive tackle, was then second-string.

"Baumhower, take your pads off," Bryant told the starter, Bob Baumhower. "Lyons, you're starting."

It was the moment Lyons had been waiting for.

"I'm thinking, 'Wow, this is pretty nice, getting recognition from Coach Bryant,'" Lyons says. "Only thing is, I ended up staying out there for like ninety-six straight plays. I don't know how I kept from crying. You're wearing like a zoot suit, almost like catcher's equipment, and you're just dragging it around. And every time they called out for a change in personnel, Coach Bryant would somehow forget me.

"I remember coming off the field just totally exhausted. He came by me and gave me a little pat on the ass and said, 'You know, Lyons, you may be a player after all.' And you're thinking, 'You know, Coach, you may be a son-of-a-bitch.' "

It was, of course, what Bryant did to all of them: pushed them to the edge.

Pushing back was not a good idea but, sometimes, players managed to make a move that spared them a little agony. Darwin Holt, who played on the 1960 and 1961 teams, went out for the school wrestling team one year just to avoid the football team's dreaded gym drills.

"I'm from Texas and it reminded me of horned frogs," Holt says. "As kids we used to take 'em in a paper sack and shake 'em up, and they would spit blood. And then you'd take the paper sack and chase the little girls around the playground. That's what those gym drills reminded you of because there was blood everywhere."

A playground, it wasn't. A training ground, it was.

"It was kind of like the Marines," Holt says. "Coach Bryant only wanted a few good men."

The few and the proud, pride being about the only thing many of the young men had that they could call their own.

"Nobody came from any money," says Chuck Allen. "That was the whole thing, whether you could tough it out. I wasn't any kind of a good player, but I survived. And there's a lot of pride in surviving."

GOOD AND NASTY

It is not enough to just say that all who stayed and played for Bear Bryant were tough. It's true, but it's not enough.

"There's four types of players," says Jackie Sherrill, who from 1963 to 1965 was a fullback/linebacker at Alabama and, for many years, a college head coach, including at Texas A & M and Mississippi State. "There's the nice player, who's gonna say 'yes, sir' and 'no, sir' and 'excuse me' on the football field. He'll go to class, never do anything wrong, and he's good enough to make a 4.0 [grade average]. But he's not good enough to win with.

"And then there's the good player, who's going be a good student. He'll be a good team player," Sherrill says. "But he's not going to beat you by himself.

"Then there's the nasty player. He's going to run some red lights, gonna miss class, and that kid's gonna beat you because he has a lot of talent. But he's not going to help you up on the football field; he may step on your hand.

"And then there's the bad player. He's not going to go to class and he's gonna do stuff on the field, like make penalties. But he has more talent than anybody else.

"Good and nasty players, that's what Coach Bryant had," says Sherrill. "He didn't have nice and he didn't have bad players. He would keep the nice kids

around, but they were not going to be players for him."

How many nasty players did Bryant have? How many good? It's safe to say almost all fell into one of these two categories and some easily floated between the two.

Darwin Holt ended up with the nastiest reputation as a hitter for leading with his elbow against Georgia Tech's Chick Graning, but there's more to that story, and this isn't about one play. It's about the way a man plays over a season and a career, the attitude he brings to every game, and every practice.

As far as Holt was concerned, the toughest of the tough was Billy Neighbors.

"Lee Roy played right side [linebacker] and I played left side," Holt says. "Neighbors played tackle on my side. Before the ball was snapped, I used to reach over and pat him on his little tush.

"He had the softest little butt in the whole world," Holt says, laughing. "And he had a 52-inch chest. It wasn't that I wanted to squeeze his butt, I just wanted to make sure he wasn't more than an arm's length away from me because I wanted his protection."

Jordan's reputation for hitting extended to practice, where it also served as a way to make a shorter day of it. "Lee Roy's just knocking heads off," recalls Jack Rutledge. "Coach would come on the big blowhorn [and here Rutledge

To be a "tough guy" during the Bryant years was to play before a full house of rabid Alabama fans.

JFK, MEET LRJ

Everybody else first remembers his 31 tackles in the 1963 Orange Bowl. If you want to summarize linebacker Lee Roy Jordan's extraordinary career at Alabama, that's the game that does it in one jaw-dropping statistic.

"To play linebacker, you've got to have that sixth sense," says Darwin Holt, who played alongside Jordan in the 1960-61 seasons. "Lee Roy had that sixth sense and no fear."

That was abundantly clear on January 1, 1963, in Miami, when Jordan chased and caught just about everyone in an Oklahoma uniform as Alabama beat the Sooners 17—0.

More memorable to Jordan is what happened before the game. He got to meet President John F. Kennedy, who was given the honor of tossing the coin before kickoff.

"Secret service people took the referee, the Oklahoma captain, and me up in the stands for the coin toss," Jordan says. "I always called tails. That was my motto back then. I won the toss and shook hands with him.

"He was very nice. But he was kind of there in support of Oklahoma. He went to their locker room and he didn't come to our locker room before the game. You think Coach Bryant didn't use that?"

He did.

As Jordan remembers it, Bryant pointed out this disparity by saying, "The president didn't see fit to come over and visit with us, but he did go see the Oklahoma guys. Y'all need to have a little extra fire in your eyes."

They did, and Jordan did, making those 31 tackles. Not that it's what he treasures most from the experience.

"I still have that silver dollar," LRJ says.

does his Bryant deep voice impersonation], 'Lee Roy, go in before you hurt somebody.' "

The guys taking the hits were good and nasty, too. Quarterbacks, especially after Bryant switched to the wishbone in 1971, were going to take their share of hits.

"Pat Trammell and Joe Namath were nasty players," Sherrill says. "They were gonna run a red light."

Running backs and receivers not only were expected to take a licking and keep on ticking, but to deliver punishing blocks.

In 1977, Ozzie Newsome was an All-American wide receiver at Alabama. But it almost doesn't do him justice to call him a receiver, because it prompts present-day images of prima donnas catching the ball and racing for the sideline, and making matador-style blocks on running plays that set teammates up as targets for hard-charging defenders.

"We made our people block," says Bobby Marks, who was Newsome's position coach. "Ozzie was a great blocker. He would just engulf defensive backs. He was so tall, so big."

Yet Newsome remembers that it was neither his blocking nor his pass receiving that first caught Bryant's attention. "Where he first got a sense of me," says Newsome, now the general manager for the Baltimore Ravens, "is one day he had me returning punts and there was a punt maybe 30 yards away from me and

I went and got it. He was amazed by my ability to track the ball." Newsome was as good as it gets, eventually making the Pro Football Hall of Fame as a tight end.

Another Alabama offensive star was much more direct with Bryant, telling the coach what he believed he could do on the front end—during recruiting. Johnny Musso, that eleven-year-old kid whose first great run for Alabama took him past the ticket takers at Legion Field, actually considered playing for the enemy: Auburn. Musso's mother, however, was pulling for Johnny to pick the Crimson Tide.

Ozzie Newsome was an All-American receiver who not only was a great pass catcher, but a brutally effective blocker.

"She'd pick up these Alabama place-mats and she'd serve his meals on that," recalls Mary Jo Lorino, Johnny's sister. "She never told him where to go."

When it came time for Bryant to close the deal on Musso's recruitment, Musso had what almost all other Alabama recruits didn't dare have: questions. This was in the late sixties. Alabama football had started to slip just as young people all across America had begun to stand up and demand that their voices be heard.

"We went over to my brother's apartment, and just the two of us talked for a couple of hours," says Musso. "And I was real frank, mainly because I didn't think I was going to go to Alabama.

"I asked some really hard questions, made some observations about the program and he got angry. One [of those observations] had to do with how they ran their running backs and used their players—a cocky high-school player talking like that to the greatest coach of all time.

"I don't think many people talked to him honestly and told them what they were thinking," Musso says. "And I think he respected that. He never mentioned that conversation, but when I went to Alabama he gave me every op-

Like quarterback Pat Trammell in the early '60s, running back Johnny Musso in the early '70s wasn't afraid to tell Bryant what he thought.

portunity to succeed. Some people had to fight and crawl to start. My freshman year, first spring training, he had me running on the first team the first day.

"Without any words to it, he just kind of threw the gauntlet back to me, 'You think you're a hotshot, well here, let's see if you can do it.' "

It was a perfect match: the good and nasty coach and the good and nasty player.

The only question is, if Musso had carried the ball more, might he have had a chance to win the 1971 Heisman Trophy over Auburn quarterback Pat Sullivan? Musso doesn't believe he would have, because "people in that part of the country weren't going to divide their vote."

He was, however, an All-American and, in the words of former teammate and later 'Bama assistant Danny Ford, "the toughest running back I've ever seen."

"Coach John David Crow helped Johnny become an excellent player," adds Ford, who also was a head coach at Arkansas. "Many times they would have a harness hooked on the practice field fence that would teach you how run with body lean. And the more you pulled, the harder it was to get your weight forward. The Italian Stallion——I can remember seeing him do that [drill] a bunch of times."

Bryant grew to love him, once telling *Sports Illustrated*, "I don't know

which I like best, watching Musso run or watching him block. He simply wipes people out when he blocks."

Although a much quieter personality, running back Major Ogilive, who played on the '78 and '79 national championship teams, was cut from the same self-made cloth.

"One year, he had a torn stomach muscle where he couldn't practice at all," recalls teammate and quarterback Steadman Shealy. "Yet he'd grade a winner [in the coaches' evaluations] every game.

"Major had this way of running where you couldn't bring him down," Shealy continues. "He'd surprise you because he was faster than you thought he was. But he also had this move where you'd kind of bounce off him."

Ogilvie isn't quite sure what to say about his own running style, but he does know this: It was no coincidence that players played through the pain. After all, enduring pain was what they most had in common.

They had no choice but to press on even when vomit was "filling the buckets" during winter workouts, so why back off on game day?

"That's what helped us to be successful, that oneness," says Ogilvie. "Not everybody was willing to go through that. Some folks lose an interest at that level.

"Those of us who did [pass] that gut check, it's kind of fun to talk about now."

ABOVE THE TEST

In four seasons playing for Bear Bryant——1958 to 1961——Tommy Brooker was certain of two things:

"Players feared him, and he controlled the coaches. They feared him."

That was the rule.

Assistant coach Ken Donahue was the exception that proved the rule. Donahue's first season on Bryant's staff was 1964. He remained through Bryant's retirement after the 1982 season, and was on Ray Perkins's staff for two years.

Donahue had played at Tennessee, the school Bryant loved to beat most. If Donahue had been anything other than what he was, as smart at devising defensive schemes as he was dedicated to his job and getting every last ounce of energy out of his players, he'd have never lasted.

"Ken Donahue was relentless," says Marty Lyons, a defensive tackle on the 1978 national title team that made the goal-line stand against Penn State. "A lot of credit for that [goal-line stand] has to go to him."

Clem Gryska, also an assistant coach during this time, says players had a love-hate relationship with Donahue. They respected him, but he could make their lives miserable. Jack Rutledge, another assistant on the staff, remembers things reaching the point where the rest of them were thinking that Donahue's dedication had to be reined in a little bit.

"The defensive tackles would have to come in and meet at eight-thirty or nine o'clock at night so they couldn't go out and get in trouble," Rutledge says. "I sat with Coach Bryant and we wondered what to do so the defensive tackles could have some kind of freedom, because Donahue wouldn't let them go."

Of course, he wasn't asking as much of them as he did of himself.

"He worked twenty hours a day," says Gryska, "probably stayed there until eleven at night. He drew up every formation."

Just as Bryant would give his teams collective challenges and would give his players personal ones, he did the same with his assistants.

"We'd be having a staff meeting, sitting around a table, and we all got tried once in a while," Gryska says.

That was the rule. Ken Donahue was the exception.

"Coach Bryant didn't mess with him," Gryska says.

LIVING UP TO
THE LEGEND

In December 1962, Tommy Brooker was a seventeenth round draft choice of the Dallas Texans of the old American Football League. When he reported to camp, his reputation preceded him.

"I walked up and introduced myself, shook hands with [running back] Abner Haynes," Brooker says. "Of course, I'd never played with black people. I'd only played against them. Anyway, the first thing he said was, 'You're one of Bear's boys.' And just the way he said it, and the rest of the players, those sitting on the bench, got up and came over and shook hands with me. They didn't know me, but the respect was there."

Because to be one of Bear's boys was to have survived and conquered. You were a tough guy.

"We were in better shape than everybody else," says Billy Neighbors.

"You'd paid the price," says Nathan, a running back on the '78 national title team. "In the fourth quarter, that's when you can put people away. We felt like the fourth quarter was ours."

Eventually, there came a time when there were no more fourth quarters. Not at Alabama, anyway. Players moved on with their football careers, or not, and moved on with their lives.

They remained tethered to what they had learned and had endured under Bryant. Through commiserating about training a bond formed between Bryant-era players, who sometimes met for the first time when returning to the Capstone for reunions and celebrations of championships past.

"They went through hell and you went through hell," says Tommy Wilcox, a safety who played on Bryant's last national title team in 1979. "But, in the long run, it paid off because we won championships."

They also won a certain status. They were a cut above former Alabama players who had not played for Bryant. Or so it seemed to some of the players from previous eras.

"Coach Bryant's players were Coach Bryant's players," says Harry Lee, who played from 1951 to 1954 and who was secretary-treasurer for the A Club during Bryant's tenure and had a good relationship with the coach. "He sort of created that gap between his players and everybody else that was before that."

All Alabama players were family, but Bryant players were the immediate family. And like the father figure he was, he warned them of the real-life gut checks he knew were waiting for them outside the white lines of the football field.

Tommy Wilcox says these warnings were a recurring theme, Bryant saying that was why he worked them as hard as he did. The coach knew there would be lost jobs, failed marriages, and family tragedies.

"He'd always use the example of

WIN ONE FOR THE BEAR

Paul W. Bryant had played at Alabama for Coach Frank Thomas, who had played at Notre Dame for Knute Rockne and with George Gipp of "Win one for the Gipper" fame.

At the Liberty Bowl in Memphis, Tennessee, on an ice-cold December day, senior cornerback Jeremiah Castille, who could be described as the strong silent type, could be silent no longer.

He had to give his own "Win one for the Bear" speech, though he was much too respectful to put it quite that way.

"I was not a very talkative person," Castille says. "It had to be the Lord that prompted my spirit, so strong, to let Coach Bryant know how I felt about him. A lot of times, as men, we don't do that."

Castille did it that day in the locker room before Bryant was to coach his last game, on December 29, 1982, against the University of Illinois. Bryant already had announced his retirement. The regular season had ended in a three-game losing streak and with defeats in four of the last six games, including to rivals Tennessee and Auburn. Bryant's last team limped into the Liberty Bowl with a 7-4 record.

Young Jeremiah Castille was thinking big picture. Because it was Bryant's last game, he knew it was going to echo into eternity.

"It was a thank-you to Coach Bryant, but it was also a message to our team that, 'Hey, guys, we're not going out and lose that game,'" says Castille, who is now chaplain for the football team. "I reckon after four years, and as a senior, I'd earned the right to stand up and say something. Looking at the changes in my life, the things the football program did for me, I needed to be able to express that. The number-one person responsible for all that was Coach Bryant."

Quarterback Walter Lewis remembers the speech.

"To hear it coming from [Castille and Eddie Lowe, a linebacker and also a senior], you never heard a peep out of them," Lewis says. "It just electrified guys."

None more so than Castille himself. In Alabama's 21–15 win, Castille intercepted three passes and won the game's Most Valuable Player Award.

"I played at the level of the speech I made," Castille says, still a little amazed.

Less than a month later, on January 26 at Tuscaloosa's Druid City Hospital, Bryant died.

Castille remains ever thankful that, hard as it was for him at the time, he did get up and say what was in his heart, adding, "I kind of gave Coach Bryant his flowers while he was alive."

Jeremiah Castille (19) was the MVP of the 1982 Liberty Bowl— Bryant's last game— as he intercepted three passes.

what are you gonna do if you come home and your wife's run off with your next-door neighbor, taken all your money, burned your house down, and taken your kids, too," Wilcox says. "He'd say you better know how to fight."

Though Bryant knew how strong they were—after all, they were *his* players—he checked on them.

"You'd get a letter from him occasionally, a phone call, to find out how you were doing," says Nathan, who played several years for the Miami Dolphins. "He wanted to see whether or not you were staying out of trouble."

Bryant was wise in his words. Trouble found his players the way it finds everyone—sooner or later.

Wilcox now has a successful outdoors TV show in which he takes well-known coaches and players from the Southeastern Conference hunting and fishing and lets them spin a few old stories. But he had a rough patch professionally.

"You're looking for a new job and you think back to that prime example he gave," Wilcox says, "and you say, 'I know he's watching me. I'm gonna tighten my bootstraps up and make it happen.'"

Lee Roy Jordan, years after he was through roaming from sideline to sideline looking for heads to rip off, was almost devoured by business debt.

"Some people advised me to give up and consider bankruptcy," says Jordan, who today owns a lumber company in Dallas. "His teachings wouldn't let me do that."

The old linebacker pauses, and then says, "It was a business goal-line stand."

Inspired by Bryant, Lee Roy Jordan learned to tackle business problems head on, just like he'd done with ball carriers.

8

IT'S PERSONAL

THE coach had gathered his team together in the locker room before the game—not just any game, but *the game*. The rivalry game that mattered most to prominent alumni, some of whom were in that locker room to hear what the coach had to say.

"Boys," the coach began, "I have but one favor to ask of you. We are getting ready to play the most important game on our entire schedule . . . we've been friends and pals for nearly two months now, and we all love and respect each other . . ."

Obviously, this was not Bear Bryant before the Tennessee game. No, this sounded much too cuddly to be the Bear. Nor was it Bill Curry before the Auburn game, though given Curry's repeated failures against Auburn, perhaps he should have asked, begged, and pleaded with his team for such a favor. Rather, this was Alabama coach Thomas Kelly in 1916. And the longer Kelly spoke, the more passionate he became.

▲ PREVIOUS PAGE
Bear Bryant respected
all of Alabama's
rivalries, but seemed
to derive more
personal pleasure
from beating
Tennessee.

154

"Now," the coach continued, "I want you boys to go out there and fight Sewanee . . . all I ask is for you to beat old Sewanee. They are our worst gridiron foe. I won't care what we do in any other game this season; you can lose them all.

"But I want you to win that game," Kelly said, "or don't come off that field alive!"

Alabama players took their coach at his word that day. They beat old Sewanee 7–6.

Because the Alabama-Auburn series had a forty-one-year hiatus—the schools didn't play after the 1907 game until 'Bama declawed the Tigers, 55–0, in 1948—Sewanee really was Alabama's "worst gridiron foe."

All these years later, the Alabama-Auburn rivalry remains a 365-day-a-year obsession. But smashing Tennessee and Coach Phil Fulmer—known to Alabama fans as "The Great Pumpkin," for the way he fills out his orange shirt—is considered vital, too. So, it is impossible to get complete agreement to this question: Which team is currently Alabama's worst gridiron foe?

The Auburn rivalry dates to February 1893 and always will be held close, because it is an intrastate competition in a place that still does not have a major-league pro team to divert fans' attention and/or to unify the Alabama and Auburn factions.

So, while the Super Bowl is a fine excuse for a party in the middle of winter, it's an exhibition game compared to the Iron Bowl.

"When you sign that scholarship, and you walk in that dorm, your main goal is to make sure you end every season with a win against Auburn," says Steve Webb, a defensive end and linebacker from 1988 to 1991. "You can win as many games as you want, but if you don't beat Auburn, it's like you haven't finalized business. That was personal."

The Tennessee rivalry has its own juice—orange, naturally, and preferably beat to a pulp. Bryant, although keenly aware of the importance, even the necessity, of defeating Auburn, found his personal vindication in beating the Vols because, when he was coach at Kentucky, he didn't beat General Robert Neyland's Tennessee teams.

Chuck Allen was on Bryant's first Alabama team in 1958. He remembers a day when they were practicing in the rain.

"He said, 'By God, you may have to play at the University of Tennessee in the rain!' It was never Georgia, never Auburn," Allen says, "it was, 'You may have to play at Tennessee in the rain.' Tennessee was big to him."

But for different periods of time and under varying circumstances, other opponents became, at least for sixty minutes and four quarters, Alabama's worst gridiron foe.

Georgia Tech was, for many years, as

Bryant takes a ride
after a win over
the Vols.

fierce a rival as Alabama had. A controversial play in the 1961 game, when
Alabama's Darwin Holt caught Tech's
Chick Graning with an elbow during a
punt return, stirred emotions to the
boiling point. After the teams met in
1964, they didn't play again until 1979.
After the Crimson Tide easily beat Tech,
30–6 in Atlanta, Bryant said the rivalry
was "not as intense as it used to be," and
it never has been.

Yet, it was still hot enough eight
years later to severely complicate Alabama's hiring of Georgia Tech coach Bill
Curry. Alabama president Joab Thomas
even received a few threats after making
the hire.

To be sure, no two rivalries are the
same. Yet they all had the same effect:
They changed the direction of the pressure. It wasn't about winning, as much as
it was about not letting down your team
and your fans.

"We just could not lose to those
teams," says Don McNeal, a defensive
back in the late 1970s. And they did not
lose to those teams.

From 1971 through 1981, Alabama
beat Tennessee eleven straight times.
From 1973 through 1981, the Tide defeated Auburn nine times in a row. Halfback Major Ogilvie, who played from
1977 to 1980, is still proud of that 8-0
record against the chief rivals.

"The group I signed with, we were
the most successful four-year group that
went through there," Ogilvie says. "We
lost one SEC game [in 1980 to Missis-

sippi State] and the other games we lost were to Nebraska, Southern Cal, and Notre Dame—storied and traditional football schools."

And as such, they were rivalry games of a different order—higher, perhaps, but for the most part less personal, too. Games against Nebraska, Notre Dame, and Southern Cal usually carried national championship implications. But, because Bryant's Alabama teams never beat Notre Dame, and because poll voters had chosen the Irish over Alabama after the 1966 and 1977 seasons, the Golden Dome represented a beacon of bias to Alabama fans.

When the Irish came to Birmingham's Legion Field in October of 1986, the Crimson masses were beyond ready to extract a little revenge. One banner in the stands captured the attitude perfectly: NEVER AGAIN NOTRE DAME.

All-American linebacker Cornelius Bennett seemed to have that very sentiment in mind with his violent, but clean, first-quarter sack of Irish quarterback Steve Beuerlein. It was a "wow" hit, and sent a shiver through the crowd. It sent a shiver through Notre Dame too. Alabama beat the Irish, 28 to 10.

Crimson Tide coach Ray Perkins brushed aside the historical significance by saying "this team" never had lost to Notre Dame, adding, "The past had nothing to do with it."

But Bennett understood, even if Perkins didn't. "I can tell my kids I was

part of the first Alabama team to beat Notre Dame," he said.

Hoss Johnson, an offensive lineman on that team, believes defeating Notre Dame was even more important than the Tennessee and Auburn games. "Nobody had ever beaten them," says Johnson, whose father-in-law, Jim Davis, was an offensive lineman for Alabama in the early 1950s. "They had Tim Brown, a new coach in Lou Holtz, Steve Beuerlein . . . to beat them was my number-one thing."

Meanwhile, throughout the SEC, beating Alabama has been the chief goal for just about everybody. Not just for Auburn or Tennessee, but for other schools and, perhaps, particularly at Ole Miss where fans always have had a chip on their shoulder about Alabama.

"It was a good feeling to beat Alabama," says Archie Manning, who as a sophomore quarterback in 1968 did just that with a 10–8 victory in Jackson, Mississippi. A year later, Manning set a national record for total offense with 540 yards—436 of them passing—in the 1969 game at Legion Field. Alabama survived this Manning massacre for a 33–32 win, but Archie's sons would work their own magic in the coming years.

Peyton Manning led Tennessee to three straight wins over Alabama. Eli Manning guided Ole Miss to two wins in three tries over the Crimson Tide. But the father does not boast. Archie Manning is from a time when to be in the same southern football conference was to be in the same southern football family, a time when, from his perspective at least, the larger feuds were with those outside the family, outside the South.

"I'm an Ole Miss guy," Archie says. "But you've got to think of Alabama and Bear Bryant and his legacy, and the multiple national championships representing the SEC. I cherish my time playing against Alabama, and I cherish my sons' games playing against them."

FAMILY FEUD: ALABAMA VS. AUBURN

On November 26, 1964, between puffs on a cigar, Governor George Wallace was, for once in his life, a diplomat.

"I love both schools," he said on the occasion of the annual Iron Bowl at Legion Field.

If that's really how he felt, he was the only one.

Everyone else picked a side. Oh, families try to be nice sometimes, but

Linebacker Cornelius Bennett's savage sack of Irish quarterback Steve Beuerlein in the first quarter set the tone for the Tide's 28–10 victory.

Alabama and Auburn first met on the gridiron in February 1893.

158

their true allegiances have a way of shining through.

DeMeco Ryans, a senior linebacker on the 2005 season and Cotton Bowl winning Crimson Tide, is from Bessemer, Alabama, near Birmingham.

"I'd go back home and it's like I'm getting hounded all the time," Ryans says. "I'd have family members saying they're pulling for me and they've got an Auburn hat on."

At least the family stayed together.

"Husbands and wives actually get separated because of the game," says thirty-four-year-old 'Bama fan Thomas Kendrick, who showed up at the 2006 Crimson & White spring game wearing a T-shirt that read: FRIENDS DON'T LET FRIENDS GO TO AUBURN."

Of course, separation has been part of the tradition for a long time. The schools divorced themselves of this series for forty-one years; even the first game of the series is a point of contention. Played in February 1893 before more than 2,000 fans, and won by Auburn, 32–22, Auburn considers it the first game of the 1893 season; Alabama lists it as the last game of the 1892 season.

In 1894, however, Alabama and Auburn found something they could agree on: Each believed the other was using ineligible players. After much protest from both sides, the game went on and Alabama scored its first victory in three tries, 18–0.

When Alabama beat Auburn 10–0 in 1906, with Auxford Burks kicking the

ALA–6 AUBURN–6

The 6–6 tie between Auburn and Alabama in 1907 was the last game between the schools for forty-one years.

first field goal in the series off a mound of dirt, according to John Chandler Griffin's book, *Alabama vs. Auburn: Gridiron Grudge since 1893,* it became the Crimson Tide's last win in the series for more than 40 years.

Auburn and Alabama played to a 6–6 tie in 1907, then the football cold war began.

A lot happened between 1907 and 1948: World War I (1914–18); the stock market crashed (1929); *The Star-Spangled Banner* was adopted as the national anthem (1931); the first minimum wage, twenty-five cents an hour, was established (1938); Japan attacked Pearl Harbor (1941); the U.S. dropped atom bombs on Japan (1945); and the CIA was formed (1947).

So, why did Auburn and Alabama stop playing?

The answer is two words that cut both ways: stubborn pride. What began as a disagreement over how much Auburn would be compensated for two days of hotel and meals for players, and over whether a suitable Southern man could be found to referee the game, ultimately became a pissing match between the schools' decision makers.

In his book, Griffin details various efforts that were made at renewing the series, including when, late in 1911, Hugo Freidman, graduate manager of athletics at Alabama, wrote to the Birmingham papers to suggest three possible dates to Auburn for a 1912 football game.

Legion Field in Birmingham was
the site of many great Alabama-
Auburn contests.

Friedman's letter, however, was an odd mix of challenge and peace offering. At one point, he wrote that it was up to Auburn to "play the game or back down." But Friedman also said: "We hold not the slightest ill will towards Auburn, and all the old scores are forgotten."

It proved the start of another feud. Griffin wrote that the schools entered into serious discussions about re-establishing the series in 1923 and 1932 but, again, to no avail. Then, in 1933, Alabama's American Legion offered Legion Field in Birmingham free of charge, provided the teams would meet on Thanksgiving Day for five straight years, with the proceeds going to a scholarship fund for children of deceased veterans. Still, there was no game.

It would take a legislative measure in August 1947 by the Alabama House of Representatives to inspire action. The following May, the two schools announced they had reached agreement and would play on December 4 at Legion Field.

The economic impact was significant. Hotels were sold out months in advance. The emotional impact was perhaps beyond measure. Some 46,000 fans packed Legion Field, in what was then the largest crowd to attend a sporting event in the state. Tickets went for the then-princely sum of five dollars. The game, however, soon ceased to be much of a competition.

Ed "Big Shoe" Salem, a 187-pound sophomore halfback for Alabama, threw three touchdown passes, ran for another, and kicked seven extra points in a 55–0 Tiger thrashing. It was the most lopsided win in the series, surpassing Auburn's 53–5 win in 1900.

Alabama Coach Red Drew subbed liberally in a fine show of sportsmanship but, as he said afterward, "Everybody got in and everybody wants to score."

Auburn Coach Earl Brown took consolation where he could, saying, "There'll be another year."

Thankfully, he was right. The series would continue unabated.

Harry Lee, a guard and linebacker at Alabama from 1951 to 1954, vividly remembers the 10–7 win over Auburn in 1953.

"We kicked a field goal to win the SEC championship," Lee says. "We were marching down the field and they had this left tackle. We'd come out of the huddle and tell him we're coming straight at him, and we just kept getting three, four, five yards at a time.

"Finally, he got so disgusted with it, he just stood up and started swinging when the ball was snapped. He got a 15-yard penalty and that set up the field goal."

In time, Auburn would have its fun, too. When Auburn blasted 'Bama 40–0 in 1957, it was Alabama's fourth straight loss to the Tigers and third under Coach J. B. "Ears" Whitworth.

Bryant and 'Bama players celebrate their 34–0 waxing of Auburn in 1961.

Alabama 10-yard line. The starters had long since been out of the game. Bryant put them back in.

"The reason I remember is I didn't have any pads on; I'd taken them off," Neighbors says. "I thought he was crazy [Alabama would win, 34–0]. I mean, what difference does it make? But I forgot they hadn't scored on us [since 1958]."

Bryant hadn't forgotten. And Auburn fans, throughout the Bryant era, would have much that they would have loved to forget.

"Before Coach Bryant came back to Alabama, Shug Jordan was the coach at Auburn and a very good coach, too," says John Pruett, who is sports editor of the *Huntsville Times,* and who has covered both schools for forty years. "They had won a championship in '57 and, from the middle fifties to the late fifties Auburn was the team that kind of ruled the state.

"Then Bryant came in—this kind of towering personality—and quickly took over. It was very tough to be an Auburn fan back in that time. And the seventies were toughest of all because Alabama won nine in a row [from 1973 to 1981]. The attitude from Auburn was, 'Hope we can get lucky and pull out a win every once in a while.' "

It was, of course, exactly the thing that Bryant plotted against.

"He prepared for Auburn all year long," says Jack Rutledge, an assistant

Chuck Allen played in that game. And it still stings.

"Your coach is over there, and he's got tears coming down his face," Allen remembers. "It's cold as hell, all the Alabama fans have left, and the Auburn student body is chanting 'We want 60!' What a good time. That'll make you hate somebody."

Bear Bryant arrived the next season and, though Alabama didn't beat Auburn in 1958, it won four straight, from 1959 to 1962. It wasn't about getting mad, it was about getting even, and then running far ahead. All four of those wins were shutouts.

Billy Neighbors, a senior defensive tackle on the 1961 team, remembers Auburn finally making a push inside the from 1966 to 1982. "Coach Bryant himself would even look at clips and put a play or two in."

In the series he wrote for *Sports Illustrated* with John Underwood, "I'll Tell You About Football," Bryant remembered placing a call to Auburn's football offices at 7:00 A.M., and a secretary informing him that no one was in yet. Bryant thought that pretty rich, asking the young lady, "What's the matter, honey, don't your people take football seriously?"

Still, there were some things for which even Bryant could not account—great plays that couldn't be scripted, terrible, unbelievable plays that belonged in a horror film.

The 1967 game was played in a marsh disguised as a football field. Only one touchdown would be scored that day, and it came with Alabama trailing, 3–0, the Crimson Tide 47 yards away from the end zone.

Quarterback Ken "Snake" Stabler made a mad fourth-quarter dash for a touchdown that is now simply known as the "Run in the Mud." Alabama won, 7–3.

"The thing I remember most about that game was not that play," Stabler says, "but what Coach Bryant said before the game. Coach Bryant said we weren't going to throw very much and play for field position and Auburn would eventually screw up the kicking game. And if you look back, they mis-

handled two field-goal snaps, they snapped the ball over the punter's head. They screwed up exactly like Coach Bryant said."

The '72 Iron Bowl played out very differently. Auburn blocked two Greg Gantt punts in the fourth quarter to rally from a 16–0 deficit to win, 17–16. When Iron Bowl week came around in 1973, Gantt had a full mailbag.

"Some of the milder [letters] say things like, 'Punt, 'Bama, Punt,'" Gantt said of the line that still lives in infamy. "Some of the others, you couldn't put in your newspaper."

While Alabama couldn't overcome the blocked punts in 1972, it was able to overcome what quarterback Steadman Shealy called "fumbleitis" in 1979, when the Crimson Tide entered the game 10–0 and on track to defend their national title.

"It's not up to me," Bryant said the week before the game, "but if we can't beat Auburn, I'd just as soon stay home and plow."

Alabama did beat Auburn, 25–18, despite losing four fumbles. The Crimson Tide trailed, 18–17, when Shealy led them on an 82-yard drive that culminated with his 8-yard scamper around left end for a touchdown and his run for the 2-point conversion.

The play of the game was yet to come. On the ensuing kickoff, Auburn's James Brooks made a 64-yard return to the Alabama 31. It was very nearly a touchdown.

THE KICK HEARD 'ROUND THE STATE

A 52-yard field goal is a long field goal. The ball has to carry a long way. Alabama kicker Van Tiffin never dreamed his 1985 game-winning kick against Auburn would carry across the years, but it has.

Auburn-Alabama week rolls around and it's like its own season. But, instead of leaves falling from trees, Van Tiffin's kick falls from the sky on the game's last play and between the uprights to upset seventh-ranked Auburn, 25—23, all over again.

"It's kind of a time of year," Tiffin says. "Everybody's calling, the media wanting to talk. I kind of thought it would wear off by now. But that's what everybody remembers.

"People tell me all the time, before the ballgame, they play the tape of that whole game. People want to tell me what they were doing, or how they acted, or how their uncle acted. I've heard about people crawling on the floor and running up and down the street. And I believe I've talked to everybody that was in that end zone."

How elated was Alabama?

Coach Ray Perkins rushed onto the field to find his 5-foot-10, 160-pound kicker, hugged him and, well, basically went nuts.

"I love you, Van Tiffin!" Perkins shouted. "I love you!"

Van Tiffin's 52-yard field goal on the game's last play beat Auburn in 1985 and made the All-American kicker one of 'Bama's enduring heroes.

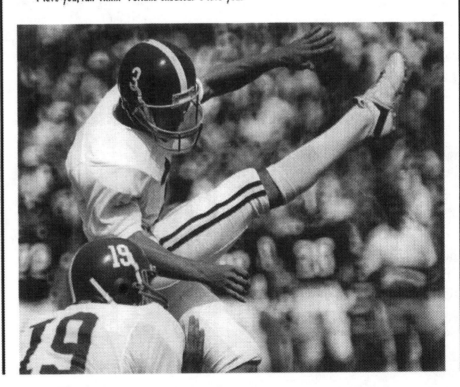

How devastated was Auburn?

"Auburn players, it'll eat their guts out the rest of their lives," Auburn coach Pat Dye said.

How did the kick come to be?

Quarterback Mike Shula, on third-and-18 from the Alabama 12, hit running back Gene Jelks for a nice gain to set up fourth-and-2 with twenty-three seconds to play, Alabama trailing 23—22. Wide receiver Al Bell, on a reverse, of all things, gained 20 yards for a first down. Then Shula passed to Greg Richardson, who ran out of bounds at the Auburn 35 with six seconds left.

Tiffin Time.

"I knew he was going to make it," says Wes Neighbors, Alabama's center that day. "I never had a doubt. That's the truth. He ran on the field, I ran off and said, 'Game over for them.'"

There was a slight wind blowing in that day and Tiffin told reporters afterward, "That always messes up my mind."

But he says now he was helped by the rush of it all.

"A timeout wasn't called, so there wasn't much time to think," he says. "So that worked in my favor. It was more of a reaction——just get the ball in the air and see what happens.

"It was one of those you really didn't feel it," Tiffin says. "And, when it's like that, it's usually a good thing. When I looked up, I could tell it was going to make it because it was traveling very well right down the middle."

End of a great game, and beginning of a sweet season: Tiffin Time.

Although statisticians credited Don McNeal with tackling Brooks, freshman Jeremiah Castille actually made the saving tackle, catching Brooks from behind at the 40 and dragging him down.

"I knew I could catch him," Castille said in the happy locker room. "I just didn't know if I could get a good enough hold of him to make the tackle."

Fittingly, Bryant's 315th career win, the one that broke Amos Alonzo Stagg's all-time wins record, also came against Auburn, in 1981.

In twenty-five years as coach at Alabama, Bryant was 19–6 against this "worst gridiron foe." It was a distinguished record his immediate successors would not begin to approach.

Former Tide player Ray Perkins went 2-2 against Auburn from 1983 to 1986. The 1985 win was as dramatic as any in the series' history, Van Tiffin's 52-yard field goal beating Auburn on the game's final play. But there was much sweetness in the 17–15 win in 1984, too. That Tide team finished 5-6. However, the victory, sealed with a goal-line stand, kept Auburn out of the Sugar Bowl. Alabama safety Rory Turner stopped Brent Fullwood inside the 1-yard line. Or, as Turner famously said, "I waxed the dude."

Beating Auburn is a 365/24/7 obsession.

Turner also granted his coach a reprieve from twelve months of misery.

"This damn sure makes living here easier the next 364 days," Perkins said.

The next Alabama coach, Bill Curry, wouldn't know. Curry, who never beat Auburn when he was at Georgia Tech, was 0–3 against them at Alabama. But worse, Curry never seemed to get it, to feel what long-time Alabama people felt.

"I think Coach Perkins had a hatred for it, and Coach [Gene] Stallings had a hatred for it, but I don't know if Coach Curry really understood it," says Roger Shultz, an Alabama center from 1987 to 1990.

Perhaps Curry should have read what Bryant's wife, Mary Harmon, once told *Sports Illustrated:* "We don't have riots, or folks don't burn each other's cars or anything like that, but an awful lot of people get their feelings hurt."

Shultz could relate. Until Stallings came in for the 1990 season, Shultz was just like Curry: 0-for-3 against Auburn. That changed with a 16–7 win.

"I'd hate to think I went my whole time at the university and not beat

Bear Bryant's Alabama teams went 19-6 against Auburn. Reason enough for Auburn people to want to change the status quo, to get the annual Iron Bowl game out of Birmingham.

"They were always fearful of playing him, to be honest with you," *Huntsville Times* sports editor John Pruett says of Auburn fans' attitude toward Bear Bryant. "As time went by, I think Auburn Nation as a whole wanted to get that game out of Birmingham. It was supposedly a 50-50 split [of fans], but in Auburn's mind they were always at a disadvantage playing Alabama in Birmingham.

"Auburn felt like whenever they'd go to Legion Field, even all the ushers and concessionaires were wearing red. When Pat Dye got the job, he pretty quickly started maneuvering to get that game home and home and he eventually did."

Steve Sloan was athletic director at Alabama when Auburn's quest to have some of the games played on its campus became the issue that just wouldn't go away. Sloan took the position that, if the contract didn't prohibit Auburn from picking the site for its home game, there was nothing to be done.

"It's certainly possible my position was wrong," says Sloan. "It certainly was a very unpopular position to take. I got maybe one letter of support."

In 1989, the Iron Bowl was played at newly renovated 85,000 seat Jordan-Hare Stadium. Auburn fans got what they wanted: a 30-20 victory in their own backyard over a previously unbeaten and number-two-ranked Alabama team.

"There's nothing like going into the hostile environment of Jordan-Hare as an Alabama football player," says Shannon Brown, who was on that '89 Alabama team and whose older brother, Steve Brown, had played at Auburn. "I can remember the buses being rocked, guys mooning the bus, crazy stuff like that."

Crimson Tide quarterback Gary Hollingsworth says, "That's the loudest place I ever played, that day in Auburn. It was unbelievable. That was something Auburn fans had been waiting for to happen and wanting to happen, I guess ever since the series started——to have a chance to play us there and upset our season."

Worth noting: With the game played in Birmingham the next three years, and with Gene Stallings on the sideline instead of Bill Curry, Alabama won each time. And in 1999 under Mike DuBose and in 2001 under Dennis Franchione, Alabama won at Auburn.

Best of all, through 2005 Alabama leads the series with a 38-31-1 record.

As 'Bama fullback Steve Whitman, a Birmingham native, said before winning the 1979 game over the Tigers, "If we don't beat Auburn, I don't want to be seen in public."

Auburn," Shultz says. "I mean, that's just unacceptable."

Steve Webb, who played defense for both Curry and Stallings, recalls that what Stallings told them before that game carried so much more weight than anything Curry had ever said. There was just more urgency to it when Stallings told them: "Don't come back in the locker room without a win."

Says Webb: "He let us go, he freed us. Alabama's never been known to be a dirty team, but we could play hard, play reckless, without worrying if we make a mistake, or if we hit somebody late, the coach is gonna pull us."

Unfortunately, Stallings's departure after the 1996 season signaled a shift of power in the series: Auburn has won six of the last nine meetings, including the three meetings against Mike Shula's teams.

"I think Mike's done an excellent job," Stallings says. "I know he's going to feel a bit more comfortable when they beat Auburn."

Because what happens on Iron Bowl day can bring happiness the other 364 days. Everyone has always understood that, including the woman who married Paul W. Bryant.

"Auburn, Alabama," Mary Harmon Bryant once said, "well . . . it's just *everything.*"

Dennis Riddle romps into the end zone for the winning touchdown near the end of the '96 Auburn game.

THE SATURDAY
EVENING ENEMY

"How much is a year of a man's life worth?" Bear Bryant once wrote. "I don't know, but the *Saturday Evening Post* took 10 years of my life, and I billed them $10 million for it."

It is not stretching the truth to say that from October of 1962 until February 4, 1964, the *Saturday Evening Post* was the worst foe, gridiron or otherwise, that Bryant and his football program had.

In October of 1962, the magazine published an article about brutality in college football. The story turned on one play from the previous season's Alabama-Georgia Tech game (a fierce rivalry under normal conditions), in which the Crimson Tide's Darwin Holt hit and injured Tech's Chick Graning with a forearm on a punt return.

Then, on March 23, 1963, the *Post* published "The Story of a College Football Fix," in which it was alleged that Bryant and Wally Butts, the athletic director at the University of Georgia, had rigged the 1962 Alabama-Georgia game.

Taken separately, each story, each accusation, was more than enough to take years off a man's life.

The saga began on November 18, 1961, when Alabama beat Georgia Tech, 10–0, in Birmingham, when as Benny Marshall of the *Birmingham News* later wrote: "Paul Bryant's first step toward

the pages of the *Saturday Evening Post* was taken, not by his choice, nor by Butts'."

The first step in question was taken by Darwin Holt. He had the task of blocking on an Alabama punt return. Chick Graning was coming down the field to cover the return. Film of the play does show Holt leading with his arm—Holt says he used a "club block"—but it also shows Graning to be strangely unaware that a player on the other team might be about to block him.

"There was nothing flagrant about the play at all," says Holt's teammate, Lee Roy Jordan. "Darwin was hustling his butt off to get a block. And it so happened that Chick was kind of loafing and looking up in the sky.

"When you go hit somebody," Jordan explains, "you don't think about hitting them with a certain part of your body. And certainly not your forearm or your elbow. And that's what happened with Chick, Darwin's forearm caught him when he had his head turned."

The play and the reaction to it still haunt Holt.

"Darwin needs to make peace with himself and the good Lord above," Jordan says. "He'll never stop being asked about it."

Today, Holt describes his hit this way: "When he turns, the only difference with the club block is you're catching him on his blind side. You drive your head and shoulder up inside his shoulder and chin and drive him out . . . then you release."

Holt adds, "He hit the ground like a bullet."

The hit broke Graning's nose and jaw and Graning lost several teeth. What is seldom mentioned is that several officials had a clear view of the play, and not one of them threw a flag. In fact, Graning's teammates didn't immediately see the hit as anything unusual. No one rushed to his side.

Game reports seemed to miss the play altogether. But once reporters in Atlanta became aware of the extent of Graning's injuries, they started throwing some pretty strong shots at Holt and Bryant.

In a Monday column for the *Atlanta Journal*, Furman Bisher wrote that it was practically required that all of Bryant's players behave in a "violent manner."

That got the masses jacked up pretty good.

"They unloaded on me the next week," Holt recalls. "They had to deliver my mail in bags. I'd get two bags a day—I'm talking tall bags. Three times I was threatened to be killed. They had two or three people from the Alabama Bureau of Investigation dressed as coaches. For a while they put all my phone calls through the police department. It was pretty bad."

And only the beginning.

Bisher also wrote the story for the *Post* on brutality in college football.

Bryant later noted that Bisher had been to Alabama practices "maybe twice in his life." In fact, the claim that Bryant wanted his players to hit first and think later contradicted Bryant's insistence on playing smart football.

"He never taught anybody anything but tackling," says Billy Neighbors, a defensive tackle in 1961. "And you better not get any penalties—especially one that was unnecessary roughness, or if you took a cheap shot at somebody. He wouldn't play you if you did that."

When Alabama played at Georgia Tech in 1962, more than one whisky bottle went flying past Bryant on the sideline. The next time he came back, in 1964, the last time the teams would play until 1979, Bryant's lawsuit with the *Post* had been settled. So the coach tried to have a sense of humor about things: Bryant wore an Alabama football helmet as he walked past the Georgia Tech student section. Some students hurled insults, but others just laughed.

Bryant, and Wally Butts, too, ultimately got the last laugh. In August 1963, Butts won a $3,060,000 judgment in federal court against Curtis Publishing Co., the owner of the *Post*.

In hindsight, it's amazing it all went this far. The *Post's* story was built from the word of an Atlanta insurance man who claimed to have accidentally been cut in on a telephone conversation between Butts and Bryant; the man said he heard Butts pass on confidential infor-

DON WADE

mation to Bryant that helped Alabama beat Georgia, 35–0.

It would take longer for Bryant's official vindication and, in the interim, he would go on statewide television to defend himself against the magazine's charges of game fixing. Looking back, Linda Knowles, Bryant's secretary in the football office, wonders if the whole thing didn't take years off his life.

As Bryant admitted later, he had nightmares, night sweats, and sat up for hours at a time worrying about what this was doing to both his blood family and his football family.

It was personal on another level, too.

"He was devastated," Knowles says. "Devastated that anyone would question his integrity."

When the verdict from the Butts trail came in, "That was the first time that I saw any joy on his face in several weeks," Knowles recalls.

Bryant settled out of court in early 1964 for $320,000. The game, if you want to call it that, was finally over.

He had won.

After he'd paid his bills, Bryant said, he even had enough money left over to buy his mother a new dress.

ORANGE MADNESS

We ought to have to pay property taxes on Neyland Stadium, because we own it.
—Center Roger Shultz, 1990

Shultz said that after Alabama had beaten Tennessee in Knoxville for the third straight time. It was a quote so good that it even threw Alabama Coach Gene Stallings for a loop.

"I'll never forget Coach Stallings saying, 'I can't believe you said that,'" says Shultz, who was a senior that season.

Bryant wore an Alabama helmet when he walked past the Georgia Tech student section in 1964; the helmet was good for protection, but for a laugh, too

"And I go, 'Hey, I don't have to play them anymore.'"

An Alabama defensive back later did a "cover" of that quote. "Antonio Langham tried to use it a couple of years later," says Shultz. "Sorry rascal tried to lay claim to my quote."

There's just *something* about beating Tennessee.

It isn't that it's necessarily better to beat Tennessee than to beat Auburn, it's just different. The love Alabama has for beating both rivals is, depending on your age and preferences, sort of like having two favorite flavors of ice cream or two favorite brands of scotch.

Until Tennessee Coach Phil Fulmer's involvement in an NCAA investigation

that resulted in serious sanctions against Alabama, the rivalry was fierce, but not ugly.

Now, a man on his way to Denny Chimes to celebrate 2005 team captains Brodie Croyle and DeMeco Ryans leaving their hand and cleat prints in the Walk of Fame carries with him a sign that reads: VOL HATERS. And this is only April, on the day of Alabama's spring game.

Another man wears a T-shirt that carries an eternal reminder. The front of his shirt reads: THE BEAR'S LOOKING DOWN . . . The back of the shirt reads: AND HE STILL HATES TENNESSEE.

Yet, long ago, respect flowed from both sides. Vols Coach General Robert

Tennessee Coach Phil Fulmer, shown with former Tide Coach Gene Stallings, went from fierce rival to most hated man in Alabama when word leaked out he had been a secret witness for the NCAA in its investigation into the Alabama football program.

Neyland once said, "Tennessee sophomores don't deserve citizenship until they have survived an Alabama game."

Likewise, Alabama players prepared for the hardest-hitting game of their season.

"All week long we'd talk about playing Tennessee and about keeping your head on a swivel because you were gonna hit until the whistle blew," says Jackie Sherrill, a fullback/linebacker in the mid-sixties. "The Tennessee game was the most physical game Alabama had every year."

Perhaps the most famous Alabama-Tennessee game from the early days came in 1932. Tennessee beat Alabama that day in Birmingham, 7–3. The only touchdown was scored on an end run in the fourth quarter by Beattie Feathers.

The game is considered a classic because of the magnificent punting duel between Feathers and Alabama All-American Johnny Cain. Feathers averaged 43 yards on 21 punts. Good as that was, Cain was even better, averaging 48 yards on 19 punts.

Why all the punts? The weather was terrible. Rain, wind, and mud all conspired to make the coaches (Neyland and Frank Thomas) wary of even trying to run the ball. Thirty years later, in 1962 and on the day Neyland Stadium was dedicated, Alabama beat the Vols, 27–7. It was Bryant's first win at Tennessee.

At least in Bryant's early years at Alabama, beating Tennessee meant more to him than beating Auburn. Bryant started the tradition of playing UT's anthem, "Rocky Top," in the Alabama locker room the week before the game. Gene Stallings did the same when he became coach, and also had the song piped in at inhumanely loud levels in Alabama's indoor practice facility. The latter was for practical reasons. Crowd noise in Knoxville could be a problem and the players had to get used to using hand signals.

"We played it over and over in the locker room hoping it would irritate them," Stallings admits.

It did. Not only did the players have to hear "Rocky Top" in their own locker room, they also had to hear it once they reached Knoxville. And everything, everywhere, seemed to be colored prison-yard orange.

"Orange potatoes, orange drinks, orange cake, and 'Rocky Top' blaring everywhere you go," says Shannon Brown, a defensive lineman from 1992 to 1995, who then mockingly breaks into song:

"Rocky Top, you will always be . . ."

"I can sing it verbatim right now," Brown says. "It's stuck in my head. It just got to where you hated it."

Baxter Booth, who was on Bryant's first Alabama team in 1958, hated the practice that came after they lost to Ten-

IT'S BROKEN—HONEST

There have been others, Alabama players who played in rivalry games with braces on their knees or casts on their hands, players who played with pain.

Quarterback David Smith strapped on a knee brace in 1988 to lead Alabama to a 28–20 over Tennessee in Knoxville. His coach, Bill Curry, was awed by this.

"It's amazing he's even walking," Curry said.

In truth, it was perhaps a little bit much to say given Alabama history—not that Bill Curry ever had a good handle on that, anyway.

In 1935, Alabama was playing Tennessee in Knoxville. The rivalry was important enough in those days that, when it was reported that end Paul W. Bryant had a broken leg and wouldn't play, university President Dr. George H. "Mike" Denny became involved.

"Dr. Denny sent for Coach [Frank] Thomas," recalled Young Boozer, a halfback on that team.

According to Boozer, Denny had read of Bryant's injury in the newspaper and decided this course of action wouldn't do.

"I just wanted you to understand that you've got to play him to have a chance," Boozer said Denny told Thomas. "You're just going to have to play Bryant even if he has a broken leg."

Bryant's own memory of the event, some thirty years afterward, was that he really didn't have any choice but to play. Yes, he knew he had broken a bone in his leg. He was even in a cast, which a doctor removed at the team hotel the night before the game. The doctor told Bryant he could at least dress for the game. Bryant figured that's what he would do—just dress. Come game day, Coach Thomas made a little pep talk and then asked assistant coach Hank Crisp, who years earlier had lost a hand in a cotton-gin accident, if he had anything he wanted to say.

Crisp, cigarette hanging from his mouth, launched into his little speech and finished with these words: "I know one damn thing, Old 34 will be after 'em, he'll be after their tails."

It took a moment for the reality to set in.

Bryant was number 34!

Thomas immediately asked Bryant if he could play.

As Bryant said, "I just ran out there." And so he played and played pretty well, too. He caught several passes and after one he made a lateral for a touchdown in a 25–0 victory. Bryant downplayed it all by saying, "It was just one little bone."

Atlanta Constitution reporter Ralph McGill wasn't so sure. He traveled to Tuscaloosa and requested to view the X-ray of Bryant's leg. It showed Bryant had a fractured fibula.

Playing against Auburn, obviously, was as important as playing against Tennessee. Probably more so to halfback Johnny Musso, who grew up in Alabama. So, in 1971, Musso didn't want to let a painful dislocated toe stop him from playing. Just as important, trainer Jim Goostree wasn't about to allow it.

Musso had injured the toe against LSU and sat out the next game against Miami.

"Coach Goostree came to my dorm room every night," Musso remembers. "He came in and rubbed that toe. But then it started looking doubtful I'd play regardless of what he did, so he started taping it up and getting it mobilized and supported. Then he started working with a plastic cast that bent, but not a lot.

"He kept working and trying until he had something he could put around my foot and actually fit in the shoe. I wore a 12½ on my right foot and a 10½ on my left foot. It got to where I could actually run. It was like a personal aim. He was obsessed that I was going to play."

Bryant, of course, was coach at this time and thinking like one. He didn't need Musso to be the hero he had been against Tennessee thirty-six years earlier. In fact, he feared if Musso tried to play and couldn't, it would be a morale buster for the whole team.

"Coach [John David] Crow told me, a good while after I graduated, they had a big argument about that," Musso says. "Coach Bryant was not going to start me, just see how the game went and then decide. And Coach Crow said, 'No, you need to play him.' He stood up for me not knowing how it was going to go."

It went well in Alabama's 31–7 win. Musso says, "I've still got some friends from Auburn that think it was a phantom injury."

Musso says he knew of Bryant having played with a broken leg.

"That was part of the lure," he says of his desire to play with his injury. "But I don't think I'd compare that with a broken leg."

In the 1935 Tennessee game, an Alabama end named Paul Bryant played with a broken leg.

FACING PAGE
Ken Stabler's ill-
advised pass out of
bounds in the '65
game with Tennessee
led to a 7–7 tie.

nessee, 14–7. Bryant's intensity was off the charts in those days. He essentially made his team play the game over.

"I was an offensive end going down the field and throwing blocks, running back to the huddle, and then running back down the field," Booth says. "I ended up in the infirmary with heat exhaustion. And that was October."

Bryant wouldn't beat Tennessee until 1961; it was the start of a four-game winning streak that ended in 1965, in Birmingham, when the teams played to a 7–7 tie. But it was the way the score ended in a tie that was so tough to take. With just seconds left, Alabama was in position for a field goal. However, quarterback Ken Stabler lost track of the downs and threw the ball away on fourth down in an effort to stop the clock.

"When Stabler threw the ball out of bounds, the stands became absolutely quiet," remembers center Paul Crane. "Then when the Tennessee people realized what had happened, there was this roar that started up—a positive roar, 'Yea!'

"Then Alabama people realized what had happened and there was this terrible sound, 'Ahhggh!' But there for a moment, just after it happened, everybody was stunned."

Bryant soon went from stunned to steamed. Although with his public words Bryant sought to protect Stabler and threw the blame on himself, his actions spoke much louder than his words.

"After the game, we went to the locker room, and the manager hadn't unlocked the door," Crane recalls. "Coach Bryant kicked the door in."

The 1966 game at Knoxville was another muddy mess. Alabama held on for an 11–10 win as UT missed a late field goal. To be a Tennessee player then was to feel that foot that kicked in Alabama's locker room door a year earlier now had hit you square in the stomach.

"I was on the ground after making my block," said Vols tight end Austin Denney. "But I heard the crowd roar and I thought we'd made it. When I looked up and saw the referee signaling no good, I have never been more disappointed in my life."

The 1972 game was also bitter for Tennessee, as Alabama scored two touchdowns over thirty-six seconds in the last three minutes of the game to take an amazing 17–10 win. Alabama offensive lineman John Hannah considered it more than amazing; it was a miracle.

"You can say what you want to about the Fellowship of Christian Athletes and all that," Hannah said afterward. "But I can tell you we all prayed in the huddle."

The issue of divine intervention aside, there weren't many things worse than the feeling of losing to Tennessee.

And victory was especially sweet for Alabama trainer Jim Goostree, who had attended UT.

"An Alabama man knows he's supposed to excel against Tennessee," Goostree said after the Crimson Tide won 30–17 in 1978. "And they feel the same way about us."

The next season, when Alabama was defending its national title, it carried a 5-0 record into the UT game at Legion Field. After having given up only nine points in the first five games of the season, Alabama fell behind 17–0 in the second quarter.

As has often been the case in the history of the series, the game carried ramifications beyond the rivalry. Often, the game meant survival for one or both teams in the national championship race. Alabama made five turnovers that day, but still pulled out a 27–17 win in what would be a 12-0 season.

"We win that game, we can play for the national championship," says halfback Major Ogilvie. "We don't win that game we can't play for the national championship."

Pressure set to the tune of that infernal "Rocky Top"?

Ogilvie says no.

"We had a little different approach to big games. We played big games all the time," he says. "It was just another day of the week to us."

When Ray Perkins succeeded Bryant in 1983, it started a period of struggle against Tennessee. Perkins went 1-3, not beating the Vols until 1986, his last season. Center Wes Neighbors vividly recalls the '83 game, which Tennessee won 41–34 in Birmingham, because just thinking about it leaves him short of breath.

"The offensive linemen, we were over there on the sideline fighting for the oxygen masks," Neighbors says. "Because they were scoring in two- or three-play drives and we were scoring on twenty-play drives. Their noseguard was Reggie White and they had some big hosses."

Bill Curry followed Perkins, and while Curry couldn't beat Auburn—0-3 from 1987 to 1989—he beat UT all three times. Mathematically, that should have evened things out for 'Bama fans, but it never did.

Clyde Bolton, a retired sportwriter from the *Birmingham News* and author of the 1972 book *The Crimson Tide: A Story of Alabama Football*, says the fact Curry's success against Tennessee didn't balance his failures against Auburn is further proof that "Auburn's always been the number-one rivalry."

"You'll hear people say Tennessee was a bigger rivalry, but it never was," says Bolton, who covered Alabama and Auburn football from 1961 to 2001. "There may have been more drama around the Tennessee game, but I think [fans] would rather beat Auburn any year and every year."

It's always been fun to beat Tennessee but, in recent years, the rivalry has been running stride for stride with the Auburn rivalry.

Yet, because the Tennessee game comes up on the schedule first, "the third Saturday in October" is the saying, although not always the exact reality, it gets first crack at defining a season. Consider Stallings's first year (1990) as head coach: Alabama started 0-3, then beat lesser teams in Vanderbilt and Southwest Louisiana. Beating a number 3-ranked Tennessee team with national title aspirations 9-6 in Knoxville was huge, the game that saved the season, as Alabama finished 7-5.

"I remember we were having a hard time making a first down, but they were, too," says Stallings. "They were gonna kick a field goal and probably go ahead, and Stacy Harrison blocked a field goal and we made more yardage on the blocked field goal than it seemed like we did that entire game. And it put the ball back where Philip Doyle could kick a field goal."

"It was a big, big win—cigars all around."

The 17–10 win in 1992 was even

Barker and Stallings, per the tradition, celebrate with cigars after a 17–13 victory over the Vols in Knoxville in 1994.

bigger, because it was a game Alabama had to have in its journey to the national championship. The defense rose up to stop UT's last drive. Eric Curry sacked quarterback Heath Shuler—"He freaking T-boned him," Shannon Brown recalls—and safety Chris Donnelly made a diving interception to ice the game. Once again, cigars all around.

"This is a tradition and probably the best part of [winning]," said offensive lineman Jon Stevenson. "And I hate cigars."

Unfortunately, there wouldn't be any reason for cigars from 1995 to 2001, a stretch of seven straight Alabama losses.

That, however, is not the longest stretch in the rivalry's history. From 1971 to 1981, Alabama won eleven straight. And there have been other streaks on both sides of the ledger.

"There have been long streaks of one team dominating," Bolton says, "which to me is not the mark of a rivalry."

The truth is that Alabama-Tennessee is simply its own rivalry, its own brand, if you will.

It's taken on a nasty undercurrent in recent years because of Vols coach Phil Fulmer's role in the NCAA investigation that landed Alabama on probation. An elephant never forgets, so there is a segment of Alabama fans that live to figuratively stomp the coach they call "Fat Phil."

In 2003, when Mike Shula's first 'Bama team prepared to play Tennessee, the schools' athletic directors couldn't even disguise the feelings that were swirling. Tennessee's Mike Hamilton wouldn't concede the entire rivalry was running with bad blood, but did say, "There is some ill will on the perimeter." Alabama's Mal Moore told the *Tuscaloosa News:* "We are in a period of finger-pointing among fans and boosters."

Most former players would like to see the rivalry get back to the way it used to be.

"In our day, they were respectful of us and we were of them," says Johnny Musso, an All-American Alabama running back in 1970 and '71. "It's a little sad with what's gone on recently. It should get back to where there's more respect."

Not that Musso's holding his breath.

Alabama's victory over the Vols in 2005 came down to Jamie Christensen's game-winning field goal, his second of the season after beating Ole Miss the same way.

Make no mistake: The kid understands these game-winning kicks were not created equally.

"If I'd missed the Ole Miss kick, I'd have been hated by many people," says Christensen. "Tennessee? I probably would have been hated by the whole state. "

9

AFTER THE BEAR

People in Alabama love Coach Bryant. They just tolerate the rest of us.

> —Gene Stallings, the third man to
> follow Paul W. Bryant as coach of the
> Crimson Tide, and the last Alabama coach
> to win the national championship

FOR years, there had been great speculation over the first coach to follow in the outsized footsteps of Bear Bryant.

And, for years, it had been a moot exercise. At the end of the 1960s, Bryant didn't take his three national championships at Alabama and go to the Miami Dolphins, although it's safe to say the Dolphins at one point had Bryant on the hook and all but reeled in to shore.

He didn't retire after his sixth and final national championship following the 1979 season. Amos Alonzo Stagg's all-time record for wins (314) was within reach and the Bear would hunt it down and surpass it, finishing with 323 career victories.

After the 1982 regular season ended, Bryant announced he would retire as coach, but continue as athletic director. Everyone wanted Bryant to win his last game, which he did, as Alabama beat Illinois in the Liberty Bowl, but the real competition was for his job.

To this day, the debate over whom Bryant most wanted to replace him continues. Some versions of what Bryant supposedly wanted then are only shared off the record.

The on-the-record accounts of how former Alabama player Ray Perkins became the first coach after Bear Bryant's twenty-five-year reign are like fingerprints: No two are exactly alike.

Former Crimson Tide player Jackie Sherrill was just finishing his first year as coach at Texas A & M when Bryant announced his retirement. And though Sherrill says he was not a candidate at that time, he says in a conversation with Bryant about a year earlier Bryant had told him, "I'm gonna recommend three, and you're one of them."

It doesn't take much of a detective to come up with four obvious names for that list of three: Perkins, Gene Stallings, Sherrill, and then-offensive coordinator, now Alabama athletic director, Mal Moore.

Stallings, however, was under contract as an assistant coach to Tom Landry with the Dallas Cowboys. One story has it that because Stallings wouldn't commit to Alabama before talking with Landry, the administration soured on him.

Billy Neighbors, who played on the '61 national championship team and maintained very close ties with Bryant, says, "He called me one day and told me [the administrators and trustees] were fighting among themselves. I always thought he wanted Gene Stallings. That's what he told me, but I don't know. He wasn't real happy. He told me they were going to screw it up, and they screwed it up."

Perkins was coaching the NFL's New York Giants. Even back in 1979, his first season coaching the Giants, Perkins couldn't ignore the possibility of returning to his alma mater.

"For several years, I always had in the back of my mind that I wanted to be the guy who followed Coach Bryant," says Perkins, who is retired and residing in his native Mississippi. "In fact, before we went to training camp and I was first head coach of the Giants, a writer for the *Newark Star-Ledger* and I were on my back porch and he asked me, 'Ray, what about a time when Coach Bryant gets ready to hang it up and the phone rings?' "

Eventually, that call would come. Waiting for it would prove difficult.

After Bryant announced his retire-

ment, but before the Liberty Bowl, he came to New York for the College Football Hall of Fame banquet. There was a separate cocktail party for those with Alabama connections, Perkins recalls, then the dinner that night.

"I came kind of expecting him to say something, but he didn't," Perkins says. "And I never did know how to approach him. I mean, I've got him on a pretty high pedestal.

"How do you tell a guy like Coach Bryant that you want his job?"

You don't. You wait for the mountain to come to you, which is what Perkins did.

"I'm in my office the next morning at about nine-thirty and the phone rings and it's Coach Bryant," says Perkins. "And he says, 'Raymond'—and he's the only person that ever called me Raymond; he could call me anything he wanted to—'are you interested in this thing down here?'

"And I said, 'Coach, I would walk to Tuscaloosa.' He said, 'Well, I figured you was off up there making so much money you wouldn't be interested. Thank you. Bye.' "

The next day, Perkins says, school president Joab Thomas called and invited him down for an interview that was "more of a formality than anything else." Ray Perkins would become Alabama's next coach, and there seems little doubt he was on Bryant's list. The questions are: How long was the list and what was the name at the top of that list?

Sportswriter Clyde Bolton says Thomas told him that Bryant offered a list with two names and that Perkins was one of them.

"He wouldn't tell me who the other one was," says Bolton, who weighed in on this changing of the guard.

"I remember writing a column that said Alabama football will never be the same," Bolton says. "I thought Coach Bryant was the best college coach that ever lived and you couldn't have it both ways. You couldn't lose the best college coach that ever lived and your program go right on being what it had been before.

"I was deluged by letters and calls

Ray Perkins said for years he hoped to be the first coach to follow Bryant, but his tenure got off to a rocky start when he made sweeping changes.

from Alabama people. I remember one said, 'You'll never live long enough to see Alabama football skip a beat.' Well, I didn't have to live very long. In 1984, Ray Perkins had a losing season."

Perkins had been an All-American split end at the Capstone and played on the 1964 and '65 national championship teams yet, early on, he lost a significant segment of the Alabama faithful.

Perkins, as new head coaches often do, changed the staff. Men who had been loyal to Coach Bryant were told their services were no longer needed, and assistant coach Bobby Marks says this was done unceremoniously with Perkins simply telling him, "I'm not gonna keep ya." Adds Marks: "Ray wasn't a man of many words."

The staff changes extended to Linda Knowles, who was reassigned from her position as secretary to the head coach. She says even the décor in the football offices changed: "No pictures of Coach Bryant."

Beyond staff changes, Perkins spoke boldly about his own role in history.

"Anybody who says he would rather follow the coach who follows the legend is not up to the challenge," Perkins said upon arrival.

Perkins's first game was on September 10, 1983, in Birmingham against Georgia Tech, an old rival. Bryant was there only in spirit, of course, having died on January 26, 1983, twenty-eight days after coaching his last game.

The new Alabama coach wore a houndstooth hat decal on his lapel for the first game and players wore the decal on their helmets that season. Alabama won the first game A.B. (After Bryant). The next day, September 11, would have been Bryant's 70th birthday.

"I felt like my biggest challenge was to win that first game," Perkins says now.

It was a respectable, if unspectacular, first season. Alabama went 8-4 and played in the Sun Bowl, but it lost the most important games to Tennessee and Auburn. In Perkins's four seasons at Alabama, he would compile a 32-15-1 record. In 1986, Alabama rose to a number two ranking and held it for several weeks. The Crimson Tide was 7-0 and coming off a rout of Tenneessee, at Knoxville, when Penn State came to Tuscaloosa and beat 'Bama, 23–3.

"The Lions came in and kind of spoiled things," says Perkins.

In hindsight, no one blames Ray Perkins for losing to Penn State and finishing the season with a 10-3 record. There are those, however, who will always blame Perkins for what they perceived as a disrespectful attitude toward Bryant's legacy and for committing one unforgivable sin: taking down Bryant's coaching tower on the practice field.

"That was sort of like your rock from the Bible," says Hoss Johnson, an offensive lineman recruited by Bryant and who played for Perkins. "It didn't need to be moved."

Ray Perkins is not a man given to speaking of regrets, but when he recalls the 1985-86 seasons at Alabama, when his linebacker corps included both All-American and Lombardi Trophy winner Cornelius Bennett *and* future All-American and Butkus Award winner Derrick Thomas, the coach will concede this much: "It was really a shame we didn't win more than ten games with Derrick on one side and Cornelius on the other, or Cornelius in the middle."

The history of lethal linebackers at Alabama is long and glorious. Lee Roy Jordan once made 31 tackles in a bowl game. Barry Krauss made the hit in the goal-line stand play at the 1979 Sugar Bowl. And the 2005 Crimson Tide team included All-American DeMeco Ryans.

But never were there two more outstanding linebackers on the field at the same time than when Bennett and Thomas played together. And it might never have happened. In high school, Bennett was a running back/linebacker. Perkins still says he recruited him with the idea that Bennett would become the "motion guy at tight end. He was going to catch 75 balls a year."

As Perkins tells it, he watched Bennett practice for an upcoming high school All-Star game to be played in Tuscaloosa; that changed the coach's mind.

"I call him into my office——and I had to meet like three different times to get the idea across to him——and I said, 'You have impressed me so much. You remind me a lot of a linebacker I had with the New York Giants named Lawrence Taylor.'"

Perkins told Bennett that he wanted him to try playing linebacker for three days during spring practice.

"If you don't like it," Perkins told him, "you can play any position on this team that you want to play."

So, Perkins says, "I was walking off the [practice] field and I just asked him, from a distance, 'What do you think?' And he said, 'Leave me alone.'"

From then on, Cornelius Bennett was a linebacker, all the way through a long and successful NFL career.

Thomas, who was from Miami, was being recruited by Florida State when Perkins hired away assistant coach George Henshaw from the Seminoles.

"So, there was that connection and George knew his high school coach real well," Perkins says. "And Derrick really liked our place. But he also went to Oklahoma the week before us."

In 1988, Thomas recorded an Alabama-record 27 sacks and finished tenth in Heisman Trophy balloting——quite a feat for a linebacker.

"Derrick was like a big brother," says Steve Webb, a linebacker and end who was a freshman when Thomas was a senior. "You were just fascinated by his athletic ability, but he took time to talk to guys, tell them what they were doing wrong, and how to be a better player."

(continued on next page)

Thomas played eleven years for the Kansas City Chiefs and was the 1993 NFL Man of the Year. Tragically, he died from injuries suffered in a car accident at the age of thirty-three.

Says Perkins: "It was awful, such a great player and a young man of his caliber . . ."

Bennett was a three-time All-American and finished seventh in 1986 Heisman voting. He played in five Super Bowls, four with the Buffalo Bills and one with the Atlanta Falcons. He recently was inducted into the College Football Hall of Fame.

Lemanski Hall, who played linebacker at Alabama from 1990 to 1993, grew up idolizing Bennett.

"He was just a maniac," Hall says. "He made all the plays."

Not just on the field, but off the field, too.

"He was a great leader," says Perkins. "I could bring him into my office and say, 'Cornelius,' or 'Biscuit,' I've got a problem with this guy and I need you to take care of it.' And he'd say, 'Yes, sir.' And it was taken care of.

"The thing about players like Derrick Thomas and Cornelius Bennett," Perkins says, "you didn't have to spend any time worrying about those guys.

"They were going to play every down like it was their last."

Says Perkins: "I told them at the time the reason I took it down. I felt like that tower needed to be at the College Football Hall of Fame. It deserved to be there. We took it down and, boy, I caught all kinds of crap."

There was more to catch after the 1984 season. The school yearbook, the *Corolla,* wrote: "Alabama football fans were faced with a cold, hard fact: the Crimson Tide was no longer a football powerhouse. Posting a weak 5-6 record, Coach Ray Perkins was the butt of ridicule and hotly criticized."

The *Corolla* asked students what they thought about Perkins.

Student David Scott's response was typical: "Ray's not Bear Bryant. He's doing the best he can do."

Center Wes Neighbors played all four seasons for Perkins and portrays Perkins as a coach with obvious strengths and weaknesses.

"Coach Perkins was very good to his players, very fair with us, and the players that played for him liked him," Neighbors says. "Coach Perkins had a problem with communication—communication to the press, communication to his coaches. If he had had a PR person, he'd have been a lot better off. He made a lot of big boosters very angry."

One word comes up time and again when Alabama people discuss Perkins: abrasive. Johnson believes Perkins arrived from New York with battle scars, saying, "He was a guy that could look

holes through you; I think he got roughed up in that media."

Kicker Van Tiffin remembers Perkins this way: "There was no gray area with him. You had to really know how to talk to him because he analyzed what you said.

"But fans had unrealistic expectations," Tiffin says. "They were going to be negative toward whoever filled that position, unless they walked in their first year and won a national championship."

Gene Bartow, later the basketball coach and athletic director at the University of Alabama-Birmingham, was the first basketball coach at UCLA after John Wooden.

"Every time Alabama lost, he was scrutinized," Bartow says of Perkins. "Just like every time I lost, I was scrutinized."

It wasn't that anyone necessarily thought Ray Perkins was anything other than a pretty good football coach. Joe Kines, Alabama's current defensive coordinator, was on Perkins's staff and remembers him for his fine-bead focus.

"Of everybody I've ever worked with," says Kines, "he seemed to have that ability to block everything out and concentrate on one task."

And as Tiffin says, "The funny thing about it is, in '86 when he went on to Tampa Bay, nobody wanted him to leave. He could have been close to a national championship. He had things going the right way."

DON WADE

Although he arrived saying Alabama was his dream job, Perkins returned to the NFL after four seasons to become coach and general manager of the Tampa Bay Buccaneers.

Not long after Perkins left to coach the NFL's Tampa Bay Buccaneers, he told the *Orlando Sentinel:* "I don't mind admitting I can be a moody person . . . if you catch me when I'm intense, I can be arrogant. I guess I'll have to work on that. But what you see is what you get. I'm not going to change."

In the end, perhaps Ray Perkins had rethought the idea of following the legend. Or at least he'd concluded that there is a shelf life for such things.

Today, he says only that it was a "tough decision" to leave Alabama. His departure angered the Crimson masses but, when he returned to town for the annual football banquet in April of 1987, he received a standing ovation.

He was, after all, still family.

FAILURE TO CURRY FAVOR

From afar, hiring Bill Curry to be the next Alabama football coach was considered a master stroke.

The *New York Times* praised Alabama president Joab Thomas for hiring Curry, head coach at rival Georgia Tech, as a leading example of "national academic movement to discipline college sports."

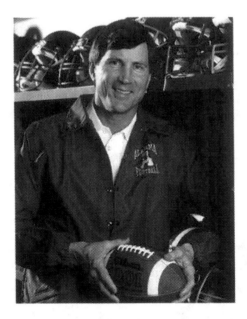

Bill Curry won points for his public speaking ability, his professed concern for academics, and won twenty-six games in three seasons, but he never was a good fit as Alabama's coach.

Obviously, the Gray Lady knew nothing of the color, passion, and pageantry of southern football. Not to mention loyalty.

While Thomas received long-distance affirmation through the national press, at home he received death threats. The fan in the stands was more concerned about Alabama's football tradition than the school acting as a lead blocker for academic reform.

Predictably, former Bryant players were not silent about their displeasure, either. Lee Roy Jordan, who applied for the job, was an outspoken critic of the hire. Tommy Brooker, like Jordan a member of the '61 national title team, was particularly angry over the process through which Curry became the coach.

"I wrote an editorial in the [Tuscaloosa] paper about it being a one-man

selection," Brooker says, referring to Thomas.

Brooker was one of many pushing for Florida State coach Bobby Bowden to get the job. Bowden was born in Birmingham and grew up as a huge Alabama fan. He even came to campus, as a freshman quarterback, for a semester before transferring to Howard College (now Samford University) in Birmingham. He also was a proven coach and, best of all, was someone of whom Bryant would have approved.

"Bobby Bowden would have been a heckuva choice," Brooker says.

Bowden even met with Thomas and other high-ranking Alabama people before Florida State played in the All-American Bowl in Birmingham.

But the choice already had been made before the meeting. In fact, Thomas ended up hiring Curry to be his football coach, and former 'Bama quarterback Steve Sloan to be his athletic director at roughly the same time.

"During my interview they asked who I thought would be best for the job and I said, 'Bobby Bowden,'" says Sloan, adding he had no real say in the hire. "I didn't know Bill would even be interested, being at Georgia Tech."

That about summed up how Alabama fans felt about things: They didn't know their school would even be interested in Curry, him being at Georgia Tech.

In published interviews at that time,

The hiring of Curry, who came from rival Georgia Tech, incensed some 'Bama fans.

Lee Roy Jordan repeatedly made references to Curry's hiring being an effort to "end the Paul Bryant era." With time, however, Jordan changed his stance. At that same April 1987 football banquet at which Ray Perkins received a standing ovation, Jordan voiced support for Curry.

The new coach almost immediately began winning converts with every public speaking appearance he made. During a February rally at the Birmingham-Jefferson Civic Center, Curry started by saying, "I'm not here to dazzle you with talk." He then proceeded to do just that—dazzle them with his charm and charisma.

He spoke about playing for famed Green Bay Packers coach Vince Lombardi, pro football's closest equivalent to Bear Bryant.

"He said religion came first, family second, and the Green Bay Packers third," Curry told the crowd. "But you know, as soon as we hit the practice field, he got confused about the order."

Curry also spoke of the two times he appeared on the cover of *Sports Illustrated:* once as a center for the Packers, and once as a center for the Baltimore Colts.

"The first time it happened, they allowed Bart Starr to be on the cover with me," he said, invoking the name of the former Alabama quarterback. "The second time, they allowed Johnny Unitas to be on the cover with me."

When there was a microphone in front of him, Curry talked a good game; there was no doubt about that.

That spring, Bryant's coaching tower was returned to the practice field, Sloan saying during a luncheon that, "I think it will serve as a bridge between the coaching staff and alumni . . ."

While the most visible symbol representing Coach Bryant went back up, the trust between Curry and former players went down. Curry wouldn't allow former players to attend practice. Nor would Curry allow some high-ranking officials in the athletic department to come to practice.

"I called Bill Curry up and said, 'Bill, what's going on?' says Brooker, who is just one of many former players who still resides in Tuscaloosa. "He said, 'We just don't know anybody.'"

Brooker countered that former Alabama player and long-time Bryant assistant coach Clem Gryska was acting as gatekeeper at practice and that Gryska "knows anybody in America that has anything to do with Alabama football."

Brooker says Curry briefly relented and opened things up, only to close practices off a few weeks later.

"They were paranoid, thinking we're gonna come in here and call Tennessee and tell them what they're doing," Brooker says. "It had never been like that around here."

After accepting the job, Curry had told reporters: "I realize I didn't play at

Alabama, or coach at Alabama, and for that reason I'm not considered one of the Alabama family. I accept that. That's how it should be. But I'd like to earn a spot in the Alabama family, and you do that by what happens on the field."

Even what happened on the field was more complicated than Curry had imagined. He had a three-year record of 26-10. And, in 1989, his last season, he had the Crimson Tide ranked second in the country.

During his tenure at Alabama, Curry's teams went 3-0 against both Tennessee and Penn State. "Which ain't exactly chopped liver," notes retired Birmingham sportswriter Clyde Bolton.

Curry's legacy, if you will, was that his teams always left Alabama fans hungry for more. He couldn't beat Auburn. And there were other defeats that fans just would not, or could not, accept.

In 1987, with Alabama 4-1 and the number fifteen team in the country, the Crimson Tide lost, 13–10, to a dreadful Memphis State team.

"It was a loss Alabama fans would not let Curry forget," Donald F. Staffo wrote in his 1992 book, *Bama After Bear: Turmoil and Tranquility in Tuscaloosa.*

"He would wear it around his neck like an albatross . . ."

Although each of Curry's teams was better than the one before it, and he was SEC Coach of the Year in 1989 when he won ten games, he never did overcome his outsider status and kept losing the very games he could not afford to lose.

Mark McCarter, who, in 1989, was covering the team for a newspaper in Anniston, Alabama, and is now a sports columnist in Huntsville, says, "Curry used to joke, when talking about how he was treated by the media, that he could be out fishing, his boat could capsize, he could walk across the water all the way to shore, and the headlines would read: CURRY CAN'T SWIM. That was about the position he was in here."

Alabama fans always seemed to have another game to hold up as evidence, too. In 1988, it was homecoming in Tuscaloosa against Ole Miss, a 22–12 debacle in which Alabama did not complete a pass all day. That night, someone

Curry was 0-3 against Auburn, which didn't sit well with the 'Bama faithful, and canceled out his successes.

armed with a brick found his target just fine: Curry's office window in the football building.

The school newspaper, the *Crimson White,* denounced the person or persons responsible, calling the incident "shameful" and "disgusting."

While most Alabama fans believed throwing a brick through the coach's window was certainly going too far, they might very well have used those same words, *shameful* and *disgusting,* to describe how they felt about Curry losing to Auburn every year.

"It was a hardship on him," says Gary Hollingsworth, who played quarterback for Curry's 1989 team. "It's like you hear in golf—the best guy never to win a major."

Steve Webb, who played on the defense during the 1988 and 1989 seasons, says the controversy over Curry began to wear down the players, too.

"We felt the pressure," Webb says.

This was especially true during Auburn week, when Webb recalls Curry and his staff being in disarray.

"We get to Auburn, and it seemed like they changed the whole philosophy as far as how we prepared for the game," says Webb, who's now a city councilman in Northport, Alabama. "We added more stuff, changed a lot of stuff."

Center Roger Shultz, who played three seasons for Curry, says: "He kind of oversaw the program like a CEO of a company. I think he'd have been a better fit now than he was then."

Curry has perhaps found his best fit in the broadcast booth. Since 1997, he

Bobby Humphrey was an All-American running back on Curry's first team and led Alabama in rushing.

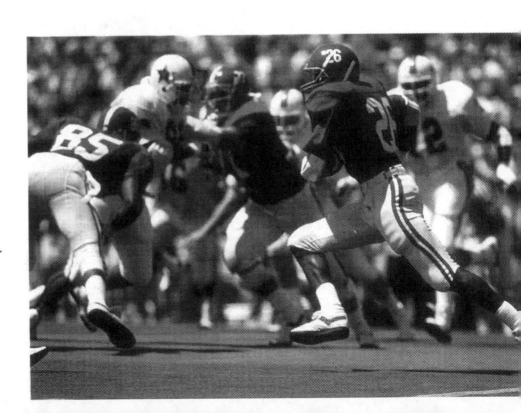

has been a college-football color commentator for ESPN.

What's certain is that he was not a good fit at Alabama, at least not once the games started.

"Fans loved him [at first] because he was charismatic, a very good speaker," says Webb. "But you lose to Auburn, that welcome mat can be pulled away."

Curry could feel the mat moving beneath his feet after his third and final loss to Auburn. The coach who liked to wear dark sunglasses on the sideline could no longer hide from the obvious: He was never going to be accepted into this family.

Amid the reworking of his contract at Alabama, Curry accepted the coaching job at Kentucky. During his introduction at a January 1990 press conference in Lexington, Curry gushed over the reception they received, saying he and his wife were "made to feel so welcome and needed."

He also told his Kentucky audience: "This is anything but a step down," and said he had merely moved from one elite program to another.

Bill Curry still talked a very good game.

THE NEXT
BEST THING

On New Year's Day 1968, in Dallas, the pupil was coaching against the teacher.

The pupil won that day, Gene Stallings's Texas A & M team beating Bear Bryant's Alabama team, 20–16, in the Cotton Bowl.

The mentor greeted the pupil on the field and hoisted him high in the air, happier for the protégé's win than he was sad about his own defeat.

"After the game, I was in the dressing room doing a press conference," Stallings recalls. "The manager came running over—couldn't hardly breathe—and saying, 'Coach Bryant's coming in! Coach Bryant's coming in!' "

Stallings excused himself from the press conference and approached his old boss.

"You looking for me?" Stallings said.

Bryant disciple Gene Stallings beat his former boss in the 1968 Cotton Bowl—a 20–16 win for Texas A & M over Alabama—but Bryant was happy for his former Junction Boy and assistant coach.

"No, I've seen enough of you," Bryant answered. "I just wanted to congratulate your players."

Says Stallings: "It just showed the class that he had."

There seems little doubt that Bryant dreamed of the day that Stallings—"Bebes"—would eventually be Alabama's coach. It didn't work out in 1983 but, when it happened in 1990, seven years after Bryant's death, Alabama football had been restored.

This was made clear when Paul Bryant, Jr., attended the press conference introducing Stallings, and published reports quoted Bear Bryant's son telling Stallings: "It's what Papa wanted."

Truly, it was what a lot of people wanted.

"You could see the old heads come back into the fold of Alabama football," says Wes Neighbors, a center from 1983 to 1986.

HE WROTE THE BOOK

With 323 career wins and six national championships, Paul W. Bryant wrote the book on coaching college football. But he did not write the book on writing the book on coaching college football. Gene Stallings did that.

When Stallings was an assistant to Bryant in the 1960s, Bryant was going to write a book with *Birmingham News* sports editor Benny Marshall. Except that Bryant really wasn't going to be very involved. He was going to pay Stallings fifty dollars to help Marshall with the technical details for a book to be called *Building a Championship Football Team*.

Stallings was excited by this prospect; he also needed the fifty dollars. So, when Marshall said he couldn't do the book, Stallings saw a great opportunity slipping away. His solution: a one-man blitz.

"I went in to see Coach Bryant and said, 'Coach, Benny Marshall can't write your book, but I can,'" Stallings recalls. And that kicked off a conversation that, when stripped of various adjectives and adverbs, went about like this:

Bryant: "Bebes, what do you know about writing a book?"

Stallings: "I don't know anything about writing a book. I've never written a book. I had a hard time passing English. But I can write your book."

And so Gene "Bebes" Stallings did just that. Bryant tore up the contract he had and said he'd split the royalties with Stallings 50-50.

"That's the contract we had," Stallings says.

And a fine one it was, too, because somewhere in the fine print there must have been something about the ghost writer winning a national championship of his own.

Linda Knowles even got her old job back as secretary to the head coach.

"I don't talk about the Perkins and Curry years," she says politely but firmly. "Coach Stallings's return was very unifying."

Bringing everyone together was exactly what then-athletic director Hootie Ingram had in mind after Alabama had become Georgia Tech West under Bill Curry.

"The beauty of hiring Gene," Ingram says, "is Gene brought in people that knew what the university was all about and loved it. Overnight, we had things going full-bore with the head coach and a group of assistants."

Although Stallings hadn't played at Alabama—he was one of Bryant's "Junction Boys" at Texas A & M—he had coached under Bryant in Tuscaloosa and was one of the Bear's favorites. And perhaps because Stallings knew he carried Bryant's blessing, and because he had seen the problems that resulted from Perkins trying too hard to make his own name, "Bebes" found a comfort zone.

One quote is particularly telling. After Stallings accepted the job, he was asked how he would handle Bryant's larger-than-life shadow. The new coach had the perfect answer.

"I love his shadow," Stallings said.

Even now, in his seventies and tending to his ranch near Paris, Texas, Stallings understands that the shadow never leaves.

"I never tried to compete with Coach Bryant in anything," Stallings says. "I wasn't interested in my record being better than his record. And I've told more Coach Bryant stories than anybody."

He also wanted his players to know the larger Bear Bryant story.

"It wasn't that he was coming in here trying to replace Coach Bryant, he more embraced Coach Bryant," says quarterback Jay Barker, who played four years for Stallings. "He took us over to the Bryant Museum when he first got here and said, 'I want you to understand about the guys who played before you and what it means to wear the crimson jersey, what it means to be part of Alabama football.'"

Stallings was the first coach after Bryant to find warmth in his considerable shadow.

Stallings mostly had a good relationship with the media, too. He was more approachable than Bryant, less abrasive than Perkins, less paranoid than Curry.

"I'd sit in Coach Stallings's office and he'd whip out the bread, mayonnaise and tomato, make us a sandwich, and we'd talk about everything on earth," recalls former Birmingham sportswriter Clyde Bolton.

As nice as this all was, none of it would have mattered one whit if Stallings didn't win.

His first team in 1990 started 0-3, but a 9–6 upset of number three Tennessee in Knoxville got the Crimson Tide back to even, at 3-3, and the team finished 7-5 to play in the Fiesta Bowl in Arizona; Ingram had hired Stallings off the NFL unemployment line, after he had been fired as coach of the Arizona Cardinals.

"That 7-5 record is so misleading," says Steve Webb, who played end and linebacker two years under Curry. "From day one, we learned there was a new sheriff in town. He didn't send us out on the field concerned about being the 'good guys' all the time. In the game of football, good guys don't always win. You've got to be tough and hard and relentless. Stallings allowed us to be that way."

In 1992, when Alabama would go 13-0, the team would need every bit of that toughness, every measure of resolve. An 11-1 finish in 1991 had raised expectations and cemented the idea that the right man was in charge.

Even Bill Curry, who was coaching at Kentucky, understood this.

"He fits the criteria that people want in a coach—and you know what I mean," Curry said during the '92 season, referring to the fact that Stallings was part of the Alabama family. "He's done an excellent job."

Stallings seemed the perfect combination of tough old coach and tender-hearted soul. Ingram would quip during the season that Stallings visits hospitals "more than most preachers."

And Stallings's relationship with his

Stallings's son, John Mark, was a huge Alabama fan when his father coached there, and remains one to this day.

adult son, John Mark, who has Down syndrome, was inspirational to all. "All his love is unconditional," Stallings said during the midst of the championship season. "He doesn't keep score."

Yet, on the football field, keeping score still mattered greatly, and mattered greatly to John Mark, who was, and still is, a big Alabama fan.

The '92 season had the usual challenges of an Alabama football season, which is to say the team was expected to win most, and preferably all, of the games, especially the Tennessee and Auburn games.

The season was complicated, however, by star receiver David Palmer's second arrest in three months for driving under the influence, and a steady drumbeat of disapproval from fans and media who wanted more scoring out of the offense.

Stallings twice suspended Palmer and it shouldn't have come as a surprise. Almost thirty years earlier, when flamboyant quarterback Joe Namath violated team rules by drinking, Bryant asked his assistants what he should do: All but Stallings voted not to suspend Namath.

"My position was, if we had a rule

During the 1992 national title season, Stallings twice suspended star David Palmer.

and somebody violated the rule, we needed to do something about it or not have the rule," Stallings says. "If I had it to do over again, I'd vote the same way."

The David Palmer controversy aside, there was almost relentless criticism of Alabama's popgun offense. After a tough 13–0 win over Louisiana Tech in the season's fourth week, *Birmingham News* columnist Kevin Scarbinsky wasted no time in writing of the potential doom and gloom that might accompany even a perfect season.

"Not even 13-0 is guaranteed to add up to a national championship for Alabama," the columnist said. "If the offense doesn't get the team beat on the field, it still can get the team beat in the polls."

It was the offense, however, that pulled out a 30–21 win at Mississippi State, and that moved Alabama to 10-0. 'Bama trailed, 21–20, going into the fourth quarter, when sophomore quarterback Jay Barker led the team on two scoring drives.

"We just had an air about us all year long that we were not going to lose," Barker says.

After shutting out Auburn, 17–0, Alabama met Florida in the SEC title game. The score was tied, 21–21 when, late in the fourth quarter, Antonio Langham intercepted a Shane Matthews pass and ran it back 27 yards for a touchdown and a 28–21 Crimson Tide win.

"Until Antonio made that play, I was about to have a heart attack," said running back Derrick Lassic. "I felt I was about to check out and join the Bear."

Now, in the season marking the one hundredth anniversary of Alabama football, Gene Stallings's team was poised to play defending national champion Miami for the 1992 national championship in the Sugar Bowl.

Miami was installed as the favorite by more than a touchdown.

"I felt like we were the better team," Stallings says, "but nobody would listen to me."

Except for the young men in his locker room.

"We never got caught up in the criticism," says Barker. "Everybody thought Miami was gonna kill us. One of the writers that week said, 'This is like David and Goliath.' And I remember telling him, 'Man, I'll take those odds.' "

Bebes' boys quieted the mouthy Miami Hurricanes with a 34–13 victory, securing the school's twelfth national championship and first in thirteen years.

As it had all season, the defense led the way.

"We prided ourselves on not giving up the big play because we knew nobody could take the ball and drive eighty yards on us," says Chris Donnelly, a safety on the team.

All-Americans John Copeland and Eric Curry anchored the defensive line. Miami's plan, of course, was to beat 'Bama deep, but defensive coordinator

Bill Oliver showed the Hurricanes every alignment imaginable, and a few that were beyond imagination, such as putting all eleven men on the line of scrimmage.

The Hurricanes believed they had finally connected on a big play in the third quarter when Heisman Trophy winner Gino Torretta completed a pass to wideout Lamar Thomas, who had beaten the cornerback with a fake and now had a lane to the end zone. But free safety George Teague caught Thomas at the Alabama 15-yard line, and reached over the receiver's right shoulder and stole the ball back. Although Miami kept the ball because Alabama was offside on the play, Teague had stopped a sure touchdown and the Crimson Tide had reclaimed the momentum. Suddenly, this Miami Hurricane had been downgraded to a tropical depression.

To think that there was a time Stallings believed he would never be the coach, never be a part of this glory. "When they hired Ray Perkins, I really didn't think I'd ever have the opportunity," Stallings says. "Not because I didn't want to, but because I didn't think they'd ever offer me the job."

The national championship party might have gone on for days, weeks, and months. . . .

"It was probably one of the most gratifying seasons Alabama fans ever had," says Ingram. "We certainly weren't

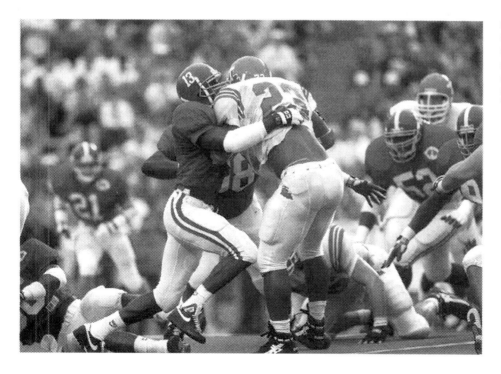

Safety George Teague (13) had a lot of great moments, but is most remembered for stripping the ball from a Miami receiver in the '93 Sugar Bowl.

supposed to go 13–0 and win the national championship. Probably, we weren't even supposed to win the conference championship."

Unbeknownst to Ingram and Stallings, there was an opportunistic party crasher in Alabama's midst: a sports agent who, in the joyous hours after the Sugar Bowl victory, had gotten All-American cornerback Antonio Langham to sign a contract and declare himself eligible for the NFL Draft.

A few days later, Langham told Stallings he had signed something to put his name in for the draft and that he wanted to remove his name and return to Alabama for his senior season; Langham apparently did not share the information about signing a contract with the agent, which would make him ineligible under NCAA rules. In fact, Langham would say he didn't even realize he had signed a deal with the agent, who weeks earlier—after the SEC title game, but before the Sugar Bowl—had made a $400 loan to Langham.

"It was an unfortunate situation," says Stallings. "I think Antonio was taken advantage of, I really do."

The NCAA's investigation reached its conclusion just before kickoff of the 1995 season: Alabama would have to forfeit all ten games in which Langham played during the 1993 season (leaving a 1-12 record), and would be put on probation. The sanctions, the first in the football program's storied history, prohibited Alabama from playing in a bowl game in 1995; the Tide also had to give up scholarships over a three-year period.

The NCAA criticized the university's handling of the entire Langham situation and, in time, Ingram and school president Roger Sayers would walk into the sunset, perhaps sooner than either man would have otherwise chosen.

"The whole thing was mishandled by all the parties involved, and I'm speaking of the University of Alabama, the Southeastern Conference, and the NCAA," Ingram says. "The university, we were kind of naïve."

In many ways, this was the beginning of the end for Stallings, too. Sayers and Ingram were the ones who brought Stallings back to 'Bama. Suddenly, they were gone and in their place were outsiders: Dr. Andrew Sorensen as president and Bob Bockrath as athletic director.

Stallings's last team, in 1996, would finish 10-3, but the season's story was about if and when he would leave. A 17–16 loss to Mississippi State in Starkville near season's end fueled the speculation when word leaked about a postgame locker-room exchange between Stallings and Bockrath, who had foolishly greeted the coach moments after this heartbreaking defeat by saying, "We've got our work cut out for us now."

Bockrath and Stallings later tried to

smooth things over publicly, but then-MSU coach and former 'Bama player Jackie Sherrill is right when he says, "That was it. After that, there was no relationship left."

So, after Alabama edged Auburn, 24–23, Stallings announced he would retire after that season's bowl game. He choked up while delivering the news to his players and many of his players shed tears, too.

"Everybody," quarterback Freddie Kitchens said, "respects him."

Although Stallings played the diplomat while making his exit, saying it was simply time for him to pass the torch, there is no point in pretending the situation was anything other than what it was: impossible.

"It's always been my position that if you don't respect the guy you're working for, you need to step aside," Stallings says now, deep into retirement. "Just as simple as that. Rank has its privileges.

"The athletic director and I just weren't on the same page. As far as being ready to quit coaching, I wasn't really ready to quit coaching."

And Alabama fans weren't really ready to see him go.

True, Stallings was right about Alabama fans loving Coach Bryant and just tolerating the rest of them. But the last football coach to win a national championship at Alabama, the one who's still comfortable in Bryant's shadow, forgets to mention one thing: They tolerated Bebes best of all.

Stallings announced his resignation after the Auburn game in 1996; he says now he wasn't ready to quit coaching.

10

FIELD GENERALS

In the state of Alabama, probably your five most recognizable names are your governor, your two head coaches at Auburn and Alabama, and your two quarterbacks.

—Former Crimson Tide QB Gary Hollingsworth, who, in 1989, threw for more than 2,000 yards.

TYLER Watts finished his career in 2002, handing off the starting job to Brodie Croyle.

Watts grew up in Alabama, so he knew the drill, or at least he thought he knew the drill. College football was king. He remembers playing football in his backyard on Sundays when the Atlanta Falcons were on television—"Nobody cared about them," he says—and watching the games that mattered on Saturdays.

Still, when that was him under center, when he was one of the five most recognizable names in the state, he wasn't entirely ready.

"Regardless of what kind of preparation you

feel like you've done to get yourself ready for playing quarterback at Alabama," Watts says, "there's nothing you can do that will prepare you. It's life changing."

Watts was early in his Alabama career, walking through a mall in Tuscaloosa one day, when a couple of fans stopped him. "They came up to me and told me they named their kid after me," he says. "I absolutely could not fathom that."

So, who knows how many little Tylers are running across playgrounds today?

Or how many Brodies are just learning to walk?

Or how many Jays (as in Barker, 1992 national championship) are in junior and senior high schools all across Alabama?

Of course, Crimson Tide coach Mike Shula, an Alabama quarterback in the 1980s, can top all that, even though he's not aware of any baby Mikes.

"I did have a bull named after me," he says. "They called it 'Shula.' It looked pretty athletic."

Nice line. All kidding aside, there really isn't a way to be prepared for being quarterback at Alabama.

"If they put Brodie Croyle's face up behind the TV anchorman, they don't

Brodie Croyle is one of the most beloved quarterbacks in Alabama history.

have to explain who that is," says *Tuscaloosa News* sports editor Cecil Hurt. "That's the kind of celebrity you have in this state, and that's a lot for a twenty-year-old to have to deal with."

Says Croyle: "Everybody wants you to come to their birthday party and wear your uniform and your helmet."

He's not joking. Repeat, he is not joking.

"Brodie Croyle has got rock-star status," says Ken "Snake" Stabler, an All-American quarterback for Alabama in 1967, who now does color commentary on the team's radio broadcasts. "He's a magnet."

Alabama history shows its best, or most beloved, quarterbacks falling into one of two categories: great athletes, which is really a two-man class made up of Stabler and Joe Namath, and great leaders who weren't great athletes, which is a really a two-man class consisting of Pat Trammell and Jay Barker.

Other quarterbacks also made their mark, including: Steve Sloan and Scott Hunter in the 1960s; Terry Davis, Gary and Jeff Rutledge, Richard Todd, and Steadman Shealy in the '70s; Walter Lewis, Shula, and Hollingsworth in the '80s; Barker and Freddie Kitchens in the '90s; Andrew Zow from 1998 to 2001; and Watts through 2002.

Brodie Croyle gets his own category. He's beloved, but is too good an athlete to be lumped with Trammell and Barker.

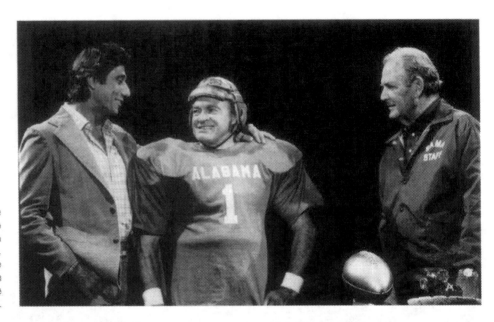

Former Tide QB Joe Namath went on to fame and fortune with the New York Jets. Here, he has a little fun clowning with comedian Bob Hope and Bryant.

Yet he's not quite in Namath's and Stabler's league, either. At least not yet. If he turns into the best quarterback the Kansas City Chiefs ever drafted, then it's a different story.

Most of all, Croyle is the quarterback who made Alabama a winner amid unfathomable trouble and turmoil. His is the modern face of Tide pride and will remain so until another quarterback steps up and makes the job completely his. If that doesn't happen in the 2006 season, then another phenomenon is likely to take effect.

"Sometimes the most popular guy," Watts says with a laugh, "might be the backup quarterback."

But any backup quarterback will have a tough time establishing himself as 'Bama's best. In 1955, first-year coach J. B. "Ears" Whitworth believed it very important to build for the future. So, he put a senior quarterback named Bart Starr on the bench and more or less left him there.

Whitworth's first team went 0-10 and Starr then lived up to his name en route to the Pro Football Hall of Fame as a Green Bay Packer. It's more proof of how difficult it is to become a starting, and outstanding, Alabama quarterback.

Even more uncommon is to be a starting black quarterback at Alabama. Walter Lewis was the first, and remembers when he was being recruited he was told he might have a chance to be the quarterback when Coach Bear Bryant won his 315th game, breaking the all-time record. That's exactly how it played out, too.

There were those who were certain that could never happen, that only a white face could peer out from the Crimson helmet and bark signals, or be shown as the face of Alabama football behind some TV anchorman.

"My parents were opposed to it because of all the negative stuff that came out of the late '60s and early '70s about Alabama," Lewis says. "They didn't have the confidence that Coach Bryant would play a black quarterback. I actually saw people make bets in front of my father that I would never play quarterback at Alabama."

Those people lost their money. And when Lewis looks at his own place in the history of Alabama quarterbacks, he doesn't restrict his viewfinder to black and white.

"I considered it an honor being associated with those men who created a tradition as it relates to quarterbacks," says Lewis. "If you're the quarterback at Alabama, it's a cherished spot."

Like Watts says, it's life changing.

So is the moment when you're no longer the quarterback at Alabama, when you pass a large measure of your fame to the next guy in line.

"I know it sounds bad," Watts says, "but it's tough not being in the limelight when it's over."

JUST A WINNER

Bear Bryant wouldn't have minded a passer, but he could live without one.

The coach wouldn't have minded a runner, but he could live without one of those, too. What Bryant could not live without was a leader. And, in Bryant's vernacular, *leader* was synonymous with *winner*. And winner, Bryant discovered, was synonymous with Pat Trammell.

"Pat was the perfect field general at a crucial time when Coach Bryant first came here," says Alabama athletic director Mal Moore, who was a backup quarterback at that time. "Pat was very smart and as mentally tough as anybody. That was the kind of guy Coach Bryant needed. He was trying to set his brand of thinking, and they thought a lot alike."

Moore's right; they did think a lot alike. They *were* a lot alike. But their backgrounds couldn't have been more different. Bryant grew up poor in rural Arkansas and struggled to get through high school. Trammell, from Scottsboro, Alabama, came from privilege and was well read.

"His daddy was a doctor," says Billy Neighbors, a teammate of Trammell on the 1961 national championship team. "He had a car. He was from an affluent family. I don't think too many doctors' sons played football back in the '60s."

On the football field, however, Trammell was more than willing to get down and dirty. That's why Bryant loved him and often said that all Pat Trammell could do was beat you.

If Bryant had been a quarterback, he'd have wanted to be like Trammell.

"He was a brilliant football man," Neighbors says. "You know, football's like a war. And Pat read every book ever written about a war. Pat Trammell was one of the best-read persons I ever knew."

Trammell, however, must have skipped the chapters on taking orders and following the chain of command. With neither the flash nor flamboyance that attended successors Joe Namath and Ken "Snake" Stabler, Trammell went about playing football and living the college life his way.

"He was as mean as a snake," says Tommy Brooker, an offensive end in those days. "If you dropped one [pass], he wouldn't throw to you again. He was going to punish you. He was kinda like Coach Bryant."

Which meant Trammell liked to have his fun, too. Brooker recalls riding around town in Trammell's convertible while Trammell smoked a cigar—away from the coaches' eyes.

In football matters, however, Trammell never hesitated to confront Bryant.

"He'd cuss him just like he was his brother," says Neighbors, who, like most of the Alabama players, was so afraid of Bryant that he usually avoided him. "He's the only one I ever heard do it. They'd get in arguments on the sidelines."

Bryant allowed those arguments because of the subject matter, how to best win the football game at hand, and because Trammell was a great leader, the closest thing Bryant could get to being in the huddle himself.

Heck, fussin' and cussin' just meant they were discussin'.

Bryant and Trammell meet General Douglas MacArthur.

212

"They had lunch together every day," recalls former assistant coach Clem Gryska.

They came to know one another very well, though not so well that Trammell could not surprise Bryant. Like that day at Legion Field, when Alabama was struggling to move the ball, but had possession on about the 50-yard line, and Trammell took it upon himself to punt—on third down.

"Coach meets him at the hash mark," Gryska remembers, "and says, 'What the hell are you doing?'"

Trammell's response: "Well, they wouldn't block. I thought the defense would do better."

"Coach looked at him," Gryska says, "and said, 'Well, you're right.'"

Center/linebacker Lee Roy Jordan remembers Trammell about the way Bryant would.

"He didn't look pretty throwing the ball, he didn't look pretty running the ball, all he did was win," Jordan says. "His decisions were the best of anybody I had seen. He knew exactly when to throw the ball out of bounds, when to go to the inside and throw, when to keep it, and when to pitch it. Pat was very outspoken and very confident and Coach Bryant respected that. Coach Bryant loved him, and respected him."

Tragically, in 1968, while in his last year of medical residency in Birmingham and just seven years after he had led Alabama to its first national title under Bryant, Trammell died of cancer. He was twenty-eight.

Said Bryant: "This is the saddest day of my life."

WILD BOYS

In a 1960 article for magazine *Coach & Athlete*, Bear Bryant wrote about quarterbacks.

"There are several basic rules by which we expect our quarterbacks to operate," Bryant said, "but I would not give a plug nickel for a quarterback who would not be willing to break every one of those rules in order to win a game."

In a way, Bryant was writing about Trammell. Though he didn't know it at the time, he also was writing about Joe Namath and Ken Stabler. They were rule breakers and risk takers supreme, on the field and off.

Of course, on the field, the results could be spectacular.

"Do whatever you have to do to win. I've always felt that," Stabler says. "It came out in my pro career [with the Oakland Raiders], the fumble play against San Diego when you roll the ball out there. And in the Auburn game, being able to make that run.

"Do whatever you have to do. That doesn't mean you do whatever you have to do off the field; you conform to his rules."

Easily said now, not so easily done then.

In many ways, Namath and Stabler were two of a kind—wild cards, jokers—"lovable rogues," says sportswriter Clyde Bolton.

Talented, lovable rogues, they were from dissimilar backgrounds. Ray Perkins caught passes from both of them.

"Namath and Stabler *were* different," Perkins says. "They really shouldn't be lumped together. Joe had a definite northeastern flair. Stabler, there's no mistaking Stabler—he's from South Alabama somewhere."

To be precise, Stabler's from Foley. Namath came out of Beaver Falls, Pennsylvania. And getting Namath to Alabama would take a lot more work than it took to get Stabler to Tuscaloosa.

Though Stabler had been recruited by Auburn, Mississippi State, and Tulane, he had been raised on 'Bama ball. His father listened to the games on radio, and so Stabler knew all about Trammell and Coach Bryant.

Alabama never would have gotten Namath, if he had not failed the college boards at Maryland.

"It would have made our program," Lee Corso, then Maryland's coach, told Mark Kriegel for his book, *Namath*.

What this meant for Bryant and Alabama was that there was a small win-

Ken Stabler liked to have his fun, too, and Bryant also suspended him. Retired sportswriter Clyde Bolton describes Namath and Stabler as "lovable rogues."

dow of opportunity. Assistant coach Howard Schnellenberger was dispatched to Beaver Falls to begin working on Namath and those close to him, including his mother and Joe's high-school coach.

It would not be an easy job for several reasons. Namath's parents were divorced, so there was that complication. Would Joe be willing to go this far from home?

There was competition for his football talents from Notre Dame, among others, and for his baseball skills from multiple major-league teams. And, had Namath decided he just wanted to play college basketball, he could have done that, too.

"Of all the players I've ever played with or coached, he's the best athlete I've ever been around," says Jackie Sherrill, a Namath teammate at Alabama, and then a long-time college football coach. "He could go baseline and dunk with both hands over his head. Whatever you wanted to do, he could beat you—baseball, football, or basketball."

Former assistant coach Clem Gryska still recalls the sorry sight that was Schnellenberger upon his return—the prized recruit in tow.

"When he got off the plane, and this was summertime," says Gryska, "his tie was untied and off to the side, and he was wringing wet. You would tell he was just exhausted. And then Joe came off and he had a little straw hat on. He looked real classy."

How did Schnellenberger get his man?

Probably two things helped more than anything else. First, he had been at Kentucky when Joe's brother Frank had been there. Second, Joe's mother, Rose, took a shine to the coach.

"Whatever Joe did," Gryska says, "he wanted to make sure it would please his mother."

And so, the quarterback who would one day be known as Broadway Joe tied on his cleats for Alabama. Freshmen couldn't play on the varsity in those days, but Namath made an impression in practices just the same. He was such a good athlete that he would have made a fine defensive back. In fact, Gryska, the freshman team's coach, initially worked him there, too.

"Coach Bryant sent a manager over to get me," Gryska remembers. "And when I got over to him he said, 'Don't mess with him in the secondary. Just let him throw the ball.' "

And, boy, could he throw the ball.

"I had never caught a ball that was so tightly wound," says Perkins.

"A beautiful passer," says Steve Sloan, a fine quarterback in his own right who was a teammate of Namath and Stabler.

"Namath was a great pure passer," says Bolton, "but Ken Stabler was probably the player I enjoyed watching the most. He was a great passer as well as a great runner. Bryant said if they'd been running the wishbone when Stabler was

216

there, they'd have had to put another digit on the scoreboard.

"He was kind of a shady character," Bolton adds. "Maybe that added a little to it. It was like watching Tom Sawyer or Huck Finn playing quarterback."

The "Run in the Mud" from the 7–3 win over Auburn in 1967 is what most fans think of when they recall Stabler's days with the Crimson Tide. It was the fourth quarter, Alabama trailed 3–0, and the ball was on Auburn's 47-yard line, on a field more fit for pigs than the pigskin.

"It was just a simple option play," Stabler says. "We had a simple I-formation type of offense then. You take the ball, go down the line, and you either keep it or pitch it.

"I cut up the field, and our wide receiver at that side, the right side, was Dennis Homan, and he got a terrific block on the safety, just cut the safety down. And I had a lane to get down the sideline. I just sloshed down the sideline to get in the corner of the end zone."

It was what had to be done to win

Stabler's "Run in the Mud" in 1967 for a 47-yard touchdown beat Auburn, 7–3, "I just sloshed down the sideline," Stabler says.

the game, same as that "forward fumble" in the pros.

Namath, too, would do what had to be done. Unfortunately, it can't always turn out with a victory. The so-close quarterback sneak in the 1965 Orange Bowl against Texas would have given Alabama a win after being voted national champions. And when the victory didn't come, there was no consoling Namath.

He had set an Orange Bowl record by completing 18 of 37 passes for 255 yards and 2 touchdowns. He had done it on a bum knee and Bryant had called his performance "courageous."

"It wasn't good enough," Namath said.

A year earlier, Namath had missed the Sugar Bowl after Bryant kicked him off the team for drinking beer.

"Joe had all the ability in the world and didn't have a lot of commitment," says Lee Roy Jordan, who had seen the signs as his teammate in 1961–62. "One of the greatest things that happened to him in his life was to come to Alabama, learn about how to be there for other people, and how to be a teammate."

Stabler, alias "Snake," says the same for his experience at Alabama. Bryant suspended him when his commitment and discipline were lacking. Like Namath, Stabler enjoyed a good time and the company of a pretty girl.

"Stabler was gifted," former assistant coach Danny Ford says of the lefthander, "but I could tell you some stories. He enjoyed himself."

Because Stabler followed Namath, and Namath had been reinstated, it's fair to wonder if Snake took that as license to shed his inhibitions.

"I never felt that because Joe was brought back that I could do whatever I wanted to do," Stabler says. "We just happened to have similar personalities, similar lifestyles, and both of us were young and dumb and not making very good decisions at the time.

"Coach Bryant made me realize you're only as good as the people around you and you're no more important than any other position on the team."

Someone else had a role in that, too: Steve Sloan, who replaced Namath in the 1964 Sugar Bowl and led Alabama to a 12–7 victory over Ole Miss, and was a senior when Stabler was in on-the-job training as a sophomore. With Namath an All-American in 1964, Sloan in '65, and Stabler in '67, Alabama had quite a run at quarterback. Bryant often used Namath and Sloan in the same game, and Sloan and Stabler in the same game.

Sloan, though overshadowed by the colorful Namath and Stabler, was an All-American in 1965, when Alabama won a second straight national title.

"The things I could do well, for me, were running the ball and the sprint-out passes," Sloan says. "Joe was more a tackle-to-tackle pocket passer. It gave them two looks, although his look was better."

Namath and Stabler were selected as the quarterbacks on Alabama's Team of the Century. They excelled in the pros, Namath delivering a win after his "I guarantee it" statement with the AFL's New York Jets before Super Bowl III, and Stabler living by Oakland Raiders owner Al Davis's credo: "Just win, baby."

So, yeah, they were Bear Bryant's kind of quarterbacks: rule breakers and winners.

They share something else as well: a love for the coach who perhaps saved their careers.

"It made you feel good to do things right [for Coach Bryant]," Namath said in a television interview several years ago. "It made you feel good to make him happy."

PERFECT PREPARATION

Mike Shula had a couple of things in common with Pat Trammell: He didn't have a big arm and didn't have great legs.

Or, as center Wes Neighbors likes to say, "Shula's the slowest white man in the history of college football. If he

Even though Namath had a bum knee, the Jets were willing to pay him whatever he wanted to come play for them in the American Football League.

started scrambling, he was going to get sacked. Every offensive lineman but one could outrun him."

With something less than total conviction, Shula denies this.

"That's not true," says the Alabama quarterback who became Alabama's coach. "I was just as fast as they were."

No disrespect to Neighbors or anyone else but, from the neck up, Shula was faster.

It's true that during Shula's four years as a player, 1983–86, he did not treat fans to a lot of razzle dazzle. But he won more than he lost, and given his physical limitations that was saying something.

"He won several games for us with

his mind," says another offensive lineman, Hoss Johnson. "Coach put a lot of trust in him."

"Coach" was Ray Perkins, who had caught passes from Namath and Stabler. Perkins knew well the differences between those quarterbacks and this one, whom he says was more like Sloan.

"Mike Shula never once tried to make a throw that he knew he couldn't make," Perkins says. "That takes a lot of discipline, you know?"

Shula was, however, more passer than runner. That's partly why he came to Alabama when Perkins came in from the New York Giants with a pro style offense.

"When Coach Perkins got the job, he hired [assistant coach] George Hen-

The media scrutiny accorded to all Alabama quarterbacks helped prepare Mike Shula for becoming coach of the Crimson Tide.

shaw from Florida State; Henshaw had been recruiting me so I sort of followed him over here," Shula says. "And I felt I had a good opportunity with the changeover. There were some quarterbacks that had been there, but they were all wishbone quarterbacks."

Shula's probably best remembered for engineering the 20–16 comeback win in 1985 over Georgia, when he threw the game-winning touchdown pass with just seconds left on the clock. He describes the play like it was no big deal.

"We had a good feeling they were going to blitz, so we used max protection," says Shula. "We caught them in the blitz, Al Bell beat the corner, and we threw it to him for a touchdown."

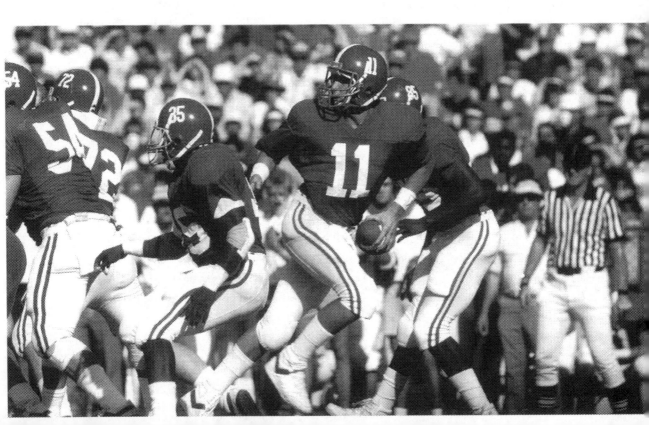

Note the *we* reference as opposed to an *I* reference. That's coach talk, which is something Shula not only learned from his famous father, but by being a quarterback at Alabama.

"I learned a lot about answering questions and making sure you never go into an interview upset," Shula says. "In my sophomore year, after a game I played badly, a writer asked me a question and I snapped at him . . . I learned from that."

AND A SOPHOMORE SHALL LEAD THEM

It is a rainy spring day in Tuscaloosa. Jay Barker is seated under an awning at an auto dealership signing autographs. Fourteen years after Alabama won its last national championship, in 1992, his signature still has value here.

A boy approaches Barker and hands him several items to sign. The boy is nervous because, after all, Barker's is a recognizable face of Alabama's last grand glory.

"What was it like to play in the Orange Bowl?" the boy blurts.

"You mean the Sugar," Barker politely corrects.

"Yeah," the boy says.

"How old are you?" asks Barker.

"Eleven."

"Wow, you weren't even around then," Barker says as much to himself as to the boy. "It's amazing how long it's been."

The funny thing about Barker's fame is that it has almost nothing to do with his 1994 season, when as a senior he finished just four yards shy of passing for 2,000 yards, four yards shy of a 400-yard passing game against Georgia, and was selected to one All-American team. As a senior, Barker was a very accomplished quarterback.

His fame, however, is from his sophomore season. He was the guy under center for a 13-0 run and a 34–13 victory over the trash-talking Miami Hurricanes in the Sugar Bowl. No matter that Barker's line from that game was downright horrifying: 4 of 13 for 18 yards with two interceptions. Alabama won the national championship. That's what matters.

"I'm a Jay Barker man," Coach Gene Stallings had said before the start of the '92 season. "Jay is far beyond where he was last year at this time."

It was the kind a thing a coach says to reassure others, and to soothe his own soul.

The '92 team had a great defense. No team scored more than 21 points against Alabama, and only two teams scored more than 13.

"What Jay did great, was he knew what he had to do to win," says Chris Donnelly, a safety on that team. "That meant not making big mistakes and putting our defense in trouble. Make the simple plays.

Jay Barker's greatest strength as a sophomore quarterback in the undefeated '92 season: not making the fatal mistake.

David Palmer was on the field was where the ball needed to be.

"I knew I could throw him a five-yard pass and it could become a 95-yard touchdown," Barker says, adding, "We never got caught up in that criticism. We were able to take care of our business and win a national title."

Stallings, however, did waver in the Auburn game. Barker was struggling, at one point 4 of 12 with two interceptions. Although Stallings didn't pull him, he came close to making a switch.

"Burgdorf crossed my mind," Stallings said of backup Brian Burgdorf, then saying of Barker, "He came back and performed under pressure. That's why he's my kind of guy."

That's why he's still signing autographs all these years later.

"He didn't do things to get us beat," says Shannon Brown, a defensive lineman on the '92 team. "There's nothing flashy about Jay. He wasn't trying to be something he wasn't.

"That's what made him a great quarterback," Brown says. "That's why he's mentioned with Joe Namath and Ken Stabler."

HE'LL NEVER STICK

Brodie Croyle was the big-time recruit from a small town, Rainbow City, Alabama. He had played for a little private school, Westbrook Christian, and had

"We didn't ask him to win the game for us or make big throws. Later in his career, he grew into more of a threat. But, at that point, he was a sophomore and I think Stallings coached into that, too. If it was third and nine, he was going to make a simple running play, punt it, put the defense in good field position, and wait to get the ball back."

Naturally, this conservative and careful offense spawned criticism. Fans wanted more points. At times, they almost seemed to lose track of the fact that the team was undefeated. Barker remembers the offensive line and the blocking backs doing an excellent job so Alabama could control the clock, and give that vaunted defense a little rest. He remembers, too, that wherever receiver missed his senior season of high school with a knee injury. And he was 6-2 and, at that point, weighed less than 200 pounds. So, despite his being considered one of the top quarterback prospects in America, there were skeptics.

Croyle met one early on at Alabama, in the apartment of a friend. This guy, this stranger, was running his mouth about the hotshot quarterback from little old Rainbow City.

"He said he was too skinny and he'll never play at Alabama," Croyle recalls the guy saying of him. "He went on and on and I didn't say anything. Finally, he says, 'Why are you so quiet?' I pulled out my wallet and showed him my ID."

The irony is that not only did Brodie Croyle make it, or *stick* as they say, he became one of the chief unifiers from 2001 to 2005, a period during which Alabama was hit with probation, had one coach for two seasons (Dennis Franchione), another for four months (Mike Price), and a young, first-time head coach in Mike Shula.

"He was the glue," says his father, John Croyle, who played for Bryant.

Croyle finished his career as Alabama's all-time passing leader. At one level, that speaks to his ability, which Stabler believes is considerable.

"I like comparing quarterbacks," says Stabler, who gets to see all the Alabama quarterbacks as the color commentator for the radio broadcasts. "Watching Brodie Croyle, I compare

Because he was skinny and came from a small private school, some people questioned if Brodie Croyle could make it at Alabama and in the SEC.

him to Joe Namath. Great arm strength, ball comes out of there in a hurry. They look alike."

It's a weighty comparison, perhaps, but then Croyle carried a heavy load in his time at Alabama. Namath had to dodge tacklers on a bum knee, but he didn't have to worry about the NCAA sacking the program and taking away bowl trips for two years, or endure a revolving door of coaches.

Just as Shula was bred to play the game and coach the game, Croyle was prepared to witness adversity firsthand. Soon after John Croyle finished college, he opened a ranch for abused and neglected children.

That's where Brodie grew up, and where heroes of Alabama football were often dropping by. To Brodie, legends such as John Hannah and Johnny Musso were "just my dad's buddies."

Brodie was young when he first met Namath and Stabler and was, he says, "awestruck." But later, not so much. They wore number 12 in their day and now he was wearing it in his.

"They tell you to represent their number well," Brodie says.

When he was injured, he heard from them and Starr.

"It's like a brotherhood," says Croyle. "Joe was like, 'Just roll with the punches. All your dreams are still intact.' At the time, I was like, 'Right.' But those guys always know what they're talking about."

Croyle brought his own style to the playing field. And a will to win that doesn't have to take second billing to anyone.

"When a play was needed, I wanted the ball," he says. "I made that known to my coaches and teammates. For the most part, when the game was on the line, they wanted me to have the ball."

At the Cotton Bowl, with less than three minutes to play and the score tied, 10–10, and more than 80 yards to go, Croyle confidently strode onto the field.

"I had a little smirk on my face," he remembers.

Up in the stands, his mother and father looked at each other and agreed: This is perfect. One more obstacle, one more chance to fall apart, only they knew Brodie wouldn't come unglued.

In the huddle, he told teammates how it was going to be.

"He just said what he always said, 'We're gonna get it done,' " recalls offensive lineman Kyle Tatum. "We were confident. It was time to go get that 'W.' "

Which they did. Croyle led them into field-goal range, the kick was frightening but on target, and Alabama had a 13–10 win over Texas Tech and an end-of-year number-eight national ranking.

Croyle had been cool, calm, and collected, again.

"You can be a king one day and a goat the next," he says of playing quarterback at Alabama. "That's why it's so special."

PRESSURE COOKER

What was it Stabler said about Brodie Croyle?

Oh, yeah, he has "rock-star status."

That's not necessarily a good thing for the first guy to follow in his cleat prints, but every Alabama quarterback has to make his own way and the paths are not created equal. Expectations are not parsed out evenly, or fairly, or even logically. Memories and reputations are not divided evenly, either.

Some quarterbacks always stood on their own two feet. Pat Trammell was The Man. Joe Namath and Ken Stabler were the stars. Steve Sloan was Mr. Dependable.

And, as the 1960s came to a close, Alabama on a downturn, perhaps

Scott Hunter was something of a scapegoat.

"He set passing records, but he got blamed a lot," says Bolton.

"Of any position that probably glorifies mistakes the most, in any sport, it's quarterback," says Richard Todd, an all-SEC quarterback in 1975 for the Crimson Tide who followed Namath to the Jets. "You can be a point guard, make 10 of 20 shots and it's considered awesome. If a quarterback is 10 of 20 and throws three interceptions, he's a losing quarterback."

"You can play your worst game, and as long as Alabama wins, you're a hero," Croyle says. "You can go 25 for 25 with 400 yards and three touchdowns, lose by one point, and you should have made that extra throw."

Croyle loved the pressure, including having to engineer a last-minute drive to get in field-goal range at the Cotton Bowl. Shula trusted Croyle to get it done.

CENTER OF ATTENTION

At first, Sylvester Croom didn't understand what was going on. He was a tight end, or at least that's what he wanted to be. And now, every day before practice, Croom and three or four other players, who didn't necessarily seem to fit together, were being drilled on their stances and starts.

Strange, very strange indeed.

"None of us knew what it was for," says Croom, now the head coach at Mississippi State. "Finally, I got wind of it, heard one of the coaches talking about it."

Coach Bryant was looking for his next center. This was not a small thing.

"About all the centers at Alabama made All-American, going back to [Paul] Crane and Lee Roy Jordan," Croom says of two from the 1960s.

Actually, the tradition goes back much farther than that, to at least 1942 when just about everyone in the free world voted Joe Domnanovich All-American. Three years later, Vaughn Mancha was an All-American center and, as Mancha likes to say even now, "I was a mean SOB."

So, yes, this was important. Jim Krapf had followed Jordan and Crane and would become an All-American in 1972. But this was before then. Bryant was looking ahead, to what he would do when Krapf had left.

"I didn't want to play center," Croom admits.

Initially, he didn't have to play center. He also didn't get to play anything else. So, after injuring his hamstring as a sophomore, Croom was more receptive, if also somewhat skittish toward the idea of switching positions.

"I'd always heard my high-school coach say guys that went to college and couldn't play anything else, they moved them to center," says Croom. "I wanted to prove I was a good player."

What he didn't know then was the high esteem in which Bryant held centers.

"I think Coach felt like he had to have a good athlete in that position," says Crane. "Because that's where everything starts on the offensive side of the ball. That's why that position has been pretty strong. He felt the center, quarterback, and fullback were kind of the core group on offense. Sylvester was a great one. Dwight Stephenson [1979 All-American] was a great one."

Coach Bryant placed a high value on the center position, and he had some great ones, including 1979 All-American Dwight Stephenson.

> After Croom's sophomore season, Bryant called Croom into his office to tell him of his plan to move him to center and what it meant.
>
> "In the wishbone, I never realized how important the center was," Croom says. "The fullback, in the wishbone, is the first option. The fullback goes nowhere if the center doesn't make his block. I asked him point blank: 'Coach, do you think I can do this?' And he said, unequivocally, 'Yes, I think you can be good at it.'"
>
> He was more than good. The next year, in 1974, Croom's teammates voted him a captain and he made All-American. He was, in his own right, a field general.
>
> "The fact he thought I could do it," Croom says, even now, "that motivated me to get it done."

In 1978, Steadman Shealy had played behind Jeff Rutledge as Alabama won the national championship. In 1979, Alabama went undefeated and won the national title again, this time with Shealy as the full-time starter.

"My senior year, when it was all mine, I wanted us to run the table," Shealy recalls. "It was a very intense year for me. I probably didn't enjoy any of it. I wanted to do nothing but win an outright national championship."

The most harrowing time that season: the 3–0 victory at LSU in the rain and sleet.

"I felt like I was running on skates," Shealy says.

He was also mindful of the great quarterbacks who came before him. "Namath and Stabler, they were my heroes," he says. "And Terry Davis, I was number 10, too."

Barker remembers feeling the pressure to produce in his junior and senior seasons after having won the national championship. After going 13–0 in '92,

and not losing until the ninth game of the '93 season against LSU, there was still criticism over the offense.

"That's Alabama football," Barker says with a chuckle. "That's expectations. If you're winning or losing, people are not going to be happy."

Certainly, some quarterbacks have had it tougher than others. Lewis, as Alabama's first African-American quarterback, received a double dose of pressure.

"I got some hate mail," he says matter of factly. "Not a lot, but some. And I got some normal criticism if we didn't perform well."

It could have been worse if Bryant and Perkins had not looked to intercept as much criticism as possible.

"Coach Bryant and Coach Perkins did that for me," Lewis says. "They were willing to take the darts and arrows."

More difficult to stop are the rumors. More recently Tyler Watts, who is white, and Andrew Zow, who is African-American, were competing for the quar-

terback job, which is just the kind of thing that talk radio and Internet message boards feed on.

"One year, our quarterback coach, Les Koenning, pulled me and Andrew into his office and said, 'I just want to know one thing: Which one of you won?' And we said, 'What are you talking about, Coach?'

"I heard y'all got into a fight this weekend," Koenning said, "and Tyler, you broke Andrew's nose, and he gave you a black eye."

"I don't know where you heard that from," Watts told him, "but you can look at us and see we ain't touched each other."

No, but it was a good story, wasn't it?

"Same kind of thing happened to Brodie his last year," says Watts. "There was a rumor he was in a car accident or a hunting accident. People will say stupid things."

It comes with the territory.

Same as the expectations, the thrill of sun-splashed Saturdays, the pressure, the glory when Alabama wins, and the misery when Alabama loses.

"Alabama's a great place to play, if you can handle it," Croyle says.

From 1998 to 2000, Andrew Zow led the Tide in passing.

Tyler Watts still can't believe that some 'Bama fans named their children after him.

"It's not life and death to us," Watts says, by way of explaining how they handle it, "but to a lot of people it's pretty close."

Or maybe it's just more personal than a twenty-year-old kid can fathom.

After all, if these people are going to name their kids after you, and they are, the least you can do is go undefeated, pass for 5,000 yards and 25 touchdowns, and win the national championship.

11

THE PRIDE GOES ON

NOBODY was any more proud of quarterback Brodie Croyle and linebacker DeMeco Ryans than Coach Mike Shula.

It was A Day, 2006, at Denny Chimes, and the 2005 Crimson Tide team captains were leaving their hand and cleat imprints in wet cement, to be forever preserved in Alabama's Walk of Fame.

Although it's a short walk on campus from Bryant-Denny Stadium to Denny Chimes, it had been anything but a leisurely stroll for these two young men. They had to walk through adversities they never could have imagined. They had to step around messes made by grown men who were supposed to have their best interests in mind. They had to "hold the rope," as Coach Dennis Franchione had put it while walking in the door, even as Coach Fran let go of the rope while running out the door.

Croyle and Ryans played but a single season

In 1999, Shaun Alexander rushed for almost 1,400 yards and helped lead Alabama to the Orange Bowl.

for Franchione before a newspaper headline read FRAN DUMPS ALABAMA. The coach, after just his second year at the Capstone, showed up in College Station to coach Texas A & M. He never even told his players at Alabama goodbye; some alumni were angry enough to tie said rope into a noose.

The players' next so-called leader, Mike Price, coached his only so-called game on March 29, 2003. Final score: Crimson 47, White 0.

On May 3, 2003, Alabama fired Price for inappropriate conduct that, at minimum, included Price having too much to drink after a golf outing in Pensacola, Florida, going to a strip club, and a woman not his wife running up a huge tab in his hotel room.

So, long before Croyle and Ryans made it to the wet cement at Denny Chimes, they and their teammates were swimming in quicksand.

Former Alabama star running back Shaun Alexander had been watching all this from Seattle, where he plays for the NFL's Seahawks. Alexander couldn't believe what was happening back at Alabama, telling reporters: "You're taught to think that you're the best, walk like you're the best, to be classy . . .

"Then all of a sudden, you see things pop up that are not characteristic of your school and you wonder: 'What in the world is going on?' "

It was the question that Ryans and Croyle must have asked themselves, and each other, countless times.

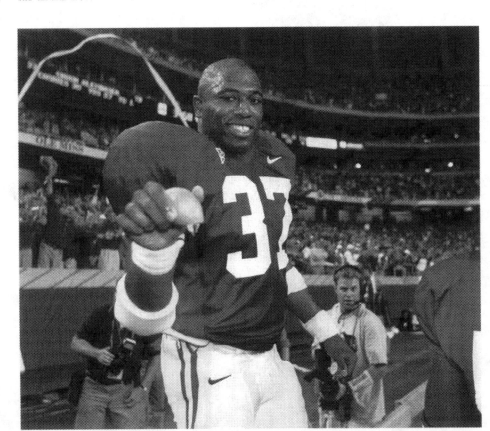

Yet they not only survived, they thrived. Croyle finished his career as Alabama's all-time leading passer. Ryans was an All-American. Better than what they did for themselves was what they did for their school: They brought an entire team with them, following in their cleat prints, to a remarkable and restorative 2005 season that ended with a number-eight national ranking.

Coach Mike Shula had a lot to say that day at Denny Chimes.

"These guys and what they represent—this whole senior class—and what they've been through . . . kept this whole university together through some tough times," Shula said to a crowd that numbered in the thousands. "And I couldn't

be happier about that [Cotton] bowl win for them and to get ten wins . . .

"I say this to our football team already: These are the guys we're gonna keep in mind as we go on and build this program and build and build it and go win our national championship [crowd erupts in cheers]. It's gonna be because of guys like these two . . ."

Next, Croyle took his turn at the microphone.

"This right here is the reason you come to Alabama," said Croyle, whose father, John Croyle, played for Bear Bryant. "You don't come to break records. This is the biggest honor you can get—to be elected by your teammates as a captain. And to put your foot

Alabama's 1983 team captains, Randy Edwards and Walter Lewis, followed the great tradition of leaving their handprints at Denny Chimes.

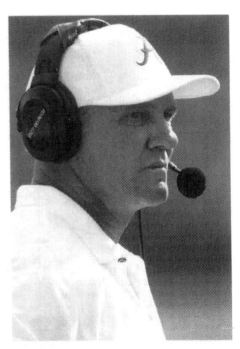

next to the Joe Namaths, the Kenny Stablers . . .

"We went through a lot . . . but y'all stuck with us. And we got Alabama back where we needed to be, and y'all are the reason we did that . . . It's been a great ride."

Said Ryans: "This is just a blessing . . . first day you get on campus, they show you all the hand prints and footprints at Denny Chimes, all the legends. My dream [was to] one day have my handprint and footprint out there . . .

"I'll miss this place. I love Alabama.

"I'll always have Alabama in my heart."

READY OR NOT

Mike DuBose had Alabama in his heart. So much so that, when he was promoted from defensive coordinator to replace the retiring Gene Stallings after the 1996 season, a giddy DuBose said, "Sometimes I have to pinch myself to make sure it's real."

His pedigree was perfect, too. DuBose had played for Bear Bryant and even became the first head coach in the program's history to have been born in Alabama, in Opp, a hamlet in the southern part of the state. So, for this time and this place, DuBose was, in many ways, the logical choice. Certainly, he was the people's choice.

"People were happy with the amount

of success under Stallings—seventy wins in seven seasons," says *Tuscaloosa News* sports editor Cecil Hurt. "From that standpoint, they didn't want to rock the boat. And as [Stallings's] staff went, Mike was probably the most qualified."

Still, DuBose had never been a college head coach. Athletic director Bob Bockrath and school president Dr. Andrew Sorensen not only were new to their jobs, they were outsiders. Even DuBose now looks back at the environment in which he was hired and says, "I think they were forced into that situation."

DuBose was Alabama through and through. As a boy, he had worked cotton fields for a penny a pound. He aimed for making a dollar a day, but found that to be impossible. So he cheated—just a little.

"I picked from sunup to sundown and I never picked 100 pounds," he said in one newspaper interview. "I'd put a water jug in my sack and any kind of rocks or melons—anything I could find I'd put in there to add some weight."

Now, however, he had a weighty job 365 days a year. And though he had been an assistant for both Ray Perkins and Stallings, DuBose perhaps didn't fully understand the challenge before him.

"Part of it was my arrogance, thinking I had all the answers," says DuBose, who in 2006 became head coach at Division III Millsaps College in Jackson, Mississippi. "One of the biggest mistakes I made was not setting aside some time and going out to Paris, Texas, to sit down and get Coach Stallings's opinion."

DuBose's first team, in 1997, slogged through a mistake-filled 4–7 season; it was 'Bama's first losing season since Perkins's second team in 1984 went 5–6. The 1998 team went 7-5, finishing the season with a lopsided loss to Virginia Tech in the Music City Bowl.

Then the spring and summer storm of 1999 hit: rumors that the coach, who was married, was involved in an improper relationship with a female employee from the football office. The story heated up even more when the woman claimed sexual harassment and sexual discrimination.

At first, DuBose denied any relationship with the woman. By early August of 1999, the coach was standing before cameras and admitting he had misled people about the relationship.

DuBose survived the scandal, albeit with two years removed from his contract; the former secretary would be paid $350,000 to settle her sexual harassment and sexual discrimination charges, and the money would come out of DuBose's salary. Bockrath called the penalties for DuBose "harsh" and the coach said, "I know I've hurt this university and the people who love it."

Tuscaloosa News sports editor Cecil Hurt believes DuBose retained his job for the same reason he got it in the first place: The school's administration was afraid to go in a different direction.

"[DuBose] had some relationships that had been built over twenty years with boosters," Hurt says.

The coach's relationships with his young players were more fragile, but the players were, for the most part, willing to stand by DuBose.

"He's human and everybody makes mistakes," says Tyler Watts, a quarterback from 1999 to 2001. "That team, we were willing to forgive him. That all came out before the 1999 season, and there's an old saying that winning takes care of everything.

"We went 10-3 and nobody was worried."

Yes, winning proved to be a cure-all. After the regular season ended, Alabama restored the two years to DuBose's contract. The Crimson Tide won the SEC title and DuBose was named the SEC Coach of the Year. Again, it was perhaps time for him to pinch himself and make sure it was real. After nearly being

sacked, DuBose had scrambled free and saved himself.

"Football was my god," DuBose says of those days. "I'd always loved the game. I had no hobbies. Football came before God, before family, before everything."

The successful 1999 season had also quieted critics of DuBose's coaching ability. Those critics would not be silent for long.

Alabama was expected to be as good or better in 2000, but opened the season with a loss at UCLA, then got shut out in Birmingham in week three by Southern Mississippi, 21–0. The team was 1–2 and DuBose had it right when he told reporters afterward: "One of two things are about to happen. We're about to separate and fall, or pull together and become a football team."

The Crimson Tide finished that season 3–8, on a five-game losing streak. After a homecoming loss to Central

A 10-3 season and SEC title in 1999 gave DuBose a reprieve from off-the-field troubles, but it didn't last.

Florida, athletic director Mal Moore told DuBose he would not be coach beyond the end of the 2000 season.

"That team just totally imploded," says sportswriter Clyde Bolton. "That was the most underachieving football team I've ever seen."

DuBose doesn't really debate the point.

"There was enough talent," he says. "We divided from within."

Much of that division came from within DuBose's staff. He blames himself, saying if he had it to do over, "I'd be more in control, more hands-on, have a tougher approach."

Unfortunately, DuBose and his off-the-field problems weren't the only ones Alabama had. By November, the NCAA had begun investigating possible recruiting violations and the name of a prominent Alabama booster from Memphis, Tennessee, had surfaced: Logan Young.

"I'd love to talk to [NCAA investigators]," Young told reporters. "I'd be the happiest person in Memphis."

Meanwhile, back in Tuscaloosa, DuBose was soon taking his leave and defensive lineman Kenny Smith was taking stock after DuBose's last game—a 9–0 loss to Auburn—by saying, "He lived out his dream. But his dream didn't go the way he wanted. I guess that's part of life."

That chapter of his life now closed and a 24-23 record forever beside his name in the record book, DuBose is

In hindsight, DuBose wonders what might have happened had Stallings not retired when he did, and had he remained in the background.

grateful for the opportunity but does wonder one thing: How might the pages have turned in the next chapter of Alabama football had he not been the coach?

"If Coach Stallings had not decided to retire and stayed on, I think the won-loss record would have been different," DuBose says. "I thought I was ready for that job. But, when I look back, I wasn't ready for that job."

HOLD THE ROPE

The next coaching search would be different. The next Alabama coach would not necessarily have to have Alabama

Coach Dennis Franchione arrived telling players they needed to "hold the rope" but, ultimately, he was the one who let go.

roots. He would have to have a proven track record as a head coach.

After a 3–8 season, says Hurt, the focus was squarely on finding "a competent football coach."

Athletic director Mal Moore reportedly made runs at then-University of Miami coach Butch Davis and Virginia Tech coach Frank Beamer, but neither gave Alabama serious consideration because of the now very public NCAA investigation.

Moore turned his attention to Dennis Franchione, the Texas Christian University coach who had his team up to thirteenth in the national polls.

"Dennis was a hot property at TCU," says Hurt, "and that's a popular thing with fans."

On December 1, 2000, Franchione became the fifth coach to follow Bear Bryant and said just what he was sup-

posed to say: "I'm honored to be the head coach at a school like Alabama with the tradition they have, with the people like Paul 'Bear' Bryant in their history. It's a tremendous thing for me."

The first meeting went well, with Franchione getting a laugh when he brought his wife, Kim, to the lectern and said, "Anyone who thinks I can't recruit should look at her."

In a few weeks, the new coach would no longer be the big story. An assistant high-school football coach in Memphis, Tenneessee, Milton Kirk, told the *Commercial Appeal* of Memphis that he and his head coach, Lynn Lang, essentially had sold defensive lineman Albert Means to the highest bidder, and that $200,000 had been paid to get Means to sign a national letter of intent with Alabama.

Once the story broke, in January 2001, Means, who played for the Crimson Tide in 2000, withdrew from school. By early September, as Franchione's first team was beginning its season, the NCAA was hitting Alabama with an official letter of inquiry charging that Logan Young had paid Lang in excess of $100,000 (not $200,000) to ensure Means signed with Alabama.

Franchione and his players were focused on the task at hand: improving the Alabama football team after the disastrous eight-loss season in 2000. Meanwhile, Franchione made a good first impression with his players.

"It was a completely different atmosphere from what we had experienced," says quarterback Tyler Watts. "There was a definite presence in the leadership role. He took charge from day one. It was a breath of fresh air because we were in a downward spiral. He was exactly what the program needed."

The Franchione motto: "Hold the rope."

At the time, it seemed like the perfect sound byte.

Players such as linebacker DeMeco Ryans, quarterback Brodie Croyle, and defensive back Charlie Peprah, all of whom were seniors on the 2005 team, held the rope in a tug of war with challenge, trouble, and turmoil.

"We stayed strong and survived,"

Peprah says. "I want us to be remembered for turning the program around."

Franchione's first team, in 2001, started the turn by finishing 7-5. But the coach never seemed to find a balance, either. Franchione was a workaholic by nature, saying upon arrival that, "I love the grind."

However, from the outside looking in . . .

"He was a control freak," says *Huntsville Times* columnist Mark McCarter. "His schedule was set to the minute, months in advance."

Control freaks do not do so well when pressure is applied from the outside.

"There's no question that Fran was uncomfortable there because of all the scrutiny, because of the daily pressure,"

Alabama's tremendous fan support can be a double-edged sword: tremendous daily scrutiny that some coaches just can't handle.

says Jackie Sherrill, a former Alabama player who was then head coach at Mississippi State. "And if you don't understand, then it gobbles you up."

Early in 2002, the NCAA exponentially increased the pressure by hitting Alabama with five years of probation, a two-year bowl ban, and scholarship cuts over the next three years. Peprah, who's from Plano, Texas, had committed to Alabama when the NCAA investigation was just getting started and hadn't expected this.

"I'd figured if we were going to be put on probation, it'd be a one-year bowl ban and I'd redshirt anyway," he says, "so it wouldn't affect me. But they hit us with two years and scholarship cuts. I didn't think they'd hit us that hard for something this class had nothing to do with. A lot of people want to see 'Bama fall."

The sanctions apparently are what felled Franchione's personal resolve.

By October 2002, the school had a new contract ready for Franchione's signature. As the contract remained unsigned, speculation grew about Franchione's intentions. In November, with the team 7-2 and sitting eleventh in the national polls, Franchione said: "It took some time to make this my team."

Still, he didn't sign the new and enhanced contract. The week before the Auburn game, rumors of Franchione's imminent departure spiked. In person,

the coach played dodgeball with reporters' questions on the subject. On his Web site, he played hardball.

"Give it a rest, please," Franchione wrote. "I'm under contract for five more seasons . . . I refused to answer the phone today after an idiotic story about Texas A & M in the San Antonio paper crossed my desk first thing this morning. I don't know how on earth these rumors get started and there's nothing I can do about them."

Except make them come true.

On December 5, in a telephone call to Mal Moore, Franchione resigned to become coach at Texas A & M.

"Fran Dumps Alabama. Contract

Worth Reported $11 Million Over Five Years," read the headline in the *Tuscaloosa News.*

Coach Fran also hadn't bothered to inform his players.

"He told me and [another player] personally he wasn't going anywhere," says Peprah. "We didn't even approach him about it; he came up to us to reassure us. 'The media or anybody asks you any questions, I'm not going anywhere.'

"The next thing I know, I'm looking at the newspaper and he's getting out of some limo or SUV in College Station."

John McMahon, Jr., president pro tempore of the UA board of trustees, was livid. He said the university had reached a "gentleman's understanding" with Franchione a month earlier, adding, "What I think about [this] you could not print in a publication read by women and children."

Quarterback Brodie Croyle's father, John Croyle, had played for Bear Bryant and had watched Brodie become Franchione's first big-time recruit. John Croyle was very upset, mentioning Coach Fran's hold-the-rope credo, and saying, "He couldn't do it himself."

Brodie, however, says he wasn't unhappy to see Franchione leave.

"I didn't particularly agree with it, but I had a hunch and I honestly wasn't terribly upset," he says. "And I don't know if that was me or my body— my 205 pound body might have been abused running the option for four years."

For his part, Franchione released a statement through Texas A & M: "It was beyond [the school's] control to provide the one thing that I [was] tired of dealing with, the NCAA. When the Texas A & M opportunity arose, I felt it was best for my well-being and peace of mind, for my family, and for my career to accept it.

"I created the situation I'm in," he concluded, "and it's mine to live with."

Long-time and often controversial Birmingham radio sports-talk-show host Paul Finebaum says: "I'd be the last guy to stand on top of a building and defend Dennis Franchione, but he had every right to go."

Hurt, the Tuscaloosa sports editor, sees it differently.

"Where I think Dennis miscalculated was in assuming if he went through a down year or two [because of the NCAA sanctions], his support and fan base would have abandoned him. Which I don't think would have been the case . . . but I don't think he believed that."

Despite Franchione's awkward departure, many of his former players at Alabama still speak well of Coach Fran.

"He was a great guy," Peprah says. "He could have handled leaving better, but that's the coaching business. When I saw him at the East-West Shrine Game, I told him I still love him."

Peprah, like so many Alabama players, had the rope burns to prove it.

PRICELESS

Franchione had gone 17-8 in two seasons at Alabama. In this era, when winning perhaps doesn't come as easily as it did in Bryant's day, or even in Stallings's day, that was good enough to keep hope alive amid the NCAA-sanctioned nightmare.

And so, as whistle-blower Milton Kirk was receiving a sentence in federal court that included six months in a halfway house after pleading guilty to one count of conspiracy, Alabama was looking for the key to its future: its next football coach.

New Orleans Saints assistant Mike Riley, a former 'Bama defensive back, was offered the job but turned it down. Several candidates—and, again, Beamer was on the wish list—were skittish because of the NCAA probation. Washington State coach Mike Price, fifty-six, was not so wary.

On December 18, 2002, Price was introduced as Alabama's new coach. He had been a college head coach since 1981 and had guided WSU to two Rose Bowls. So, as the saying goes, this would not be his first rodeo. Former Tide players liked the looks of the new coach, too. Everyone from Lee Roy Jordan to Ozzie Newsome to Joe Namath had praise for

Price, with Namath calling this a "perfect fit."

Price, naturally, thought so, too.

"This is a dream," he said. "I feel like I'm in football heaven."

Price brought with him the West Coast offense and another dream: scoring points in bunches.

Quarterback Brodie Croyle liked that notion and said of the new coach, "I know he's wide open and likes to throw it around."

All too soon those words would take on a more dour double meaning.

Then there was Price's comment after he purchased Franchione's old house by a golf course in the North River subdivision.

"I'm not afraid of bad karma," Price

said, "unless you mean ten wins . . . and finishing eleventh in the nation."

Of course, it wasn't bad karma that did in Price. It was horrendous decision-making. On April 17, 2003, he played in a pro-am golf tournament in Pensacola, Florida. Exactly what happened that night and in the wee hours of the next morning we might never know. What's certain is Price had too much to drink and went to a strip club. *Sports Illustrated* wrote a story that claimed Price had sex in his hotel room with an exotic dancer; Price denied this and filed a $20 million lawsuit against publisher Time, Inc. In 2005, the lawsuit, according to a statement from the publisher, was "amicably resolved." Terms of the settlement were not disclosed.

Alabama, however, had not waited for the *Sports Illustrated* story to determine Price's fate. Yes, university officials knew the story was coming, but they'd already heard enough to take action. And so on May 3, 2003, they fired Price without him ever having coached a game and without him ever having signed the agreed-to $10 million coaching contract.

"Coach Price had been warned several weeks before about his public conduct," said university president Robert E. Witt. "His conduct in Florida was not consistent with the warning he received."

While responsibility lies with Price for the decisions he made in Pensacola, Finebaum, never one to hesitate in criticizing Alabama, raises a valid point about the hiring of the coach: Did Alabama really know what it was getting?

"I've heard every day that they 'checked it out,' " says Finebaum, who also writes a column for the *Mobile Press-Register.* "But what's checking it out?"

Yet, in just the four months Price had been with his players, he had connected. When Price apologized to his wife and his players in a press conference, running back Shaud Williams cried and couldn't even stay to hear all his coach had to say.

Quarterback Brodie Croyle publicly defended Price.

"Coach Price and I bonded when he first got here," Croyle says. "After what went down, I was one of the first to

Quarterback Brodie Croyle was excited about Price's West Coast offense, had bonded with the coach, and asked the university to give Price another chance.

stand up and say he's the coach we want, give him another chance. I basically got blasted in the media for it."

Price read a statement, but took no questions.

"To the university and the entire 'Bama Nation, I admit mistakes and at times inappropriate conduct," Price said in part.

However, he also believed he should have been allowed to stay, asking, "Whatever happened to a second chance in life?"

Price would get a second chance, but it would come the next season and at the University of Texas-El Paso of Conference USA, a non-Bowl Championship Series league.

Surprisingly, Price and his family remained in Tuscaloosa through much of the 2003 football season. Price's sons Eric and Aaron were on his staff at Alabama.

"It was neat. Being from the west, I never imagined myself and my dad coaching at Alabama," Eric Price told the *Commercial Appeal* of Memphis he and Aaron had joined their father at UTEP. "The whole Bear Bryant thing, the tradition . . . it was definitely a cool place to be."

In fact, even after the firing, the family Price watched Alabama football games.

"We'd have a party at one of our homes in Tuscaloosa," Eric said. "And we'd cheer like [crazy]."

It was as close as Mike Price got to being on the sideline on a Saturday. Those were "his" players he was watching. That's how it felt. And he still cared about how they did.

"Oh, yeah," Price told the Memphis newspaper. "Those kids didn't have anything to do with anything. They were great kids."

Kyle Tatum, a senior offensive lineman on the 2006 team, was one of those kids.

"Two coaches in a few months," says Tatum, who had been recruited by Franchione. "I mean, it hurts you. You look at your program and go, 'Are we gonna be all right? And who's gonna come in?'

"We fought for Coach Price and maybe the situation was handled a little harshly, but this is Alabama. You've got to look back and see the standards. He was fired and we moved on.

"Coach Shula came in and wanted Alabama back on top. That's the best thing that could have happened to us," Tatum says. "We're blessed to have a man that really loves this place."

RIDING THE STORM OUT

It's difficult to fully describe what it is to coach at Alabama, but *Huntsville Times* columnist Mark McCarter comes pretty close.

"Coaching at Alabama," McCarter

says, "is like being on a WaveRunner. You've got both hands on the handlebars, and you've got to be ready to hop a bunch of waves. You've got to respect the history, and you have to have a tolerance for the fans."

Mike Shula's job, then, was to hang on for dear life, and yet make it look like he had everything under control from the start, like Alabama football again was back on course.

Shula was hired on May, 8, 2003; the Crimson Tide was high and rough when he came on board. The son of Pro Football Hall of Fame coach Don Shula, Mike Shula had been bred for this. He had been around the game all his life. Still, he had never been a college head coach. And he was young, just thirty-seven at the time of his hiring.

Of course, Wallace Wade and Frank Thomas were each in their early thirties when becoming head coach at Alabama. They combined to win five national championships. Bear Bryant was in his early thirties when he accepted his first college head coaching job at Maryland.

Age and inexperience could be overlooked given Shula's obvious attributes: He was family, having played quarterback for Alabama from 1983 to 1986. Just as important in the wake of recent embarrassing events, Shula's reputation was pristine.

His former roommate at Alabama, noseguard Curt Jarvis, told one newspaper: "I've seen him when no one else is watching. He behaves like someone is watching him all the time. I was a little bit wilder than Mike when I was in

Mike Shula, son of Pro Football Hall of Fame coach Don Shula, was just thirty-seven years old when named Alabama's coach on May 8, 2003.

school. Mike would say, 'You can do that, but it's not right.' He kept me in line, and I owe him a lot."

Shula was coming from his father's old team, the Miami Dolphins, where he had been quarterbacks coach under Dave Wannstedt. The NFL had long been familiar territory for Mike Shula. He was in junior high school when he started charting plays for his father's Miami team, when another Pro Football Hall-of-Famer, Bob Griese, was still playing quarterback. And Shula was a senior in high school during the 1982 NFL players' strike, which meant that Dad had shorter days at the office.

"I'd come home from school and we'd watch film together," Shula remembers.

Without question, then, Mike Shula returned to the Capstone with a sound football mind. He also had played for Alabama during a time of transition, for Ray Perkins, the first coach after Bryant.

This time, however, Shula walked into an unmitigated mess. And he had just 115 days from his first day to the season opener.

"People were looking for direction," he recalls. "This was Alabama, and these kids didn't sign on for probation, and no bowl games, and three coaches in one year.

"These kids, most of them, grew up as loyal, loyal Alabama fans. They loved Alabama. And whoever the coach was, they were going to make it work. But there was a thirst for stability and leadership."

With so little time, Shula and his staff were not able to ease their way into things or spend much time meeting and greeting the masses. They had to go to work. Once practice started, they were all business. They had to be.

"Shula is building this program back just like Coach Bryant did, and keeping control," says longtime Bryant assistant

Jack Rutledge. "Shula has got it so squeaky clean, it's unreal.

"We can't even go to practice unless we've got a coach with us. And those coaches are tight-knit. They're like Coach Bryant's [staff] was. They're taking care of each other."

One of those assistants is defensive coordinator Joe Kines, who also was on Alabama's staff for two years when Shula was a quarterback.

"If you go to the racetrack, every once in a while a horse walks out there that's just a cut above," Kines says. "Same thing with a coach. This guy's been older than his years since he was a junior in college and getting the wide receivers together in the dorm and making sure everything was done right."

Still, as expected, the 2003 season was a rough ride: a 4–9 record, though six of the losses were by eight points or less and two came in overtime: to Arkansas, and in the incredible five-overtime, 51–43 heartbreaker to Tennessee. Auburn beat Alabama by just five points.

"I've said 'close' too many times this year," Shula said after the Auburn game. "I'm tired of saying it and our team is tired of hearing it."

Fans, however, mostly understood the set of unusual and painful circumstances that had conspired to make the season so difficult. Finebaum says the collective mindset now is not like it was when he arrived in the early 1980s and "every loss was Armageddon."

From within, that didn't make the losing any easier to take.

"I'd never been part of a losing season in my life," says Croyle. "Just to be handcuffed like we were . . . that was the toughest year."

Handcuffed is a good word. The NCAA had basically put 'Bama's hands behind its back.

"The first year they will have none of their classes affected by probation would be 2008," says *Tuscaloosa News* sports editor Cecil Hurt. "It's a gradually diminishing thing that was designed by the NCAA to have long-term effects, and it's had long-term effects."

There were constant reminders in the news, too. In October 2003, a federal grand jury indicted wealthy booster Logan Young on three counts, including bribery of a public servant, in the Albert Means recruiting scandal. Young pleaded not guilty.

In January 2004, papers released in the federal case indicated Tennessee head coach Phil Fulmer had been a secret NCAA witness in the investigation into Alabama's football program. The following summer, Fulmer skipped SEC media days in Birmingham for fear of being served a subpoena in a lawsuit accusing him of snitching on Alabama in exchange for the NCAA overlooking rules violations at Tennessee.

All of this represented an undertow that made turning the program around that much more difficult and kept Shula

◀ FACING PAGE
Under Shula's guidance, Alabama won its first nine games in 2005, was part of the national title picture for a time, and received a Cotton Bowl invitation.

at a distance from the media. Although he didn't have the harsh exterior that his coach, Ray Perkins, sometimes had, Shula's quiet dignity could make him come off as cold and robotic.

The 2004 season, however, had been a success, given the circumstances. With the bowl ban now lifted, Alabama's 6-5 record in the regular season earned the team an invitation to the Music City Bowl in Nashville. McCarter recalls a representative from the bowl coming to Tuscaloosa and giving Shula a guitar.

"It was like handing an infant to a bachelor," McCarter, a columnist, says with a laugh. "He didn't know which end to hold."

McCarter got a few minutes alone with Shula, and decided to ask some different questions. Shula was receptive and, among other things, McCarter learned that Mike's brother David once received a set of drums for Christmas, that Mike's late mother had sung in the church choir, and that Shula himself recently had become a Parrot Head [Jimmy Buffett fan] and was working his way from Buffett's new material back to the old stuff.

"It was like, 'OK, he's human,' " McCarter says.

That quiet, businesslike cover could be deceptive in other ways, too.

"Shula has a fire," says Wes Neighbors, a former center who snapped many a football into Shula's hands. "He looks like he'd be mild-mannered. He's soft-spoken away from football and puts it in the proper perspective; even Coach Stallings had a problem with [perspective], and getting a big head.

"You're treated like a god here," Neighbors adds. "And you do have to realize how to handle it. I think Mike, with his dad, knows how to put it in the box it needs to be put in."

Maybe part of it is the fact Shula is younger, and is married and has three young daughters. To the extent that the football coach at Alabama can have a balanced life, and he really can't, Shula is trying to make sure he doesn't miss out on being a dad.

Shula was happy with a ten-win season in 2005 and a Cotton Bowl victory, but far from satisfied.

Yet nobody questions his work ethic and one would be hard-pressed to find an NFL coach that was more dedicated than Don Shula. As the elder Shula said when he came to Mike's first spring training camp in 2003, "He knows Alabama football. He's been there. He knows expectations."

Expectations were right there in front of him on the first day he set foot on the practice field. Expectations that stood tall in the form of that famous coaching tower.

"Just for a second, I thought about Coach Bryant being on those fields all these years," Shula says. "To me, [the tower's] a reminder of what our standard is: excellence."

"I think all of us ought to look over there and say, 'Hey, we're not gonna be satisfied with just being average.' "

'BAMA IS BACK

In February 2005, Logan Young was convicted on money laundering and conspiracy charges. If Alabama Nation considered the verdict a loss, it would be the last one for many, many months.

The 2005 season started with a nine-game winning streak, and nothing Phil Fulmer had to say to the NCAA or anyone else would stop it. To keep the streak going, Alabama would have to pull out a 13–10 win at Ole Miss and a 6–3 victory over Tennessee in successive weeks.

The offense did not light up the scoreboard in those games or in most games during the 2005 season. Alabama relied on its defense, and defense first is as much a tradition as Bryant leaning against the goalpost before the game and wearing a houndstooth hat during it.

"I think Coach Bryant would have been smiling a quite a few times [in 2005] with the way we won some games on defense," says former linebacker Lee Roy Jordan.

The Tennessee game is as good an example as any. Roman Harper forced a fumble late in the game, Croyle drove Alabama into field-goal range, and then Jamie Christensen hit from 34 yards out with thirteen seconds left for perhaps the sweetest victory of the Shula era.

"What a way to win the game," a jubilant Shula said. "Our guys hung in there for the whole game. Whenever it looked like things were going against us and nothing was going to go our way, our guys stepped up and made some plays."

It was the theme of the 2005 season, a 10-2 season that ended with similar heroics in the Cotton Bowl—the NCAA-record fifty-third bowl game in Alabama's history. The defense did its job all day, holding Texas Tech without a touchdown until less than three minutes remained in the game. Croyle and the offense got the ball at the Alabama 14-yard line with 2:56 left on the clock, the score tied 10–10. Croyle coolly guided the Crimson Tide downfield.

GOING FORWARD

For a rich tradition to remain a viable asset, there has to be as much attention paid to the future as to the past.

Under the leadership of athletic director Mal Moore, Alabama has been making major improvements to its athletic facilities. The most celebrated of these improvements——the expansion of Bryant-Denny Stadium——was to be complete by opening day 2006.

The stadium expansion, which includes the addition of sky boxes and club seats, will increase capacity from almost 84,000 to more than 92,000. Other recent improvements in football include a new locker room, a state-of-the-art weight room, a new sports-medicine area, a renovated football administration building, and a Hall of Champions, celebrating Alabama's football tradition. The upgrades in football were crucial, given the competition in recruiting from inside and outside the Southeastern Conference.

Other improvements made as part of the overall project: renovations to Coleman Coliseum and Bryant Hall, and new tennis, golf, and soccer facilities.

"All this had to be done," Moore says. "Not to go ahead of people, but to bring us up. Other people had pulled away in the last ten or fifteen years."

Charlie Peprah, a senior defensive back on the 2005 team, remembers that Alabama was behind when he was recruited out of Texas.

"Everything's here now," Peprah says. "You've got top-notch facilities."

Says Lemanski Hall, a linebacker on the '92 national championship team who went on to play in the NFL: "It's very important because we were losing guys to other teams on [facilities] alone. I walked through the fieldhouse and was just blown away.

"I don't think we have any excuses now," Hall adds. "We should get the player. We've got the finest facilities in the country."

As athletic director, Mal Moore has spearheaded the move to improve football facilities in particular, and athletic facilities as a whole.

Jamie Christensen's 45-yard game-winning field goal in the Cotton Bowl wasn't pretty, but it was effective.

Christensen had connected on back-to-back game-winners against Ole Miss and Tennessee, but this time he would have to be true from 45 yards. By all accounts, his kick was a cross between a wounded duck and a knuckleball that hits the outside corner at the knees. It seemed to take the ball forever to reach its destination . . . through the uprights and just over the crossbar in the lower left-hand corner.

But it was a fitting end to the season—a 13–10 victory and one last rally for Croyle and all the other seniors, one more challenge against all odds.

"We couldn't have picked any better way to go out," Croyle says. "We didn't want a blowout. We wanted a close game and a two-minute drill, win or lose. And then we got the ugliest kick in

Alabama history, and that was the story of our career. It wasn't pretty, but we got it done."

And so everyone who was part of the glorious 2005 season and the end-of-year number eight national ranking was part of Project Restoration Red Jersey.

"We set the bar," Ryans says. "These guys who are still there, they understand that when we said, ''Bama is back,' that wasn't just for one year. We want to keep the tradition rolling."

ALWAYS ALABAMA

How do you put a tradition like Alabama's into words? One small story at a time.

It's hearing Ray Perkins say that hav-

Ryans, drafted in 2006 by the Houston Texans, says the 2005 'Bama team's achievements were just the beginning: "We want to keep the tradition rolling."

ing his hand and cleat prints at Denny Chimes means more to him than his Super Bowl rings.

It's listening to Tyler Watts recall visiting Denny Chimes when he was a boy, and placing his hands and feet in the prints of all the captains who came before him.

It's learning that Don McNeal still makes a point to visit Denny Chimes.

"I go out there and clean my name off, right beside my man Tony Nathan," says McNeal.

And it's knowing that a national championship ring truly is priceless.

"I've got a ring from '79," says former equipment manager Colin MacGuire, who though small in stature remains as big an Alabama fan as there is. "And I'd be the first to say I'd like to be a millionaire, but if somebody offered me ten million dollars for this ring I ain't

going to take it. It's just got too many memories behind it."

Those priceless memories are what keep the tradition going. It's why Perkins and a group of guys from the 1964-65 national championship teams get together at a hunting lodge almost every year. It's also why you can find Perkins at most home games. Shula played for him at Alabama, coached for him at Tampa Bay.

"Mike's kind of like a son to me," says Perkins.

Just as Bear Bryant was like a second father to so many players, including Sylvester Croom.

"I like to stand down by the goalpost before the game, and I'll get real close," says Croom, head coach at Mississippi State. "But I tell myself, 'I'm not leaning up against that goalpost.' Not just at Alabama, not anywhere. Now that goal-

senior offensive lineman on the 2006 team. "I hate to keep bringing it up, but you just gotta look at the facts and what happened with our football team due to that.

"I feel like no other program could have come back from such a hard hit, other than us," says Tatum, who's from Prattville, Alabama. "That's what's so special about our class—me, Chris Harris, Ken Darby, Jeremy Clark, all of us were being recruited and committed when [everything] came out.

"I kind of had second thoughts," Tatum admits, "but then I went to a game and I never looked back. When I saw the players run on the field and put on that crimson helmet, I didn't want to go anywhere else."

According to the NCAA and the federal government, the guy delivering that hard hit was booster Logan Young. His conviction was on appeal when, in April of 2006, he was found dead in his Memphis home. Police, after initially suspecting homicide, ruled his death accidental. And so closed an unpleasant, and, at times, almost unbelievable, chapter of Alabama's history. After his death, charges against him were dismissed.

"Most fans would just as soon never hear his name again," says Birmingham radio sport talk show host Paul Finebaum.

Meantime, the names of Alabama's heroes live on. And many times, even the heroes themselves are left in awe. All-

Only Bear Bryant could lean against the goalpost and make it look right, says former 'Bama center Sylvester Croom.

post is pretty comfortable and you may see me doing it at our practices, but you'll never see me leaning up against the goalpost before a game.

"That's out of respect for him," Croom says. "Ain't nobody else that can pull that one off."

To be sure, Bryant is still the face of Alabama football, and always will be the face of Alabama football.

The tradition did not stop when he retired, or die when Bryant passed on. And in recent years, when trouble seemed to come in tidal waves, the program kept its head above water because so many people cared enough to commit.

"It was a real tough situation, the probation and all," says Kyle Tatum, a

American placekicker Van Tiffin made the most famous field goal in school history, yet he looks back and says, "It was so great to play at Alabama, if I'd just gotten to kick off I'd have been fine."

Linebacker Lemanski Hall was hardly the biggest name on the '92 national championship team. But he was a solid player and, thus, memorable.

"My wife and I went to a game a couple of years ago, and this lady came up to me and said, 'Lemanski Hall,' and she just talked to me about how much I meant to the school and said, 'I enjoyed watching you play.'

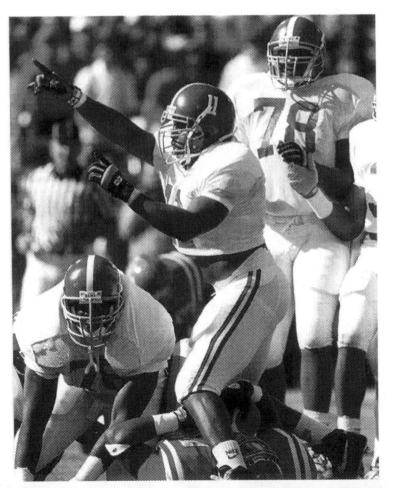

Former linebacker Lemanski Hall (1990-93) says he tried to play like he was representing all the players who had come before him.

"When I played," continues Hall, "I wanted to make sure I represented the players before me because I knew they were watching. I wanted people to say, 'That Lemanski Hall, he played his butt off.' But that lady, she gave me chills."

Darwin Holt, also a linebacker, played on the 1961 national championship team.

"Having played at the University of Alabama is the biggest ego trip in the world," Holt says. "There's not a day goes by that you don't have someone talking to you or wanting to take your picture. And I'm sixty-seven years old.

"It's beautiful," he says. "It just keeps going on and on. It never stops."

No, it doesn't.

And there is always another generation of fans growing up in the rich tradition and putting down deep roots. Ben Faucett is a four-year-old from Birmingham. His grandfather went to Vanderbilt. He has uncles who pull for Tennessee.

"His uncles tried to teach him 'Go Vols,' but he turned cold on them," explains the grandfather, Charles Martin.

Why does little Ben love the Crimson Tide?

"Because my dad likes Alabama," he says. "And because they win. Roll Tide!"

Winning, everyone understands. It's the mission. It's the reason for the season.

That most recent Cotton Bowl victory was the thirtieth in school history.

The Tide rolls on . . .

It's an NCAA record. And it was achieved amid obstacles that would have brought a lesser program to its knees and left it there interminably. It just goes to show, you can't keep a good school down; and you can't keep a great football program from its rightful place.

"We stand atop all the elite programs," Tatum says. "If you want to win, you come to Alabama."

Always.

Printed in the United States
By Bookmasters